FLORIDA STATE
UNIVERSITY LIBRARIES

JUL 1 1 2001

TALLAHASSEE, FLORIDA

INTERNATIONAL POLITICAL ECONOMY SERIES

General Editor: Timothy M. Shaw, Professor of Political Science and International Development Studies, and Director of the Centre for Foreign Policy Studies, Dalhousie University, Nova Scotia, Canada

Recent titles include:

Pradeep Agrawal, Subir V. Gokarn, Veena Mishra, Kirit S. Parikh and Kunal Sen
ECONOMIC RESTRUCTURING IN EAST ASIA AND INDIA: Perspectives on Policy Reform

Solon L. Barraclough and Krishna B. Ghimire
FORESTS AND LIVELIHOODS: The Social Dynamics of Deforestation in Developing Countries

Kathleen Barry (*editor*)
VIETNAM'S WOMEN IN TRANSITION

Jorge Rodríguez Beruff and Humberto García Muñiz (*editors*)
SECURITY PROBLEMS AND POLICIES IN THE POST-COLD WAR CARIBBEAN

Jerker Carlsson, Gunnar Köhlin and Anders Ekbom
THE POLITICAL ECONOMY OF EVALUATION: International Aid Agencies and the Effectiveness of Aid

Steve Chan
FOREIGN DIRECT INVESTMENT IN A CHANGING GLOBAL POLITICAL ECONOMY

Paul Cook and Frederick Nixson (*editors*)
THE MOVE TO THE MARKET? Trade and Industry Policy Reform in Transitional Economies

O. P. Dwivedi
DEVELOPMENT ADMINISTRATION: From Underdevelopment to Sustainable Development

John Healey and William Tordoff (*editors*)
VOTES AND BUDGETS: Comparative Studies in Accountable Governance in the South

Noeleen Heyzer, James V. Riker and Antonio B. Quizon (*editors*)
GOVERNMENT–NGO RELATIONS IN ASIA: Prospects and Challenges for People-Centred Development

George Kent
CHILDREN IN THE INTERNATIONAL POLITICAL ECONOMY

David Kowalewski
GLOBAL ESTABLISHMENT: The Political Economy of North/Asian Networks

Laura Macdonald
SUPPORTING CIVIL SOCIETY: The Political Role of Non-Governmental Organizations in Central America

Gary McMahon (*editor*)
LESSONS IN ECONOMIC POLICY FOR EASTERN EUROPE FROM LATIN AMERICA

David B. Moore and Gerald M. Schmitz (*editors*)
DEBATING DEVELOPMENT DISCOURSE: Institutional and Popular Perspectives

Juan Antonio Morales and Gary McMahon (*editors*)
ECONOMIC POLICY AND THE TRANSITION TO DEMOCRACY: The Latin American Experience

Paul J. Nelson
THE WORLD BANK AND NON-GOVERNMENTAL ORGANIZATIONS: The Limits of Apolitical Development

Archibald R. M. Ritter and John M. Kirk (*editors*)
CUBA IN THE INTERNATIONAL SYSTEM: Normalization and Integration

Ann Seidman and Robert B. Seidman
STATE AND LAW IN THE DEVELOPMENT PROCESS: Problem-Solving and Institutional Change in the Third World

Tor Skålnes
THE POLITICS OF ECONOMIC REFORM IN ZIMBABWE: Continuity and Change in Development

John Sorenson (*editor*)
DISASTER AND DEVELOPMENT IN THE HORN OF AFRICA

Howard Stein (*editor*)
ASIAN INDUSTRIALIZATION AND AFRICA: Studies in Policy Alternatives to Structural Adjustment

Deborah Stienstra
WOMEN'S MOVEMENTS AND INTERNATIONAL ORGANIZATIONS

Sandra Whitworth
FEMINISM AND INTERNATIONAL RELATIONS

David Wurfel and Bruce Burton (*editors*)
SOUTHEAST ASIA IN THE NEW WORLD ORDER: The Political Economy of a Dynamic Region

Latin America's New Insertion in the World Economy

Towards Systemic Competitiveness in Small Economies

Edited by

Ruud Buitelaar
Chief, Industrial Development Unit
Economic Commission for Latin America and the Caribbean (ECLAC)
Mexico

and

Pitou van Dijck
Associate Professor of Economics
Center for Latin American Research and Documentation (CEDLA)
University of Amsterdam

First published in Great Britain 1996 by
MACMILLAN PRESS LTD
Houndmills, Basingstoke, Hampshire RG21 6XS
and London
Companies and representatives
throughout the world

A catalogue record for this book is available
from the British Library.

ISBN 0-333-64527-8

First published in the United States of America 1996 by
ST. MARTIN'S PRESS, INC.,
Scholarly and Reference Division,
175 Fifth Avenue,
New York, N.Y. 10010

ISBN 0-312-12823-1

Library of Congress Cataloging-in-Publication Data
Latin America's insertion into the world economy : towards systemic
competitiveness in small economies : edited by Ruud Buitelaar and
Pitou van Dijck.
   p. cm. —(International political economy series)
Includes bibliographical references and index.
ISBN 0-312-12823-1 (cloth)
1. Latin America—Economic policy.   2. Competition—Latin America.
3. Competition, International.   4. Foreign trade promotion—Latin
America.   I. Buitelaar, Ruud.   II. Dijck, Pitou van.   III. Series.
HC125.L35365   1996
338.98—dc20   96-2581
                                                                                  CIP

Selection, editorial matter and Chapter 16 © Ruud Buitelaar and
Pitou van Dijck 1996
Chapter 1 © Pitou van Dijck 1996
Chapters 2–15 © Macmillan Press Ltd 1996

All rights reserved. No reproduction, copy or transmission of
this publication may be made without written permission.

No paragraph of this publication may be reproduced, copied or
transmitted save with written permission or in accordance with
the provisions of the Copyright, Designs and Patents Act 1988,
or under the terms of any licence permitting limited copying
issued by the Copyright Licensing Agency, 90 Tottenham Court
Road, London W1P 9HE.

Any person who does any unauthorised act in relation to this
publication may be liable to criminal prosecution and civil
claims for damages.

10   9   8   7   6   5   4   3   2   1
05   04   03   02   01   00   99   98   97   96

Printed and bound in Great Britain by
Antony Rowe Ltd, Chippenham, Wiltshire

This book is dedicated to the memory of Fernando Fajnzylber

Contents

List of Tables ... ix

List of Figures ... xi

List of Maps ... xii

List of Abbreviations ... xiii

Notes on the Contributors ... xv

Foreword by Gert Rosenthal ... xviii

Acknowledgements ... xx

Maps ... xxi

1 Towards a New Insertion in World Markets: An Introduction ... 1
   Pitou van Dijck

2 The Gains from Trade Reconsidered ... 17
   Hans Linnemann

3 The Exchange Rate as an Export-Stimulation Mechanism ... 31
   Hans Visser

4 Structural Adjustment in the 1980s: Stimulus or Setback for Private Investment in the Industrialisation Process? ... 59
   Valpy FitzGerald

5 The Scope for Industrial Policy in a Free-Trade Environment ... 75
   José Tavares de Araujo Jr

6 Export Processing Free Zones as an Export Strategy for Central America and the Caribbean ... 85
   Teresa S. Weersma-Haworth

7	The Export Processing Free Zone of San Bartolo in El Salvador *Geske Dijkstra and Carlos Rivera Alemán*	95
8	The Historical Experience: Growth Accounting *André A. Hofman*	105
9	Social Development during Periods of Structural Adjustment *Rolph van der Hoeven and Frances Stewart*	123
10	Trade Policy and Changing Trade Patterns *Cees van Beers*	139
11	Chile: from Early Liberalisation to 'Second-phase Export-led Growth' *Anne Theo Seinen*	151
12	Industrial Competitiveness and Government Policies in Uruguay *Anton Timpers*	163
13	The Competitiveness of Manufacturing Firms: the Case of Venezuela *Carla Macario*	175
14	Export Promotion in Costa Rica *Geske Dijkstra and Juut van der Wijk*	191
15	The Systemic Weakness of Guatemala's Competitiveness *Juan Alberto Fuentes K.*	207
16	Conclusions *Ruud Buitelaar and Pitou van Dijck*	225
References		235
Index		249

List of Tables

1.1	The performance of manufacturing industry in Latin America and Asia, 1985–92	3
1.2	Manufacturing production and exports in selected countries	4
1.3	Manufacturing production and international trade in selected countries, 1985–92	8
1.4	Trade liberalisation in selected countries, 1985–92	10
1.5	REERs in selected countries, 1980–92 (1980 = 100)	11
4.1	Shares of private investment in GDP in selected countries, 1970–90 (%)	63
4.2	Relative prices and public investment in selected countries	65
6.1	Incentives offered in EPFZs	91
7.1	Some indicators of EPFZ San Bartolo, 1976–92	99
7.2	Some indicators of EPFZs in selected countries, 1991	100
7.3	Exports from EPFZ San Bartolo, 1977–91	101
7.4	EPFZ San Bartolo, value added and exports, 1976–90	101
7.5	Employment in EPFZ San Bartolo, 1976–90	103
8.1	Labour inputs, 1950–89 (average annual compound growth rates)	111
8.2	Capital inputs, 1950–89 (average annual compound growth rates)	114
8.3	GDP and JFP, 1950–89 (average annual compound growth rates)	116
8.4	Explaining economic growth, 1950–89	117
9.1	Urban unemployment and wages in selected countries, 1980–91	126
9.2	Allocation ratios in adjusting countries, 1981–90	132
9.3	Tax structure, 1981–90	135
10.1	Shares of manufacturing production in GDP (1) and of manufactured exports in total exports (2) in selected countries, 1970, 1980 and 1990	140
10.2	Contributions of the five largest manufacturing export sectors to total manufactured exports in five Latin American countries, 1968–70, 1978–80 and 1988–90	145
10.3	Contributions of the five largest manufacturing export sectors to total manufactured exports in three Asian countries, 1968–70, 1978–80 and 1983–5	146

10.4	RCAs in twelve major Latin American manufacturing export sectors, 1988–90	147

Uruguay

12.1	Import tariffs, 1980–93 (%)	168
12.2	Real effective protection for manufacturing industries, 1981 and 1985 (Corden method, %)	169

Venezuela

13.1	Export to output ratios for manufacturing sectors, 1980, 1988 and 1989 (%)	177
13.2	Ten major non-traditional manufactured exports, 1992 (as % of non-traditional exports)	178

Costa Rica

14.1	Effective protection in manufacturing sectors, 1987 and 1993 (Balassa method, %)	198

Guatemala

15.1	Macro-economic indicators, 1980–92 (%)	209
15.2	Traditional and non-traditional exports, 1981–92 (annual growth rates, %)	214
15.3	Export:output ratios in manufacturing sectors, 1989 (%)	216
15.4	Private investment, 1980–91 (%)	218
15.5	Public investment, 1980–92 (%)	220

LIST OF APPENDICES

8.1	Sources of data	119
10.1	ISIC categories	148

List of Figures

3.1	Equilibrium situation in the dependent economy under fixed exchange rates	34
3.2	The dependent-economy model with free-floating exchange rates	36
3.3	Capital imports in a dependent economy with floating exchange rate	37
3.4	The foreign-exchange market with an overvalued currency	40
3.5	RER and openness of the Chilean economy, 1975–91	49
3.6	RER and openness of the Chilean economy, metals and ores excluded, 1975–91	49
3.7	RER and openness of the Colombian economy, 1975–91	53
3.8	RER and openness of the Colombian economy, coffee excluded, 1975–91	54
3.9	RER and openness of the Uruguayan economy, 1975–91	55

Uruguay

12.1	Investment as a proportion of GDP and industrial production, 1980–90 (%)	165
12.2	Total, industrial and other exports, 1980–91 (current $US)	165

List of Maps

1 Latin America xxi
2 Central America xxii

List of Abbreviations

ASEXMA	Asociación de Exportadores de Manufacturas
ATPA	Admision Temporal para el Perfeccionamiento Activo
AVEX	Asociación Venezolana de Exportadores
CACM	Central American Common Market
CADEX	Centro de Atención Directa al Exportador
CAT	Certificado de Abono Tributario
CAUCE	Convenio Argentino-Uruguayo de Cooperación Económica
CBI	Caribbean Basin Initiative
CET	Common external tariff
CIF	Costs insurance freight
CINVE	Centro de Investigaciones Económicas
CODESA	Corporación de Desarrollo Industrial S.A.
CORFO	Corporación de Fomento
DAJFP	Doubly augmented joint factor productivity
ECLAC	Economic Commission for Latin America and the Caribbean
EER	Effective exchange rate
EPFZ	Export processing free zone
EU	European Union
FINEXPO	Fondo de Financiamiento de las Exportaciones
FOB	Free on board
GATT	General Agreement on Tariffs and Trade
GSP	General System of Preferences
GDP	Gross domestic product
GNP	Gross national product
GTZ	Gesellschaft für Technische Zusammenarbeit
ICE	Instituto de Comercio Exterior
IDB	Inter-American Development Bank
IFC	International Finance Corporation
ILO	International Labour Office
IMF	International Monetary Fund
INEGI	Instituto Nacional de Estadística, Geografía e Informática
IPC	Interdisziplinäre Project Consult Gmbh
ISIC	International standard industrial classification
ITC	International Trade Center
JFP	Joint factor productivity
LAIA	Latin American Integration Association

List of Abbreviations

LDC	Less developed country
MIPLAN	Ministerio de Planificación y Coordinación del Desarrollo Económico y Social
na	not available
NAFTA	North American Free Trade Agreement
NIC	Newly industrialising country
NTB	Non-tariff barrier
OECD	Organisation for Economic Co-operation and Development
PEC	Protocolo de Expansión Comercial
PREALC	Programa Regional de Empleo para América Latina y el Caribe
R&D	Research and Development
RCA	Revealed comparative advantage
REER	Real effective exchange rate
RER	Real exchange rate
SEGEPLAN	Secretaría General de Planificación
SAP	Structural adjustment programme
UNCTAD	United Nations Conference on Trade and Development
UNCTC	United Nations Center for Transnational Corporations
UNICEF	United Nations Children's Fund
UNIDO	United Nations Industrial Development Organisation
UNDP	United Nations Development Programme
USA	United States of America
USAID	United States Agency for International Development
VAT	Value added tax
WHFTA	Western Hemisphere Free Trade Area

Notes on the Contributors

Cees van Beers is Assistant Professor of Economics at the University of Leiden, The Netherlands. He received a PhD at the Free University of Amsterdam (Tinbergen Institute) in 1991. His main fields of interest are the exports of developing countries and foreign-trade problems of economies in transition.

Ruud Buitelaar is Chief of the Industrial Development Unit at ECLAC's office in Mexico. He studied Development Economics at the Free University of Amsterdam. He has worked for UNIDO at the UNDP office in Montevideo, and at the Joint ECLAC/UNIDO Industry and Technology Division in Santiago de Chile. He has published widely on industrial development issues in Latin America.

Pitou van Dijck is Associate Professor of Economics at the Center for Latin American Research and Documentation (CEDLA) at the University of Amsterdam. His main fields of interest are industrialisation and trade policies in Asia and Latin America. He is co-author of *Export-oriented Industrialization in Developing Countries* (1987), *South–South Trade Preferences* (1992), *India's Trade Policy and the Export Performance of Industry* (1994) and author of *Sustainable Outward-Oriented Industrialization Policies* (1995).

Geske Dijkstra is Assistant Professor of International Economics at the University of Limburg, Maastricht, The Netherlands. She studied economics and sociology at the University of Groningen, where she also received her PhD in economics in 1988. She has published widely on the economic development issues of Central America and is author of *Industrialization in Sandinista Nicaragua* (1992). She has lived and worked for some four years in Nicaragua and El Salvador.

Valpy FitzGerald is Director of Financial Studies and Professorial Fellow of St Antony's College, Oxford University, Extraordinary Professor of Development Economics at the Institute of Social Studies (The Hague) and Visiting Professor of International Economics at the Universidad Complutense (Madrid). He has worked on the macroeconomics of Peru, Central America and Mexico and is currently concerned with the effects of global capital market integration on private investment behaviour in the region. His most recent work is *The Macroeconomics of Development Finance* (1993).

Juan Alberto Fuentes K. is Director of Research at ECLAC's office in Mexico. He is a Guatemalan citizen with a PhD in economics from the University of Sussex and an MA in Economics from the University of Toronto. He is the author of various articles on trade and foreign investment in Latin America and of *Desafios de la Integracion Centroamericana* (1989).

Rolph van der Hoeven is an economist and Interdepartmental Manager, Structural Adjustment issues at the ILO in Geneva. He has previously worked as a senior economic adviser of UNICEF in New York and in various positions for the ILO in Africa. He has published widely on economic planning, basic needs and structural adjustment. He is the author of *Planning for Basic Needs: A Soft Option or a Solid Policy?* (1988) and co-editor of *World Recession and Global Interdependence* (1987), *Africa's Recovery in the 1990s* (1992), *Poverty Monitoring: An International Concern* (1994) and *Structural Adjustment and Beyond in Sub-Saharan Africa* (1994).

André A. Hofman is staff member of the Economic Development Division at ECLAC's office in Santiago de Chile. He is desk officer for Ecuador and co-ordinates a research project on long-run development in Latin America. He participates in the International Comparisons of Output and Productivity (ICOP) project of the University of Groningen, The Netherlands.

Hans Linnemann is Professor (Emeritus) of Development Economics at the Free University of Amsterdam. From 1966 to 1970 he held the same position at the Institute of Social Studies in The Hague, of which he is now Honorary Fellow. His main research interest is in the international trade of developing countries. His most recent book is an edited volume, *South–South Trade Preferences* (1992). Research and advisory work brought him to a number of Latin American countries, and he lived for two years in Ecuador.

Carla Macario is a staff member of the Division of Production, Productivity and Management at ECLAC's office in Santiago de Chile. Previously she worked for the Mexican government.

Carlos Rivera Alemán studied economics at the Faculty of Economic Sciences of the University of El Salvador. He works as an investigator at

Notes on the Contributors

the Instituto de Investigaciones Económicas (INVE) of the University of El Salvador. Currently he is a PhD candidate at the University of Barcelona, Spain.

Anne Theo Seinen studied economics and international relations at the University of Groningen, The Netherlands.

Frances Stewart is a Fellow of Somerville College and Warden of Queen Elizabeth House, Oxford. She worked at UNICEF as a Special Adviser on Adjustment. She is a development economist and has published widely on technology and development, basic needs, adjustment issues and fiscal policy. She is co-author of *Planning to Meet Basic Needs* (1985), *Adjustment with a Human Face* (1987) and *Alternative Development Strategies in Sub-Saharan Africa* (1992).

José Tavares de Araujo Jr is an economist with a PhD from the University of London (1982). He has been at the IDB since October 1992. He is former Director of the Brazilian Tariff Commission (1985/1988). He is a full Professor at the Federal University of Rio de Janeiro (on leave).

Anton Timpers graduated in international relations from the University of Groningen, The Netherlands. His specialisation is the economic development of Latin America.

Hans Visser is Professor of Money and Banking and International Economics in the Department of Economics at the Free University of Amsterdam. He publishes principally on monetary economics. Among his recent publications are *Modern Monetary Theory* (1991) and *A Guide to International Monetary Economics* (1995).

Teresa S. Weersma-Haworth is an economist with an MSc in Development Economics from the London School of Economics. Her fields of specialisation are project evaluation and feasibility studies of micro-agribusiness, and institutional models and alternative forms of trading for sustainable development. She has lived and worked for many years in several countries in Latin America.

Juut van der Wijk studied economics at the University of Limburg in Maastricht, The Netherlands and the University of Zaragoza, Spain. At the time of writing she was guest researcher at the Maestría en Política Económica para Centroamérica y El Caribe at the National University (UNA) in Heredia, Costa Rica.

Foreword

The greatest challenge facing developing countries today is to improve the participation of their national economies in an intensely competitive international market. To become an active player in the globalisation process appears to be crucial to the improvement of standards of living and the achievement of greater equity. On the other hand, to sit on the sidelines entails the risk of increasing marginalisation, contributing to inequalities between income groups at the national level and between countries internationally.

This is, of course, not a new phenomenon: much of Latin America's economic history can be analysed through the prism of the efforts made to foster export commodities as a route to modernisation and economic development. Indeed, the expansion and diversification of those commodities were the main engine of growth from colonial times through the middle of the twentieth century, and have continued to play an important role in the post-war period up to the present.

However, the post-war period also offered lessons on the shortcomings of the dependence on basic agricultural and mineral commodities as the main sources of foreign exchange, suggesting the need to move into more knowledge-intensive activities that could improve the dynamic effects of exports on overall economic performance. This need was strongly enhanced by the dramatic changes in the manner in which global production, distribution and consumption of goods and services have evolved in recent times, forcing policy-makers and private agents to adapt to rapidly changing circumstances, sometimes through radical departures from the practices of the past.

All of the above is another way of saying that the broader subject of this book is a secular pre-occupation in Latin American development. What makes it so timely is the new context in which these issues are cast in the 1980s and beyond: Latin America's lengthy period of adjustment, as well as the time when the transnationalisation of most economic variables grew exponentially. Indeed, as the authors of this book argue, attaining international competitiveness in an increasing number of activities, either to export or to satisfy domestic demand, poses numerous demands on any country, and especially on developing countries. Rarely is there one single factor that explains 'success' in increasing levels of productivity among a wide range of sectors and activities; rather, simultaneous progress is required on several fronts. The latter include a stable and coherent macro-economic and regulatory environment, the development of financial and labour markets, adequate physical infrastructure, an appropriate institutional framework, suitable human resources at the entrepreneurial level as well as in the labour force, and numerous other elements. Selective public-sector interventions in support of emerging export-orientated activities appear to play a vital role as a complement to incentives derived from 'getting prices right'.

The intensive learning process of past decades is still going on and this book offers new insights, based on cross-sectoral and specific case studies. We are therefore most pleased to have been able to co-operate with the Center for Latin American Research and Documentation (CEDLA) at the University of Amsterdam, in its sponsorship. I am also happy to note that the book is dedicated to our late colleague, Fernando Fajnzylber, whose pioneering work was most certainly a source of inspiration for several of the authors.

GERT ROSENTHAL
Executive Secretary, ECLAC
Santiago de Chile,
November 1994

Acknowledgements

Many people have contributed enthusiastically to this book. Above all, the editors wish to express their gratitude to the two institutions that supported from the start the research project financially and in kind: the United Nations Economic Commission for Latin America and the Caribbean (ECLAC) and the Center for Latin American Research and Documentation (CEDLA) at the University of Amsterdam. We have appreciated in particular the encouragements by Cees den Boer, Director of CEDLA, the late Fernando Fajnzylber of ECLAC and Joseph Ramos, Director of ECLAC's Industry Division in Santiago de Chile, Horacio Santamaria, Director of ECLAC's Mexico office and Gert Rosenthal, Executive Secretary of ECLAC. We would like to thank also the secretarial and general services staff of both institutions, who supported us in particular during the 1993 seminar in Amsterdam and in the final stages of the editorial process in Amsterdam and Mexico City.

RUUD BUITELAAR
PITOU VAN DIJCK

Latin America

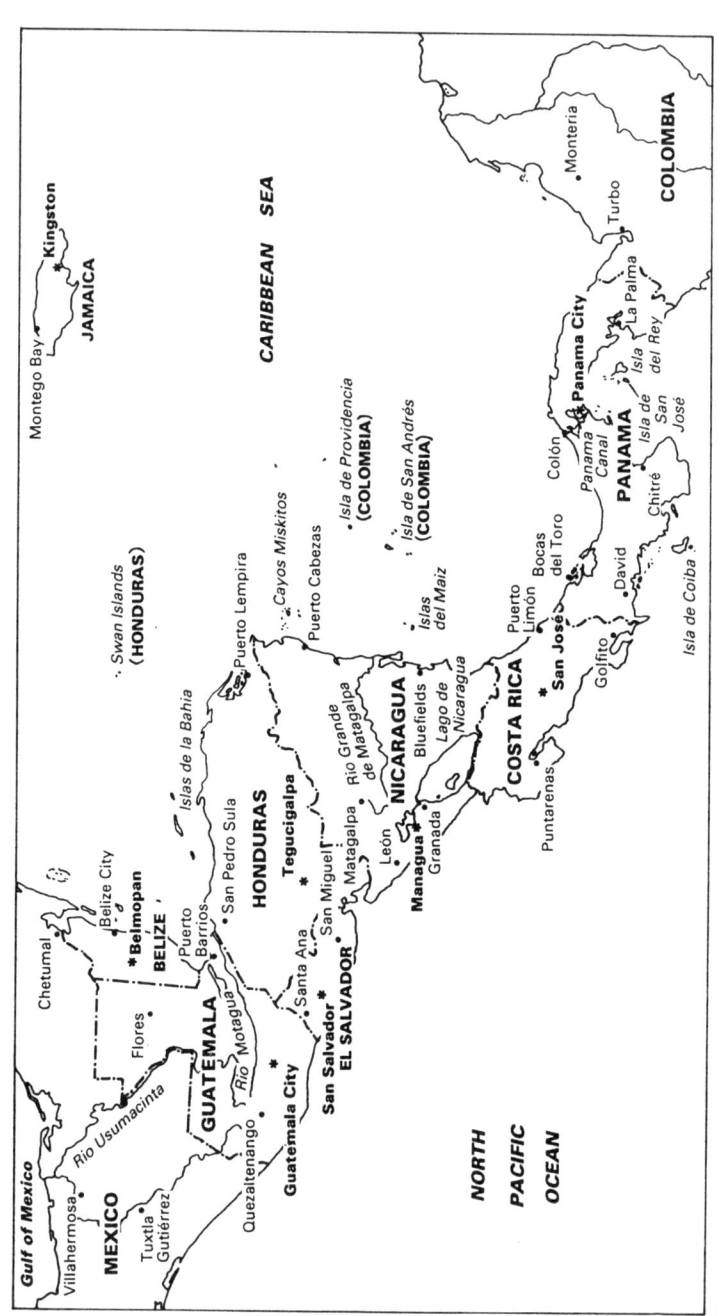

Central America

1 Towards a New Insertion in World Markets: An Introduction[1]
Pitou van Dijck

1.1 THEME AND CONTEXT

This volume examines the contributions governments can make in order to stimulate efficient and export-orientated manufacturing production in small- and medium-sized economies in Latin America in the coming years. The study focuses on the progress that has been made recently to correct policy failures of the past, the obstacles and bottlenecks that have occurred in the process of economic transition and the challenges the selected countries face in order to stimulate in a systemic way the development of an internationally competitive manufacturing sector.

In most of these economies, destabilising and ultimately unsustainable macro-economic policies as well as protectionist industrial regimes hampered the development of efficient manufacturing industries and manufactured exports for a long period of time, Chile being the first exception. A significant re-orientation in the macro-economic policies and trade and industrialisation regimes of a large number of countries took place only as recently as the second half of the 1980s and the early 1990s. Far-reaching adjustments were implemented as part of stabilisation and restructuring programmes that reflect the new priorities in the region – these are often referred to as the 'Washington agenda'. The main priorities are in the areas of fiscal discipline, a re-orientation of government expenditures, tax reform, financial liberalisation, exchange-rate adjustment, trade liberalisation, the attraction of direct foreign investment, deregulation and the establishment of property rights (Williamson, 1990). The emphasis is on 'getting prices right' and on reducing the role of government to the creation of a stable and stimulating macro-economic environment, the correction of market failures and the provision of public goods.

Notwithstanding the progress made in implementing the Washington agenda, and particularly the reform of trade policy and exchange-rate regimes, this book questions whether the mix of policies currently pursued in many of these countries will suffice to bring about the required transformation of the manufacturing sector and a new insertion in world markets. A series of critical reflections is presented on the policies that are actually pursued and arguments are put forward for governments to take a more prominent position in the development process.

This volume analyses the process of transition in a group of countries that differ widely in many respects, but which also have in common some broad structural characteristics that have a profound impact on the structure of their comparative advantages in the short term and on their options for industrial development: they are middle-income countries, well endowed with natural resources, and have a small domestic market. Their economic development is strongly related to primary production and export of commodities, and the volatility of markets for primary products tend to generate instabilities and Dutch-disease effects. To deepen the analysis, we have included five case studies, of Chile, Costa Rica, Guatemala, Uruguay and Venezuela.

1.2 THE PERFORMANCE OF THE MANUFACTURING SECTOR

To put the challenges ahead in a clear perspective, we shall start our investigation by presenting a series of indicators related to the development of the manufacturing sectors in Latin America and east and south-east Asia during the 1970s and 1980s. Table 1.1 shows in a stylised fashion three long-term developments that are particularly worrying from the perspective of some Latin American countries.

First, the growth of manufacturing production in the countries in east and south-east Asia exceeded by far industrial growth in Latin America. The industrial stagnation in Latin America during the 1980s is in sharp contrast with the dynamism shown in the Pacific Rim and other areas in Asia. Consequently, the centre of gravity of manufacturing production in developing countries is shifting very rapidly towards Asia.

Second, growth of the volumes and values of manufactured exports in the Asian newly industrialising countries exceeded by far the export performance of the manufacturing sector in Latin America during the 1970s and 1980s. Both areas managed to increase their shares in world trade in manufactures but this was particularly the case with the Asian countries.

Third, industrial development in Latin America is more dynamic in the three large countries, Argentina, Brazil and Mexico, and particularly in the latter two countries, than in the smaller countries of the continent. Also, the contribution of the three large countries to total manufactured

Table 1.1 The performance of manufacturing industry in Latin America and Asia, 1985–92

	Year	Latin America (incl. Caribbean)	East, south-east and south Asia (excl. Japan)
1. Share of region in world manufacturing production (%)	1980	9.1	4.4
2. Growth of manufacturing production (%)	1970–80	5.4	8.6
	1980–85	−0.6	7.8
	1985–89	1.8	10.2

		Latin America	NIEs (Hong Kong, Korea and Singapore)
3. Share of region in world manufactured exports (%)	1970–75	1.2	2.0
	1985–90	2.1	6.2
4. Manufacturing export volume growth (%)	1970–79	12.7	17.0
	1980–90	9.1	13.5

		Latin America	East Asia	South Asia
5. Manufactures as share of total exports (%)	1965	7	34	36
	1990	34	69	69

		Argentina	Brazil	Mexico	All other countries
6. Share of country in Latin America's export of manufactures (%)	1970–74	14.6	28.1	22.1	35.1
	1975–79				33.1
	1980–84				24.5
	1985–90	8.4	46.9	25.2	19.4

Sources: 1 and 2 taken from: United Nations (1991), *National Account Statistics: Analysis of Main Aggregates, 1988–1989* (New York: UN). Table 6, pp. 174–9; 3, 4 and 6 taken from: IDB (1992), *Economic and Social Progress in Latin America 1992 Report* (Washington, DC: IDB). Table 1, p. 192, Table 3, p. 198 and Appendix Table 3, p. 262; 5 taken from: The World Bank, *Global Economic Prospects and the Developing Countries, 1992* (Washington, DC: The World Bank) Table 1–9, p. 14.

Table 1.2 Manufacturing production and exports in selected countries[a]

		Years	Chile	Colombia	Costa Rica
1.	Value added in manufacturing (1988 $US m.)	1990	6 839	10 151	4 019
2.	Share of manufacturing production in GDP 1980 constant $US (%)	1970	24.5	22.1	15.5
		1980	21.4	23.3	18.6
		1991	21.7	21.3	18.4
3.	Growth of manufacturing production (%)	1970–80	−0.8	5.8	7.9
		1980–85	−1.9	1.3	0.2
		1985–89	7.8	4.2	4.8
4.	Value of manufactured exports (current $US m.)	1990	845	1 709	374
5.	Share of manufactured exports in GDP (%)	1970–75	0.8	1.8	4.7
		1985–90	1.8	2.5	6.1
6.	Share of manufactures in exports (%)	1970	4.4	8.1	19.7
		1980	9.7	20.4	34.3
		1990	9.8	25.3	25.7
7.	Growth of manufactured exports (%)	1970–90	13.4	12.6	9.7
8.	Concentration index	1980	0.406	0.579	0.316
		1989	0.372	0.311	0.344

Table 1.2 Continued

	Ecuador	El Salvador	Guatemala	Uruguay	Venezuela
1. Value added in manufacturing (1988 $USm.)	2 775	970	1 245	2 341	12 741
2. Share of manufacturing production in GDP 1980 constant $US (%)	15.9	15.2	16.6	26.7	17.5
	17.7	15.0	17.6	28.2	18.8
	13.6	15.6	15.8	24.7	20.7
3. Growth of manufacturing production (%)	10.5	4.1	6.2	3.5	5.7
	0.8	−2.2	−2.1	−6.2	1.8
	0.1	2.8	1.7	4.3	2.1
4. Value of manufactured exports (current $US m.)	70	125	287	663	1 851
5. Share of manufactured exports in GDP (%)	0.3	5.0	5.2	2.1	0.3
	0.3	2.5	3.1	5.9	1.9
6. Share of manufactures in exports (%)	1.7	28.7	28.0	20.4	1.5
	3.0	20.1	24.2	38.2	1.7
	2.6	22.6	23.7	39.1	10.7
7. Growth of manufactured exports (%)	10.9	2.0	5.5	14.6	19.6
8. Concentration index	0.547	0.380	0.310	0.235	0.674
	0.462	0.509	0.287	0.216	0.515

[a] Hirschmann index has been normalised to make values from 0 to 1 (maximum concentration).

Sources: 1, 5 and 7 taken from: IDB (1992) *Economic and Social Progress in Latin America 1992 Report* (Washington, DC: IDB), Table B–10, p. 291, Appendix Table 3, p. 192 and Appendix Table 2, p. 261; 2 taken from: ECLAC (1993) *Statistical Yearbook for Latin America and the Caribbean, 1992 edition* (Santiago de Chile: ECLAC), Table 58, p. 90; 3 taken from: United Nations (1991) *National Account Statistics: Analysis of Main Aggregates, 1988–1989* (New York: UN), Table 6, p.p. 174–9; 4 and 6 taken from: The World Bank (1992), *World Tables 1992* (Washington, DC: The World Bank), Country page 8 taken from: UNCTAD, *Handbook of International Trade and Development Statistics 1991* (New York, 1992), Table 4.5, pp. 241–4 export performance of the region increased. Indeed, most of the other countries are marginal suppliers of manufactures on world markets.

As Table 1.2 shows, the absolute size of the manufacturing sector is very small, the countries with the largest manufacturing base being Venezuela, Colombia and Chile. It is striking that during the period 1970–1990 the share of the manufacturing sector in GDP only increased substantially in Costa Rica and Venezuela, while in all other selected countries it decreased or stagnated, at least when measured in current domestic market prices. As will be substantiated below, liberalisation measures may have reduced significantly the difference between domestic and international prices and thus reduce the statistical illusion created by the use of domestic market prices rather than international prices. Growth of manufacturing production was relatively high in the 1970s, dropped sharply during the first half of the 1980s and recovered somewhat in most of the selected countries in the second half of the 1980s. The recovery was particularly strong in Chile.

Traditionally the manufacturing sector was strongly orientated towards the domestic market, due to the anti-export bias in government incentives and the lack of international competitiveness of domestic industries. However, the data presented in the lower part of Table 1.2 indicate that in most of the countries the contributions of manufactured exports to total domestic production and the share of manufactures in total exports increased. The average growth rates of manufactured exports exceeded significantly average growth of manufacturing production during these two decades. Growth of non-traditional exports resulted in a more diversified export structure as indicated by lower values of the concentration index that are shown in the final rows of the table.

The aggregated data presented here, however, do not necessarily reflect upon an increasing international competitiveness of domestic industries, since foreign-owned firms tend to play a significant role in the manufacturing sectors of most Latin American countries and this is even more true of exports. The number of domestic firms directly engaged in exports of manufactures in a significant and systematic manner is rather small in most of the selected countries. This is even true of Chile, which had already introduced an outward-orientated policy in the 1970s. Particularly in the Caribbean and some Central American countries, exports of manufactures are to a substantial degree generated by foreign-owned firms located in export-processing free zones.

To appreciate the changes that have recently taken place in Latin America in terms of overall economic growth, industrial development and outward orientation, a more detailed analysis is required of recent developments in this area. Table 1.3 shows in more detail changes in production and international trade in selected Latin American countries during the period 1985–92. During these years the recovery started and major shifts in macro-economic policies were implemented in those countries that had not implemented stabilisation and industrial restructuring policies before.

Table 1.3 shows, first of all, that recovery was well under way during this period. After a series of years with negative real growth rates at the beginning of the 1980s, the second half of the decade and the early years of the 1990s show positive and high annual growth rates of GDP measured in constant prices. Second, overall economic growth was not led so much by industrial recovery during these years. The shares of the manufacturing sector in GDP measured in current prices, did not increase significantly in most of the countries, while this share declined fairly dramatically in Uruguay. Substantial reductions in the levels of protection for manufacturing industry have changed domestic terms of trade for industry during these years. Third, in nearly all of the selected economies, the shares of imports and exports in GDP increased substantially, indicating that the economies were opening up rapidly, particularly in the cases of Chile, Costa Rica and Ecuador. Uruguay is the only exception, showing a constant share of imports and a declining share of exports in GDP. Fourth, the contribution of the manufacturing sector to total exports of goods increased in all countries and particularly so in Chile and Colombia.

1.3 TRANSFORMATION OF THE TRADE AND EXCHANGE-RATE REGIMES

Within the context of appropriate macro-economic policies, liberalisation of imports and an exchange-rate policy that is supportive for the sectors of tradables are crucial for the stimulation of an internationally competitive and export-orientated manufacturing sector. Traditionally, manufacturing industries received a high degree of more or less permanent protection through high and dispersed import tariff rates and quantitative import restrictions, while further stimulation was given through tax exemptions and other export and investment incentives, preferential credit schemes, foreign-exchange rationing and government procurement schemes. Thus, the predominant type of economic policy in the past created a relatively privileged position for industrialists and a strong incentive to cater for the domestic market only. Production for the small domestic market provided only limited incentive for technological improvements and product development. Moreover, the availability of subsidised credits for industry

Table 1.3 Manufacturing production and international trade in selected countries, 1985–92

	1985	1986	1987	1988	1989	1990	1991	1992
Chile								
Annual growth rates (constant prices)								
GDP	2.0	5.6	5.8	7.4	10.0	2.1	6.0	10.4
Manufacturing production	2.7	7.9	5.6	8.6	10.0	0.1	5.5	12.2
Total exports	12.3	9.8	8.8	6.1	15.7	7.6	12.8	12.3
Total imports	–10.3	9.6	17.1	12.1	25.3	0.6	8.6	22.1
Shares in GDP								
Manufacturing production	21.9	20.6	20.6	20.9	n.a.	n.a.	n.a.	n.a.
Total exports	27.3	28.7	31.4	35.7	35.5	34.3	33.7	31.4
Total imports	24.4	24.8	27.2	27.9	31.1	31.2	28.8	29.1
Manufactures in total exports of goods	6.0	7.7	8.4	8.5	9.9	10.5	12.7	n.a.
Colombia								
Annual growth rates (constant prices)								
GDP	3.1	5.8	5.4	4.1	3.4	4.3	2.1	3.5
Manufacturing production	3.0	5.9	6.2	1.9	5.6	4.2	0.8	4.8
Total exports	12.9	23.2	7.2	1.7	5.9	18.5	3.5	6.7
Total imports	–6.5	11.1	5.2	2.3	–3.6	8.2	–4.2	29.4
Shares in GDP								
Manufacturing production	21.4	22.5	20.3	21.2	20.9	19.9	20.1	19.8
Total exports	14.4	20.1	18.0	17.5	18.9	21.7	22.3	20.5
Total imports	13.6	13.9	14.9	15.4	15.2	16.1	15.0	17.6
Manufactures in total exports of goods	15.6	13.7	18.1	20.9	21.5	22.7	30.9	n.a.
Costa Rica								
Annual growth rates (constant prices)								
GDP	0.7	5.5	4.8	3.4	5.7	3.6	2.3	7.3
Manufacturing production	2.0	7.3	5.5	2.2	3.4	2.6	2.1	10.5
Total exports	–4.0	3.6	20.9	7.4	15.8	9.1	9.2	13.3
Total imports	6.0	17.6	17.6	–0.9	18.1	10.8	–3.1	24.4
Shares in GDP								
Manufacturing production	22.1	21.3	21.3	21.3	20.4	19.4	19.9	20.3
Total exports	30.7	31.3	31.6	34.0	34.9	34.3	38.5	38.6
Total imports	32.5	30.5	35.8	35.8	38.6	41.1	39.1	43.6
Manufactures in total exports of goods	21.5	20.0	23.6	24.5	28.6	28.1	25.5	n.a.
Ecuador								
Annual growth rates (constant prices)								
GDP	4.3	3.1	–6.0	10.5	0.3	2.3	4.4	3.9
Manufacturing production	0.2	–1.6	1.7	2.0	–5.0	–1.3	3.7	4.6
Total exports	12.0	8.5	–16.1	31.1	–1.7	5.5	10.5	5.2
Total imports	7.3	–0.2	15.4	–10.0	5.1	0.1	16.7	8.5

Table 1.3 Continued

	1985	1986	1987	1988	1989	1990	1991	1992
Shares in GDP								
Manufacturing production	18.9	19.8	19.5	21.4	21.1	19.7	20.8	21.6
Total exports	26.8	22.8	24.0	28.4	29.4	32.0	30.9	29.6
Total imports	20.9	22.6	30.3	30.5	31.2	28.5	31.1	33.1
Manufactures in total								
exports of goods	0.8	1.4	2.3	2.2	2.4	2.3	2.4	3.9
Guatemala								
Annual growth rates (constant prices)								
GDP	−0.6	0.1	3.5	3.9	3.9	3.1	3.3	4.6
Manufacturing production	−0.8	0.7	2.0	2.2	2.3	2.2	2.3	2.9
Total exports	3.1	−14.0	6.0	5.6	13.3	6.5	−4.8	5.7
Total imports	−12.9	−14.7	47.8	3.8	5.9	−0.7	7.0	18.9
Shares in GDP								
Manufacturing production	n.a.	n.a.	n.a.	n.a.	n.a.	n.a.	n.a.	n.a.
Total exports	18.5	16.1	15.8	16.1	17.3	19.7	17.8	17.1
Total imports	20.1	14.6	22.3	21.9	22.5	23.7	21.7	24.2
Manufactures in total								
exports of goods	19.9	16.6	22.9	23.7	24.7	23.3	26.4	n.a.
Uruguay								
Annual growth rates (constant prices)								
GDP	1.5	8.9	7.9	0.0	1.3	0.9	2.9	7.4
Manufacturing production	−1.6	11.7	9.9	−0.9	−0.2	−1.5	−0.5	1.5
Total exports	6.0	11.5	−8.5	9.1	10.3	12.7	−0.8	4.7
Total imports	−1.1	29.4	15.8	0.0	1.4	1.1	17.9	22.6
Shares in GDP								
Manufacturing production	29.4	29.7	28.9	28.2	26.2	26.3	24.9	21.7
Total exports	26.8	26.2	21.6	23.8	25.4	26.2	23.2	21.5
Total imports	21.1	20.3	19.2	19.2	19.2	20.1	20.2	21.3
Manufactures in total								
exports of goods	34.7	34.8	43.4	37.7	39.6	38.6	39.8	40.5
Venezuela								
Annual growth rates (constant prices)								
GDP	1.5	6.3	4.5	6.2	−7.8	6.9	10.4	7.3
Manufacturing production	5.0	7.1	2.5	6.9	−11.8	6.0	11.5	7.0
Total exports	−1.3	12.4	−1.7	7.9	5.5	14.5	5.0	−5.8
Total imports	−5.4	0.8	2.2	19.0	−32.5	−7.9	46.0	20.5
Shares in GDP								
Manufacturing production	22.7	23.1	21.1	20.5	21.2	20.5	19.8	19.1
Total exports	24.1	19.8	21.4	20.6	33.9	39.5	30.9	25.5
Total imports	18.1	20.2	23.4	27.2	22.3	20.2	26.2	28.5
Manufactures in total								
exports of goods	5.1	4.8	3.9	4.9	8.0	7.1	6.3	n.a.

Source: IDB, 1993.

stimulated the use of relatively capital-intensive production techniques, adding to the social costs of this type of industrial policy.

As shown in this volume, many of the small and medium-sized countries in the region have made great progress in trade-policy reform. Tariff and non-tariff barriers (NTBs) have been reduced significantly and exchange-rate regimes have become more supportive for the sectors of tradables in a short period of time. Table 1.4 presents in a stylised fashion the reductions in average import tariffs and para-tariffs and the elimination of NTBs in selected economies between 1985 and 1992. Tariff rates were cut in a shockwise fashion in many of the countries. Moreover, the coverage rates of NTBs were reduced to zero in most countries.

The policies of liberalisation and stabilisation were accompanied by significant changes in the exchange-rate regimes.

Table 1.5 presents the adjustments made in the real effective exchange rates (REER) during the period 1980–92. The index is defined as the local currency price of foreign currency, so that a rise in the index signifies a depreciation. The exchange rate tended to appreciate in real terms during the early 1980s – particularly in Colombia, Ecuador, El Salvador, Guatemala, Uruguay and Venezuela – but in the second half of the 1980s the exchange rate depreciated substantially, which stimulated the restructuring of the manufacturing sector and the expansion of exports. However, the flourishing of new export activities can be disrupted due to the very success of a credible policy of stabilisation and an early liberalisation of

Table 1.4 Trade liberalisation in selected countries, 1985–92

	Tariff rates (%)[a]		Coverage of NTBs (%)	
	1985	1991–2	1985–7	1991–2
Bolivia	20.0	8.0	25.0	0.0
Chile	36.0	11.0	10.1	0.0
Colombia	83.0	6.7	73.2	1.0
Costa Rica	92.0	16.0	0.8	0.0
Ecuador	50.0	18.0	59.3	n.a.
Guatemala	50.0	19.0	7.4	6.0
Uruguay	32.0	12.0	14.1	0.0
Venezuela	30.0	17.0	44.1	5.0

[a] Tariff rates include tariffs and para-tariffs.
Sources: The World Bank and UNCTAD

Table 1.5 REERs in selected countries, 1980–92 (1980 = 100)

	1983	1984	1985	1986	1987	1988	1989	1990	1991	1992
Bolivia	75.0	57.8	33.7	114.4	118.6	125.0	130.2	154.4	149.5	153.0
Chile	111.8	113.7	141.1	167.0	180.0	192.5	188.1	193.3	187.6	178.0
Colombia	85.2	93.0	106.7	143.2	160.5	166.5	172.7	195.8	189.5	173.5
Costa Rica	118.4	120.5	122.2	135.9	149.8	163.6	157.7	160.8	176.3	173.0
Ecuador	94.3	114.2	110.0	136.6	177.7	236.6	204.5	221.8	211.9	213.2
Guatemala	83.8	83.6	114.7	117.7	121.2	130.7	135.3	163.8	139.3	131.9
Uruguay	130.3	136.0	141.0	143.0	146.4	155.5	148.7	164.7	144.9	134.9
Venezuela	89.6	105.6	110.0	131.7	183.9	164.7	193.7	215.3	201.8	193.0

Source: IDB

the capital account. Return of flight capital and foreign investments may create a new form of overabundance of foreign exchange that may result in a tendency towards overvaluation of the domestic currency.

1.4 CHALLENGES AHEAD

Notwithstanding the significant changes in policies and the great efforts to stimulate and diversify exports, the domestic industrial basis for trade is still weak and the contribution of domestic firms to the manufactured export performance of the countries is relatively small. The chances of a successful new insertion in world markets depend critically on the relationship between government and the private sector, and particularly on the capability of government to create an atmosphere that is conducive to investment in the sectors of tradables. The small and medium-sized countries in Latin America face challenges that require new initiatives by government and the private sector that are vital for a successful industrial transformation in the long term. Here we distinguish six such challenges.

The first of these challenges fits with the Washington agenda: 'getting prices right' is in many cases a precondition for industrial development that has not yet been met and requires further policy changes. Many tariff and NTBs are still in place, domestic price regulations are in force, and market barriers frustrate the entry of newcomers into the market place, particularly of small firms. Moreover, governments are often not capable of establishing exchange-rate regimes that support industry and export diversification in a consistent manner in the longer term. This is particularly true of countries that are heavily dependent on production and export of only one or a few primary products that are potentially vulnerable to Dutch disease.

It should be noted, however, that 'getting prices right' is not identical to government abstinence but may require government interventions for at least three reasons:

(i) to do away with market imperfections created by the private sector and improve the smooth and flexible functioning of markets;
(ii) to support economic activities that create positive external effects, preferably in a first-best manner;
(iii) reduce economic activities that create negative external effects.

Second, private and government investments must be stimulated to generate growth. The Washington agenda emphasises the role of sound macro-economic policies to stimulate investment and the return of flight capital and foreign investors. A statistical analysis including 31 Latin American and Asian countries showed significant relations between changes in the shares of investment, domestic savings and exports in GDP during the 1980s. This indicates that improvement of export performance and strengthening of international competitiveness require stimulation of investment and domestic savings. Domestic savings as a share of GDP are particularly stimulated by high real interest rates (van Dijck, 1992).

During the 1980s both private and public investments declined dramatically and investments in infrastructure and education were delayed and neglected in most countries in the region. Riedel has shown that government capital expenditure and an appropriate macro-economic climate, as reflected by limited government-induced market distortions and an open trade regime, stimulates the rate of return on private investments (Riedel, 1992, p. 62). The World Bank review of best practices of trade policy reform underlines also the importance of government investments that are complementary to private sector investments to strengthen the export sector (Thomas *et al.,* 1991, p. 109). To stimulate private investment, particularly in export sectors, the expectations of the private sector must be in line with the strategy that government envisages. The structural adjustment that accompanies the opening of the economy must be supported politically by the public and by investors and producers in the private sector. The necessary preconditions for this to happen are consistency in government policies, a clear longer-term perspective for economic development, and a strong commitment of government to such long-term objectives. In view of a history of debilitating policies and the limited capabilities of many governments – particularly in the smaller countries – to interact with the private sector and steer the course of development in an efficient manner, this may be a major challenge indeed. In this area there may be important lessons to be learned from the successful east Asian countries which managed to create a reliable and stimulating general atmosphere for industry without incurring the costs to society at large of inefficiency and inward-orientation. It is true that the east Asian developmental states intervened in capital and labour markets as well as the markets for tradables, and 'got prices wrong' on the basis of long-term priorities (van Dijck, 1989 and 1992).

Third, in order to create a competitive edge in international markets, government may have to play an active supporting role well beyond the creation of a supportive macro-economic environment. Development of infrastructure and human capital formation are two major factors in creating a competitive edge in world markets. More specific interventions and types of support for industries with a potential competitive advantage have been considered at the theoretical level and have also been implemented by governments in open and competitive economies such as the so-called miracle economies in east and south-east Asia. However, selective types of intervention may be risky, the costs of failure may be high and the case for pursuing such types of industrial policies is as yet unsettled.

Fourth, new institutions are required for the transformation process to be successful. Haggard has rightly stressed the role of political and other decision-making and facilitating institutions and considers the organisation of the decision-making process key to the success of the east Asian developmental state (Haggard, 1990). Apart from such decision-making bodies, new institutions may be required to facilitate the export drive of domestic firms. There are no *a priori* reasons for government to undertake the establishment of export promotion institutions. Moreover, many government export-promotion organisations have failed, albeit that they had to operate under conditions that hampered rather than stimulated export activities in general (Hogan, *et al.,* 1991, pp. 10–15). Nevertheless, export reconnaissance and marketing institutions may have some of the characteristics of quasi-public goods and may require a government initiative to be created.

Fifth, the social costs of transforming the trade and industrialisation regimes may be high, particularly in the short term. Shockwise liberalisation may result in drastic changes in production and employment opportunities and a steep increase in unemployment. The process of re-allocation requires a high degree of mobility and adaptability of the labour force. Adjustments of the REER may result in wage cuts in real terms and a decline of purchasing power of large segments of the urban population. Additional government interventions may be required to facilitate the transition process and increase the social and political sustainability of the opening of the economy.

Sixth, government involvement may be required to contain the negative external effects of industrial production on the environment. Non-economic arguments for sustainable development stem from concepts such as the intrinsic value of nature. Apart from such arguments there are two economic arguments for government to intervene in the course of industrial development for the sake of environmental protection: welfare and exports. Negative environmental effects of manufacturing production result in a welfare loss, thus reducing the contribution of the sector to overall welfare. Moreover, entrance to third markets, particularly of OECD countries, may be hampered in case exporting countries do not comply with standards pertaining to the environmental impact of products and production processes. Pro-active government initiatives in exporting countries may be required to prevent such environmental standards in importing countries from becoming a new type of NTB to imports in the future.

1.5 ORGANISATION OF THE STUDY

This first chapters of this volume deal with some theoretical aspects of policies to support the transition towards an efficient and export-orientated industrial sector. The role of trade liberalisation, supportive exchange-rates and private and government investments are central topics in the chapters by Linnemann, Visser and FitzGerald (Chapters 2–4). In Chapter 5, Tavares de Araujo Jr reflects upon the meaning of industrial policy over and beyond what has been discussed in the preceding chapters. Weersma-Haworth (Chapter 6) and Dijkstra and Alemán (Chapter 7) then review a highly specific and localised type of export-orientated industrial policy: the export processing free zone (EPFZ).

Chapters 8–10 attempt to put the industrial developments in the small and medium-sized economies in Latin America into a somewhat broader and longer-term perspective. Hofman (Chapter 8) compares the growth performance of groups of countries in Latin America and Asia since 1950 in a growth accounting framework; van der Hoeven and Stewart (Chapter 9) analyse the social dimensions of the process of structural adjustment in Latin America and attempt to assess the contribution of industrial transformation in this particular context; and van Beers (Chapter 10) attempts to assess changes in comparative advantages of Latin American and Asian countries. In the final part of the book, five case studies (Chapters 11–15) have been included on the transformation of the trade and industrialisation regimes in Chile, Uruguay, Venezuela, Costa Rica and Guatemala. The five studies focus, again, on changes in the system of protection, the exchange-rate regimes, and incentives to invest in the export sector. Most of the studies include results of investigations at the firm levels as well, to reveal the specific export barriers that firms face and the inadequacy of supporting institutions.

Finally, Chapter 16 puts together the major findings in a concise way and attempts to draw conclusions that may be of importance for scholars and those involved in the design of trade policies in the future.

Note

1. Part of this chapter is a revised version of van Dijck, 1995.

2 The Gains from Trade Reconsidered

Hans Linnemann

2.1 DEVELOPING COUNTRIES AND THE GAINS FROM TRADE

International trade has a long history, dating back to antiquity. It brought, and brings, gains to those directly involved in it. More important, participation in international trade also brings gains to society at large – though not necessarily to all its individual members. Therefore, the general opinion, of economists and non-economists alike, is: the more trade the better. In policy terms: remove all obstacles to trade, so that it can freely spread and expand its beneficial effects.

Yet government intervention in international trade has a long history as well. Nations traditionally want to have some control, or even a great deal of control, over their international trade. Most ubiquitous are measures of all sorts to restrict imports, but most countries also use an array of instruments to stimulate exports – including financial support for industries that would otherwise not be able to export their products. Such intervention policy would seem to contradict the above notion of the gains to be obtained from free international trade.

This apparent contradiction is due to a host of factors and circumstances that are analysed in detail in the large and ever growing body of literature on international trade. In an 'ideal' and hence rather abstract world, free trade would benefit all nations; however, reality deviates so strongly from the assumptions pertaining to this ideal world that in actual fact trade intervention abounds and trade conflicts regularly occur among nations. Since free trade in the strict sense is a Utopian ideal, and the opposite case of complete autarky an utterly unrealistic proposition, the normative theory of international trade largely focuses on the best use of policy instruments to achieve gains from trade, in terms of national welfare. Given the relevant characteristics of a country's economy, what type of trade policy measures and what intensity of their application will best serve the country's interests in the shorter and in the longer run – keeping in mind the possible reactions of trade partners as well?

18   *The Gains from Trade Reconsidered*

The purpose of this chapter is to review some of the fundamental choices Latin American countries face in the process of trade liberalisation to which they have committed themselves. Within this restriction we have to limit ourselves to the bare essentials. Section 2.2 discusses the concepts of trade liberalisation, trade bias, and export promotion. Section 2.3 focuses on the links between export promotion and export growth, and between export growth and overall economic growth. Finally, Section 2.4 reviews selected aspects of implementing trade-regime changes and tries to formulate some tentative policy guidelines for Latin American countries involved in the process of trade liberalisation.

2.2 LIBERALISATION AND EXPORT PROMOTION

Traditionally, trade liberalisation has been extremely controversial in Latin America, and the trade and industrialisation regimes of most countries in the region were characterised by protection and import substitution policies during a very long period. By the mid 1960s, however, the shortcomings of this trade-policy orientation began to be recognised in broader circles. Several countries tried, for shorter or longer periods, to change over to trade liberalisation but usually reverted fairly soon to the former inward-looking development strategy. It was not until the debt crisis and its aftermath that most countries of Latin America seriously committed themselves to more or less fundamental reforms aiming at liberalisation.

The urgent need to strengthen the region's international competitiveness is now generally acknowledged. To remedy the pervasive balance-of-payments problems calls for liberalisation of imports in order to stimulate exports, an opening-up to capital inflows including foreign direct investment, and a sound exchange-rate policy. This type of measure directly related to the external economic relations of the country concerned should go hand in hand, however, with internal reforms aiming at greater flexibility and efficiency of the economy. All in all, this is a tall order for any government, and in fact for any society; adequate political support will be forthcoming only when the fruits of the inevitably painful adaptation process become noticeable for all in a not too distant future.

This chapter focuses on one element of the larger package of policy adaptations: trade liberalisation as an instrument for export promotion and economic growth. As regards export promotion, it goes without saying that it is in particular the promotion of exports of manufactures that should hold the stage. We need not dwell upon the drawbacks of a strong dependence on exports of a few primary commodities: already in 1950 the (contested) Prebisch-Singer analysis made Latin America aware of the dangers of heavy reliance on primary commodity exports, and subsequent experiences have not been encouraging – apart from the special case of oil-exporting countries, in so far as they did not fall victim to the Dutch disease. The need to diversify the export package into more dynamic product groups, as well as the successes of the Asian NICs, underline the importance of expanding exports of manufactures. Hence the interrelation between trade liberalisation and industrialisation policies.

In the past, Latin American industrialisation policy was tied in closely with the import-substitution policy pursued; in due course, attempts were made to broaden the scope of both policies by regional economic cooperation and integration – with meagre results, however. Decades of import-substitution measures created in virtually all Latin American countries an incentive structure that is strongly biased towards production for the home market and against an export orientation of manufacturing industry. The basic aim of trade liberalisation is to increase international competitiveness by changing the incentive structure; that is, the structure of prices of products as well as of production factors. The underlying notion is that, in order to maximise welfare, factor prices as well as product prices should reflect the 'true' scarcity of the factor or product concerned, and for tradable products this 'true' scarcity is indicated by world market prices. A proper price structure, based on true scarcities, would lead to the proper production and investment decisions.

The term 'incentive structure' is of crucial importance in distinguishing between trade regimes, and requires further clarification. To keep things simple, let us assume for the moment that production factor prices are the same for all industries, so that in the analysis only product prices matter. For producers of a tradable commodity, the alternatives are selling on the home market or on the world market. If producers would be indifferent as to their sales market, the trade regime would be neutral – that is, not biased for or against exports. One dollar's worth of exports would bring, against the prevailing exchange rate, the producer exactly the same earnings in local currency as one dollar's worth 'not-imported', that is, sold in the domestic market at the same price as an identical imported commodity would fetch. To the producer, the effective exchange rate for exports (EERex) would be the same as that for imports (EERim). How are these effective exchange rates defined (see Bhagwati, 1978 and 1990)?

EERex represents the local currency proceeds of one dollar export value plus any additional producer earnings (per dollar) in the form of subsidies, tax rebates, preferential credit facilities, and so on arising from export-promoting government regulations. Similarly, EERim represents the local sales price per dollar import costs – that is, the local currency parity plus import duties, other border charges and possibly a premium or rent element due to non-tariff barriers such as quantitative restrictions. If EERex > EERim, the trade regime for the commodity concerned has a pro-export bias; in the much more common case of EERex < EERim, the effective exchange rate comparison favours import substitution and the trade regime shows an anti-export bias. Assuming a single exchange rate for all foreign trade, under the neutral trade regime the above-mentioned 'plusses' in case of export are equal to the 'plusses' in the import-substitution case; in the particular situation that all 'plusses' are absent for both exports and imports – that is, when they are all zero – we have a free-trade regime, which is, of course, at the same time a neutral regime.

Note that the effective exchange rates EERex and EERim are compared at the product level: the incentive structure may for one product show an anti-export bias and for another a pro-export bias. When for most tradable products an anti-export bias exists, as is generally true for most of Latin America, a country's overall incentive structure may be characterised as an anti-export trade regime, but even in that case there may well be some products for which the incentive structure is neutral or pro-export biased. When on average EERex < EERim, and especially when EERex << EERim, a country clearly follows an import-substitution strategy. When on average the two EERs are about equal (showing a discrepancy of no more than, say, 5 per cent) the trade regime is neutral. Yet, according to Bhagwati (1990, p. 18), the literature on the subject usually refers to this constellation already as an export-promoting trade strategy, which it is, in fact, only when compared to the common situation in developing countries where import substitution is the rule. The rare cases of an average incentive structure EERex > EERim might then be labelled as an ultra-export-promoting strategy.[1]

How does the popular term 'trade liberalisation' fit into this picture? Liberalisation refers to doing away with regulations, and in the post-war period in the countries of Western Europe the term indicated in particular the elimination of administrative controls such as import licences and foreign exchange allocations. Only after the strongly binding NTBs had been abolished or considerably lowered, did the reduction of tariff levels also come to be the object of trade liberalisation. There are good reasons for this sequence, as we shall see below. Trade liberalisation is best understood as a relative concept: it is a policy of reducing government interference with foreign trade, and imports in particular, without necessarily eliminating all intervention.[2] It indicates a regime change in the direction of free trade, but not necessarily free trade itself. In a situation of strong protectionism, as in most developing countries, trade liberalisation shifts the regime in the direction of export promotion. Note, however, that a shift towards an export-promoting trade strategy does not, in theory, require a move towards trade liberalisation; as the above discussion of the effective exchange rates has shown, government intervention at the export side in the form of export subsidies and the like (raising EER_{ex}) may in principle achieve the same objective. Thus, analytically the issue of the extent of government intervention in trade can be separated from that of the degree of inward or outward orientation of the incentive structure. In actual practice, however, it may not be realistic to see them as completely unrelated.

Let us take a closer look at our earlier analysis of the incentives for producers centred around the concept of the EER, and pay attention to the role of government in all this. The characteristics and limitations of the effective exchange rates as indicators of the direction of bias in the trade regime have to be spelled out in some detail.

(i) EER_{ex} and EER_{im} as defined above are so-called nominal EERs that determine the producer's decision to sell his product abroad or at home; the word 'nominal' indicates that the EERs relate to gross output rather than value added. When investment in new production capacity is considered, EERs must be compared between products and therefore have to be computed on the basis of value added because of differences in input requirements between products.

(ii) We assumed that one exchange rate is used for both exports and imports. In the case of multiple exchange rates, obviously the relevant rate has to be applied, and similarly a bonus has to be taken into account (one of the 'plusses' on the export side) if part of the foreign currency earned accrues directly to the exporter and yields him a premium. Note that a devaluation of the currency in the first instance equally stimulates export production and import-substitution production, as both become more profitable compared to the production of non-tradables. Depending on the actual input coefficients and demand-side reactions, export incentives may ultimately increase most.

(iii) As regards the incentives for home-market production, particular attention should be given to quantitative restrictions and other NTBs creating a rent income for producers. Its magnitude may not be determined easily, but it is certainly easily earned. Lobbying to keep competing imports low, if necessary combined with

22   *The Gains from Trade Reconsidered*

bribery and other corruptive practices, is an example of directly unproductive activities (Bhagwati, 1982) induced by administrative controls over trade that are unfortunately all too common to be disregarded.

(iv) In comparing the producer's incentive structure for exports versus home-market production, only the immediate financial gains were referred to. This is a simplification, as less tangible considerations may play a role as well. In the present context they are relevant only inasmuch as they would affect the choice between the export and home market. The element of risk involved in opting for one or the other market should be mentioned in particular, as well as the existence or not of government guarantee schemes for export trade.

(v) It should be borne in mind that an EER-based analysis focuses on the incentive structure for private enterprise decisions. This focus is fully warranted in view of the usually preponderant role of the private sector in investment and production decisions. For a few particular industries or enterprises broader national policy goals may make it desirable to maintain (stronger) protection, possibly in the form of state ownership, in spite of a regime switch towards liberalisation. Note also that such a regime switch affects the government budget, particularly so in countries still relying heavily on trade taxes: a lowering of import duties and export taxes and an increase in export subsidies both enlarge the government deficit.[3]

Our short survey of the effective exchange rates for export and import activities as the key variables determining the type of trade regime should not obscure the fact that trade policy measures alone, however appropriate in themselves, will not be adequate to solve the (external) economic problems faced by most Latin American countries. They have to be part and parcel of a much broader policy reorientation including the areas of public finance, monetary stability and national savings. The important role of exchange-rate policy, in its own right and as an export-stimulating mechanism, is dealt with separately by Visser in Chapter 3. It is tempting to go a step further, beyond economics, and to discuss the role of the state in Latin America (see Fishlow, 1990) and to stress the fundamental importance of strengthening in Latin culture the civic community that generates patterns of social co-operation based on trust, tolerance, and widespread norms of active citizen participation instead of autocratic patron-client politics (see Putnam *et al.*, 1993). However, such topics would take us way beyond the theme of this chapter.

2.3 EXPORT PROMOTION AND ECONOMIC GROWTH

A policy of trade liberalisation may vary in extent and intensity, but its primary aim is always the same: to increase the efficiency and competitiveness of the economy and to promote export growth. Stronger growth in exports – in particular of non-traditional exports, that is, manufactures – is first of all required for solving the perennial balance-of-payments problems; moreover, stronger export growth is widely believed to result in stronger overall economic growth. In the literature on the subject these issues are usually discussed as two separate questions: (i) how, and to what extent, does trade liberalisation lead to export growth, and (ii) how, and to what extent, does export growth lead to overall economic growth?[4] We shall address the questions in this order.

Liberalisation of foreign trade is first and foremost a lowering of import barriers of all sorts, as these barriers are much more important than any export barriers. Consequently, the immediate effect is an increase in imports and a fall in the domestic sales prices of import-substituting industries. As exports are initially hardly affected, the trade deficit would increase instead of decrease. To prevent a worsening of the balance of trade, liberalisation measures of some significance will necessarily have to go hand in hand with a real devaluation of the national currency.[5] Suppose, for example, that the change in the real exchange-rate exactly offsets the price decrease of importables that would result from the lowering of import barriers so that in the domestic market import products do not change in price; EERim would remain unchanged but EERex would improve as a consequence of the real devaluation, thus making export production more attractive as compared to home market production. This example is an extreme case, inasmuch as the real exchange-rate adaptation need not be fully 'offsetting' for the EER to change in favour of exports, nor for the net effect of the regime change on the balance of trade to be positive.

Yet, trade policy cannot rely on an 'automatic' link between a lowering of import barriers plus real devaluation – as liberalisation measures – and a rapid increase in exports as a guaranteed consequence. Referring to the experience of the Asian NICs, Sachs (1987b) stresses the need for active government involvement in promoting exports, and wonders whether import liberalisation is in fact a required component of an outward-orientated trade regime; in Section 2.2 above we made the same observation. Helleiner has expressed similar doubts, and argued that a certain threshold level of development surpassing that of, say, sub-Saharan Africa must have been reached before export promotion policies will work

(Helleiner, 1986; see also Tyler, 1981) and that, moreover, world market conditions must be favourable at the time of the regime switch (Helleiner, 1990). Edwards (1989a, 1993) illustrates the same point by comparing the experiences of South Korea and Chile: Korea's decades of fast export growth were based on a gradual lowering of import barriers with substantial government support for export activities until about 1983, whereas Chile enforced a drastic liberalisation between 1975 and 1979, including the elimination of virtually all government intervention in foreign trade. He concludes that 'the Chilean experience of that period became one of ultra trade liberalisation without export promotion' (Edwards 1989a, p. 181). The export successes of Chile only came nearly a decade later, when in the second half of the 1980s world trade propitiously expanded.

An accurate comparison of country experiences with trade liberalisation remains fraught with tremendous difficulties, as the specifics of the policy adaptations and the details of the economic constellation both internally and externally may and will vary considerably.[6] A tentative conclusion might read as follows. Trade liberalisation, in the sense of lower and more uniform import barriers and in the form of tariffs rather than non-tariff measures, improves in due course a country's competitiveness and export performance, provided that it is accompanied by devaluation, low inflation, well-focused export-promoting government policies, and elimination of domestic distortions and rigidities – and all this under relatively favourable world market demand conditions. Even if all these provisos are satisfied, economics cannot indicate the optimal level of tariffs and government support for exports: the direction of the desirable regime change may be clear, but about the speed and intensity of change the profession's views diverge.

What about the second issue referred to above, the link between export growth and overall GDP growth? Can a stronger, more firm conclusion be reached in this area? Theoretical arguments make this plausible: obviously, export production directly contributes to GDP itself, but additionally it has a number of indirect effects that are equally if not more important. Export sectors are under constant pressure to maintain and improve productivity, they accumulate knowledge about world market outlets and technological developments in foreign countries, they generate the foreign exchange needed to obtain essential inputs in other industries and to import new technologies, they train through learning-by-doing an efficient and alert labour force and this may have spread effects on other industries, and they may exploit economies of scale unattainable for purely domestic industries and thus attract foreign private capital.

To verify empirically the validity of such arguments a host of studies has been undertaken in the last two decades.[7] Initially, most of these studies followed a very simple approach: for a sample of LDCs the average GDP growth rate over a certain period was regressed on the export growth rate over that period, and these cross-section regressions generally showed a positive and significant relation between exports and GDP growth. Later studies were somewhat more refined, differentiating between primary and manufactures exports, between favourable and unfavourable demand conditions, between different time periods and regions, and between exports to North and to South. Some studies used regressions based on annual changes rather than period averages, others introduced additional variables such as a (crudely assessed) degree of inward or outward orientation of the economy.

Only a few findings will be summarily reported here. Following a Feder-type model and using annual observations for the periods 1973–9 and 1980–5, van Beers (1991) relates the overall growth rates to the investment rate, the growth rate of the labour force and the growth rate of exports, for a group of 11 Asian and a group of 9 Latin American countries separately. For both periods as well as for the two periods combined all parameter estimates for export growth are positive, but whereas the Asian estimates are statistically significant, those for the Latin American group are not significantly different from zero. Kavoussi (1985) was the first to refine the analysis by distinguishing different sources of export growth; he found that strong world market demand is a major factor – if not a prerequisite – for a positive link between export growth and GDP growth, and subsequent studies (for example, Singer and Gray, 1988) confirmed this finding. Jung and Marshall (1985), and several researchers after them, tested the relation between export growth and GDP growth on Granger causality, and concluded that frequently the direction of causality could not be firmly established.

All in all, one may safely conclude that straightforward Ordinary Least Squares analysis of GDP growth explained by a production function augmented with some export growth variable(s) does not solve the issue. Two more recent approaches hold the promise of bringing us further, eventually. Esfahani (1991) broadened the underlying model by incorporating in it the role of imports (of intermediates in particular). Three equations are introduced and estimated, describing the interaction between production, exports and imports. He finds that export growth contributes to overall growth by relaxing the import constraint that LDC production frequently faces, and he does not find evidence of any externality effects of exports. An improvement in the econometric techniques thus far employed is made by Khan and Saqib (1993) who deal with the simultaneity between export and overall growth by using the Three-Stage Least Squares technique in estimating the parameters of a system of three simultaneous equations (augmented production function, export supply and export demand functions) from 1972–88 time series data for Pakistan. They find a strong association between export performance and GDP growth, with overwhelmingly indirect effects of exports on economic growth.

In spite of their opposite findings, the last two studies have one message in common: broader and technically more sophisticated analysis is needed to address properly the issue at stake. And it may well be that differences in economic structure, economic order and development level between LDCs are so varied and extensive that a comparative analysis of performance requires much more than a few cross-section estimates.[8] For the time being, our overall conclusion on the link between export growth and GDP growth can only be a very tentative and rather vague one: it is doubtful whether, unconditionally, exports should be seen as an actual or potential 'engine' of growth for each and every LDC,[9] and it is more befitting to see trade as a 'handmaiden' of growth, with in particular exports of manufactures as a valuable channel for strengthening the interaction with the world economy and as a means of financing the imports needed for sustained expansion and development.

2.4 IMPLEMENTING TRADE POLICY REFORM

The tenor of the preceding section was to emphasise that for countries beset with development problems trade liberalisation is not the magic key to a flourishing and rapidly expanding economy – in spite of the songs of praise often raised in international gatherings. In the complex reality of this world there are hardly any magic keys, and this applies also to overcoming economic development obstacles. However, this does not mean that trade liberalisation is an irrelevant issue or an undesirable course of action. The often contestable and inconclusive results obtained thus far in empirical studies on the trade-growth linkage are at least partly due to inadequacies and oversimplifications in the analyses; as we have seen, trade policy measures should form part of a broader set of policy changes in order to be effective, and export growth does not only depend on the trade policy pursued. For most LDCs, a policy change lowering the anti-trade bias in the incentive structure (though not necessarily 'free trade') would seem to be indicated; if there is one fact that the past record of countries tells us, it is that strongly protectionist countries have not been among the fast-growing LDCs.

It is not surprising that nowadays most of Latin America has committed itself to greater openness to trade. According to IMF data, it has been the only developing continent that experienced in the post-war decades a dramatically declining foreign trade ratio. The ratio of exports plus imports to regional GDP stood at over 28 per cent in 1959–60, and has gone down to 18 per cent in 1986–7. The corresponding figures for the other extreme, Asia, are 15 and 56 per cent, respectively (Linnemann, 1993a, p. 130). If in the past decades one region has denied itself the gains from trade, it has been Latin America. Policy-makers in the region now have come to realise this fact.

How should a regime change towards trade liberalisation be effectuated? As observed before in this chapter, such a programme will in its specifics strongly depend on the particulars of the country concerned, and one should be careful not to recommend a standard recipe. The points listed below are therefore of necessity formulated in very general terms and should even then not be interpreted as the one and only road to economic salvation. They may be seen as a sort of check list, of use both in designing trade policy reforms and in analysing a country's actual liberalisation measures. Some of these points have been referred to already in the above, others are added here.

(i) Trade liberalisation aims at increasing the international competitiveness of the economy. This can be realised only if at the same time domestic rigidities and imbalances are significantly reduced, which calls for a sound macro-economic policy and perhaps even institutional changes.

(ii) In this context it is of particular importance to establish and maintain a realistic and uniform exchange rate.

(iii) Liberalisation of international capital movements should preferably not precede but instead should follow, in due course, liberalisation of trade – in order to avoid disturbing effects of the rather volatile financial markets.

(iv) In the area of trade restrictions themselves, priority should be given to the elimination of all NTBs by replacing them by (more or less) equivalent tariff measures, in order to suppress rent-seeking activities and to create greater transparency of the impact of import restrictions.

(v) Subsequently, the import tariff structure has to be greatly simplified by bringing the highest and higher tariff rates down to a common level per type of end use, with intermediates and capital goods having a lower common tariff level than consumer goods. Uniformity of protection levels is of importance in order to reduce the extent of distortions in the domestic price structure.

(vi) Even the lower level of import duties still introduces, or rather maintains, an anti-export bias in the incentive structure. Hence, export promotion measures are needed to shift the trade regime (on an average) more towards neutrality or a pro-export bias. Such measures have to be focused on selected manufacturing industries, and should also have a maximum of transparency in order to avoid abuse through favouritism and discretionary policy-making.

(vii) Selection of the manufacturing sectors to be promoted, and of the means to do so, is obviously both difficult and of key importance. The potential for developing comparative advantage is the decisive criterion. A useful entry for such analysis would seem to be the classification of industries on the basis of the primary factors determining the competitive process in the distinct sectors, using, for example, the OECD (1987) classification into five product groups: resource-intensive, labour-intensive, scale-intensive, differentiated (that is, tailored to highly varied demand characteristics), and science-based. Given a country's (potential) resources and location, such analysis would quickly narrow down the options.

(viii) In facilitating imports and stimulating exports, the developmental need of fostering modern technology, technical know-how, and innovation has to be borne in mind – a factor stressed of late in endogenous growth theory (Lucas, 1988).

(ix) As stated earlier, and as recognised in the above points, trade liberalisation and export promotion do not require a policy shift towards free trade. The role of government in the form of discretionary intervention should indeed be reduced, and import barriers lowered, but consistent and transparent policies of export support may fit quite well in the new trade regime, thus combining import substitution with export promotion.[10] At lower levels of overall development, import substitution will most probably dominate, whereas beyond a 'threshold level' export promotion will gain in weight. In economically small countries, such as those of Central America and the Caribbean, the limits of sensible import substitution are reached sooner than in large countries with a more sizeable domestic market; this also implies that small countries are well-advised not to move too far away from a free-trade regime.

(x) Greater openness to trade may also be aimed at by discriminatory liberalisation such as in free-trade areas or customs unions, rather than at the global level. Yet, in view of the modest record of earlier attempts in this direction, including those in the Latin American region, and in view of the minor extent of such intra-regional trade today, a regime change should be implemented with respect to all foreign trade in order to be effective. Regional co-operation and integration schemes – for example, among the Central American countries or among the Caribbean countries – could be a useful complement but not a substitute. Trade liberalisation between all LDCs – covering all South-South trade and thus in principle carrying greater weight – is at this moment not more than a remote possibility in a distant future (Linnemann, 1993b).

The above list of implementation issues does not pretend to be exhaustive. Some questions of great importance remain unanswered, either due to ignorance or due to strong dependence on the country-specific situation. For instance, opinions differ widely regarding the speed and intensity of implementation: should a one-shot 'shock treatment' be practiced, or a step-wise regime adaptation according to a fixed time schedule? The reforming government should firmly and unequivocally commit itself to the implementation, whether all-at-once or phased, but what is it to do in the face of large-scale civil unrest because of initially increasing unemployment in domestic-market industries? Is the World Bank staff assertion that 'trade reforms are successful if they are bold and extensive' (Alam and Rajapatirana, 1993, p. 47) truly justified as a general rule? International institutions advocating the case of trade liberalisation have been slow in paying attention to either transitional or long-term employment effects. In this and other areas uncertainty still prevails.

Our last remark is therefore a reiteration of the need for more detailed analysis of individual countries, both in terms of their actual economic structure and institutions, and as regards their historical experiences in the area of trade policy and policy changes. This type of work is done, *inter alia*, in this volume for a sample of Latin American countries. It is through these and similar country-specific studies that we may hope to find answers to the open questions. The success of trade reforms would seem to depend first of all on a careful and solid analysis of the economic, social and political facts regarding the country concerned; the boldness and extent of the desirable regime changes must ultimately be decided upon only in the particular context of each country.

Notes

1. Referring to 'the average incentive structure' is somewhat inadequate, as an average obfuscates the variations in EER that may exist between products and sectors. Liang (1992) suggests a typology of trade strategies based on sector-wise trade incentives and disincentives.
2. For a concise overview of different interpretations of the term 'trade liberalisation', see Edwards, 1993, pp. 1364–5.

3. In Fishlow's view, in Latin American development problems the lack of budgetary balance is even the core issue: 'The principal problem confronted by the countries of the region is a fiscal shortfall, not massive inefficiency resulting from misallocation of resources' (Fishlow, 1990, p. 62).
4. Of the few studies not following this two-step approach, we mention here the cross-section analyses of Heitger (1987) and Edwards (1992) that try to relate economic growth directly to trade orientation. Note, however, that developing an overall index of 'trade orientation' is not an easy job. Edwards gives no fewer than nine alternatives.
5. A nominal devaluation results in a real devaluation to the extent that domestic prices of non-tradables are kept constant. In actual practice, at least some erosion of the nominal devaluation is likely to occur.
6. Major trade-policy studies based on comparative country experiences are Bhagwati (1978), Krueger (1978), Michaely *et al.* (1991), and in the context of debt and adjustment, Sachs (ed.) (1989). In all of these studies several Latin American countries are included. Congdon (1990) and Alam and Rajapatirana (1993) focus on this region.
7. References to some twenty-five empirical analyses are given in Linnemann (1993a). See also Greenaway and Reed (1990) and Edwards (1993).
8. Several authors have stressed recently that in-depth country analysis, with much more attention to the microeconomics behind the trade-growth links, is likely to be a more fruitful approach for future research than cross-country regressions; see Havrylyshyn (1990) and Edwards (1993). A recent growth analysis by Knight *et al.* (1993) combines cross-section and time series analyses in a panel data approach that takes country-specific effects into account. On future research lines, see also Tybout (1992).
9. Apart from the analytical findings briefly discussed above, export pessimism may be based on protectionist trends in the industrialised countries and on the so-called 'fallacy of composition' argument introduced by Cline (1982). For an example of this pessimistic view see Athukorala (1989), and for an optimistic stance see Bhagwati (1990).
10. See also Krugman (1984), with the provocative title 'Import Substitution as Export Promotion'. Note that his analysis presupposes a relatively large domestic market.

3 The Exchange Rate as an Export-Stimulation Mechanism
Hans Visser

3.1 AIMS OF EXCHANGE-RATE POLICIES

For governments there is no getting around the need to follow an exchange-rate policy. First, a decision has to be made on which system to adopt: a fixed-rate (for all practical purposes a fixed-but-adjustable peg) system, a fully-floating rate system, or something in between, such as a predetermined crawling peg or tablita system. Second, in a fixed-rate system some level of the exchange rate must be chosen and in a floating-rate system a choice must be made between fully free-floating and 'dirty' floating. The choice depends on a government's policy aims and on the economic environment.

Broadly speaking, one of two policy aims will take precedence: (i) the repression of inflation or (ii) export promotion. The exchange rate can be used as a nominal anchor as needed to fix prices in a monetary economy, or to attain real targets (Corden, 1993). Other, less respectable aims may motivate governments in actual practice. In cases where there is no full convertibility – that is, where economic agents are not free to buy and sell any amount of foreign exchange they wish in official markets or at the official exchange rate – governments have an opportunity to confer favours on groups whose allegiance they seek for their survival, or the ruling groups may simply themselves appropriate the rents created by restricting access to the foreign-exchange market. Such behaviour may take various forms. There may be one official exchange rate at which there is excess demand or there may be a multiple-rate system in force. Permits to buy foreign exchange or to buy foreign exchange at a favourable rate are valuable and can be used to distribute favours or to siphon off rents. Here we shall focus on the two policy aims first mentioned, but one should be aware that the world is a wicked place. Inconvertibility creates rents and these rents elicit morally reprehensible behaviour which, even worse in the eyes of some, is at odds with allocational efficiency and is one reason for preferring full convertibility.

Repression of inflation

It was the professed aim of the Southern Cone governments in the second half of the 1970s to fight inflation with the help of the exchange rate. Apart from Chile and Uruguay, a very serious attempt was made in Argentina by Minister of Finance José Martínez de Hoz in the years 1976–80. This attempt failed for a number of reasons (see Calvo, 1986, and Corbo and de Melo, 1987).

Attempts to utilise the rate of exchange to fight inflation rest on the assumption that the law of one price is approximately valid. For small countries, this fits in with the dependent-economy model. In this model, the law of one price applies to tradables, for which the country in question is a price-taker. Foreign-currency prices of tradables are given and the way to keep domestic price rises of tradables in check is to link the domestic currency firmly to a foreign currency. The logic is impeccable, provided the dependent-economy model is relevant, but for such a policy to succeed, domestic monetary and fiscal policies must be not too expansionary. The exchange rate in itself is clearly insufficient to contain inflationary pressure (see Dornbusch and Fischer, 1993). In Section 3.2 the relevant model will be presented.

Export promotion

If the aim of exchange-rate policy is to increase exports and improve the current account of the balance of payments, a high real exchange rate is called for. We define the exchange rate e as the price of one unit of foreign currency expressed in units of domestic currency. The real exchange rate, RER, is the nominal exchange rate adjusted for the ratio of foreign and domestic price levels: $RER = e.P_f/P_d$ (RER is a dimensionless variable in this definition; under purchasing power parity it equals unity). In the literature the reciprocal of RER as defined here has often been used, but with our definition of e the present definition of RER appears logical: a rise in e means that foreign currency becomes more expensive relative to the domestic currency, and a rise in RER means that foreign goods become more expensive relative to domestic goods. In the framework of the dependent-economy model another definition of RER is also used. RER as defined above implies an improvement of the competitiveness of domestic goods in world markets as RER rises, but in dependent-economy models the law of one price holds and similar goods have similar prices on all markets: price competition has no place in the model. Instead, in dependent-economy models RER is defined as the ratio between tradables prices P_t and non-tradables prices P_n (or its obverse). A rise in RER means that producing export goods or import-competing goods becomes more attractive to domestic producers. Here we shall use RER in the first sense. If export promotion is the driving force of exchange-rate policy, the dependent-economy model is not the only one that presents itself. In that case, one need not believe that the law of one price is a good approximation to reality. The tried and trusty IS-LM model, where prices and wages are sticky, could serve as well. For the sake of brevity, though, we shall remain within the confines of the dependent-economy model.

The economic environment and the choice of exchange rates

We have mentioned the economic environment as one factor determining the choice of exchange-rate system. This concerns the choice between some form of fixed-rate system and a more flexible-rate system. Pegging one's currency to another currency may be an attractive option if there is a dominant trading partner, especially if the currency of that country is not subject to a serious fall in purchasing power – that is, if inflation is low. If international trade is more evenly spread over a number of countries whose exchange rates are not fixed, stabilisation of the domestic currency in terms of a basket of other currencies may be the preferred option. If, however, the main export product is a commodity with a widely fluctuating world market price and consequently export revenues fluctuate strongly, a floating rate may be called for in order to provide some protection to the domestic market against external shocks. Export receipts will fluctuate less wildly in terms of domestic currency if buoyant exports imply a low exchange rate and a depressed market leads to a high exchange rate. This helps provide a modicum of stabilisation to nominal national income and may also help to adjust imports, which is especially important if foreign exchange reserves or credit lines are insufficient to bridge a significant fall in export revenues, even if it were only temporary. Generally, however, even if a stable nominal exchange rate is not feasible, a stable RER is certainly called for. With a fluctuating RER, exporters have less incentive to establish sales networks abroad and exports will suffer, most of all those of manufactures.

3.2 THE DEPENDENT-ECONOMY MODEL

We shall present a succinct graphical exposition of the dependent-economy model. This model can of course be depicted with the help of the

Salter diagram. However, a different kind of diagram offers the opportunity to depict not only the equilibrium conditions in both good markets, but also explicitly the equilibrium condition in the Walrasian money market. A graphical analysis will suffice for an understanding of the working of the system. (For the algebra, see Frenkel and Mussa, 1985.)

The fixed-rate case

We start with the fixed-rate case. The model is depicted in Figure 3.1. *NN* shows the equilibrium condition in the market for non-tradables. As the money supply increases people feel richer and spend more. Starting from equilibrium, excess demand will develop in the non-tradables market. In order to maintain equilibrium, the relative price q of non-tradables has to rise. A rise in q causes a shift in production from tradables to non-tradables and a shift in consumption from non-tradables to tradables, thus eliminating excess demand. Hence, *NN* has a positive slope. Similarly, an increase in the money supply will, starting from equilibrium, cause excess demand in the market for tradables. The relative price of tradables has to rise – that is, q has to fall – in order to restore equilibrium. *TT* is negatively sloped. A fall in q will set in train a shift in consumption away from tradables and a shift in production towards tradables. If the price mechanism functions smoothly, the economy is always on the *NN* curve – that is, the market for

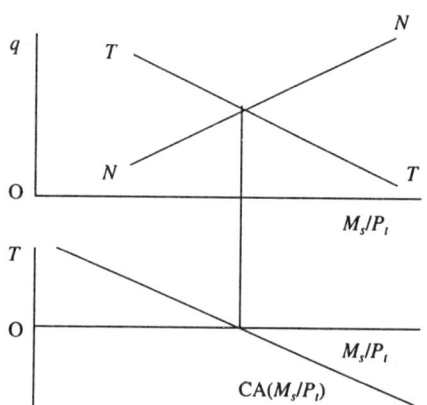

Figure 3.1 Equilibrium situation in the dependent economy under fixed exchange rates
Note: $q = P_n/P_t$, M_s = money supply,
CA = current account.

non-tradables is always in equilibrium. There may, however, be disequilibria in the market for tradables. A disequilibrium in the market for tradables is just another term for a current-account disequilibrium, neglecting international factor payments. Current-account equilibrium is found at the intersection of the *TT* curve and the *NN* curve. Note that the situation of the *NN* and *TT* curves depends on both private and public spending propensities.

Now consider an inflationary financed increase in government spending on non-tradables. The *NN* curve will shift upward, for at any level of the money supply a higher relative price of non-tradables will be necessary to ensure equilibrium in the non-tradables market. Government spending has increased and, as can be seen from the figure, the money supply has to fall in order to prevent overspending. Private expenditure is reduced in this way. Consequently, current-account equilibrium is also found at a lower level of the money supply – that is, the *CA* curve shifts to the left. However, inflationary finance means that the money supply has risen rather than fallen. Over and above the upward shift of the *NN* curve, there has been a movement to the right along the *NN* curve; q has risen too much and must fall again for equilibrium to be restored. Abstracting from net international capital flows, an automatic stabiliser is at work. The current account turns into deficit and, in the absence of net capital flows, the money supply decreases. If all goes well, the economy starts sliding down the *NN* curve towards the intersection with the *TT* curve. Two conditions must be met, though, for such an automatic restoration of equilibrium to occur. First, money creation must stop. Second, we assumed price flexibility. Given tradables price P_t, q can only fall if P_n falls. If the prices of non-tradables exhibit downward stickiness, unemployment will develop in the non-tradables market. In that case, the nominal exchange rate can be utilised as an instrument to increase the real exchange rate. The real exchange rate has fallen, but has to rise in order to restore equilibrium. This can be brought about by a devaluation. Such a devaluation will immediately reduce the real money supply (that is, in the model the money supply in terms of tradables) and so reduce spending. If net capital inflow occurs, the adjustment may be postponed, but subsequently an even higher fall in q may be necessary in order to create a surplus on the goods and services account, enabling interest and amortisation to be paid. The economy now has to move to the left of the intersection of *NN* and *TT*.

For the floating-rate case, the diagram differs slightly. The money supply is independent of the balance of payments. We drop the *CA* segment in the diagram and add a segment picturing the equilibrium condition in the Walrasian money market, in the process restricting the transmission mechanisms between the monetary and the real sectors of the economy to the interest rate mechanism (see Figure 3.2). In the absence of net capital flows, the economy must be at the intersection of the *NN* and *TT* curves, if the price mechanism functions properly. With net capital flows, the economy must still be on the *NN* curve, but it need not be on the *TT* curve, as net capital flows compensate any disequilibrium on the current account. Consider the case of fully interest-elastic capital flows (Figure 3.3). In the case of capital imports the current account will be in deficit and the relative price of tradables will be lower than in current account equilibrium. In other words, there is an excess demand for tradables which translates into an import surplus.

In the short term, capital is sector specific. An increase in spending on non-tradables will draw labour away from the production of tradables. The marginal product of labour falls in the non-tradables industry, but the relative price of non-tradables will rise to enable the non-tradables industries to match wages in the tradables industries, which have risen in terms of tradables because of increased marginal product of labour. It stands to reason that, if real wages are sticky downward in terms of non-tradables, unemployment results. If for some reason capital inflow dries up – as was generally the case in Latin America in 1982[1] – the relative price of tradables will have to rise and real balances will have to fall in order to maintain full employment in both the tradables and the non-tradables sectors. Production has to shift to tradables because import surpluses are no longer financed by capital imports and real balances have to fall because

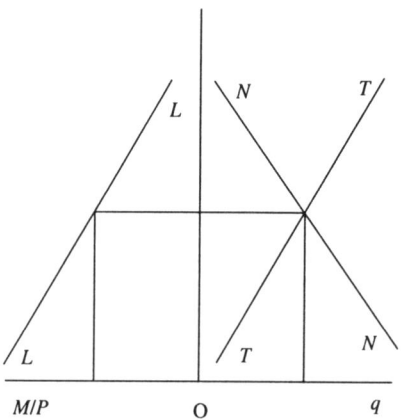

Figure 3.2 The dependent-economy model with free-floating exchange rates

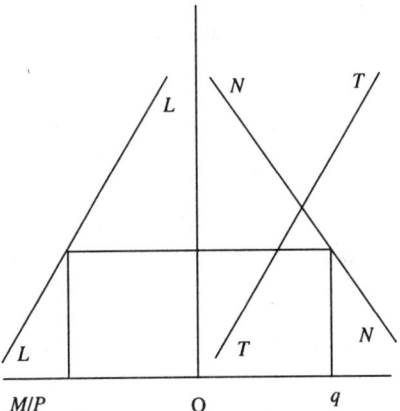

Figure 3.3 Capital imports in a dependent economy with floating exchange rate

non-tradables have to become relatively cheaper, and excess demand for non-tradables must be prevented. It will even be necessary to create an excess supply of tradables in order to fulfil debt-service obligations, which implies an even further fall of the relative price of non-tradables. Unemployment will result if real wages exhibit downward stickiness in terms of tradables. Obviously, the relative price of non-tradables cannot easily be reduced through an absolute price fall, so the common solution to the problem will be to let the exchange rate rise. Tradables become more expensive and the average price level increases, which serves to diminish real balances, as is required for maintaining equilibrium in the non-tradables market. Note that in the long term relative prices need a smaller change in order to bring about the desired change in production proportions, since factor mobility is a function of time (see Hoffmann and Homburg, 1990). If labour is sector-specific, there is no way at all to avoid unemployment.

Again, the success of the adjustment process hinges on monetary and fiscal policies being restrictive. Too expansive monetary policies would lead to continuous price increases and depreciations of the domestic currency. With respect to fiscal policy, a distinction should be made between government spending on tradables and non-tradables. In both cases, increased spending means an upward shift of the relevant curve. An increase in spending on tradables makes the *TT* curve shift upward, which leads to a higher rate of interest and, given the money supply, a higher price level. The relative price of tradables increases, which in this case can only mean that the absolute price of tradables rises. This amounts to a depreciation of the currency. An increase in government spending on non-tradables has less clear-cut results. The *NN* curve shifts upwards, the relative price of non-tradables rises and the general price level goes up again. These two movements are compatible with higher, lower and constant tradable prices, so the exchange rate may stay put or move in any direction. With fully interest-elastic capital flows, an increase in government spending leaves the rate of interest and the general price level undisturbed, given the money demand function. Higher spending results in an excess demand for tradables and a deficit on the current account which is financed by capital import.

A spending shock in the non-tradables market again does not influence the rate of interest or the general price level. Production has to shift from tradables to non-tradables, which is dependent on a rise in the relative price of non-tradables. The relative price of non-tradables can only increase, given the average price level, if absolute non-tradable prices increase and absolute tradable prices fall. This means an appreciation of the currency. The relative price of non-tradables moves beyond the point where the market for tradables is in equilibrium. Tradable prices are too low for equilibrium and, again, excess demand develops. Note that government spending shocks are assumed to be neutrally financed, for the money supply remains unchanged. An increase in private spending propensities will have similar results. If capital inflows dries up, not only restrictive monetary policies, but also restrictive fiscal policies, will help maintain full employment during the drastic adjustment to a situation with an excess supply of tradables rather than excess demand. A cutback in spending on tradables will help sustain the exchange rate, a cutback in spending on non-tradables will be accompanied by a depreciation.

A three-good economy

The dependent economy model can be extended by distinguishing two types of tradables: importables and exportables. Importables are produced domestically and imported, and exportables are produced domestically and sold in domestic and foreign markets. We stay within the framework of the dependent-economy model (see Aghevli *et al.*, 1991; for a three-goods, two-factor model using an Edgeworth-Bowley box diagram see Edwards, 1986a). For a small country, world market prices of importables and exportables are given but need not remain unchanged. Consequently, the commodity terms of trade may change. The model can be utilised to analyse a number of problems. Consider a reduction in import duties:

prices of importables fall, excess demand develops in the importables market and so does excess supply in the exportables and non-tradables markets. The excess supply in the exportables sector helps to finance increased imports. To restore equilibrium in the non-tradables market, a relative price reduction for tradables is necessary. As absolute price decreases are painful, this means a depreciation of the currency.

Sector-specificity of production factors may, again, complicate the adjustment process (see Nowak, 1989, pp. 49–52). A reduction in protection will make importables cheaper relative to exportables and non-tradables. Labour will switch to exportables and non-tradables. The marginal product of labour in terms of exportables and non-tradables will fall and, if wages are sticky downward in terms of these goods, unemployment will result. In the course of time, as capital also moves across sectors, the labour intensity of production in the exportables and non-tradables industries is reduced again. The marginal product of labour in terms of exportables and non-tradables increases and wages will rise or unemployment will decrease.

3.3 RESTRICTIONS ON INTERNATIONAL PAYMENTS

If the exchange rate is used as an instrument to stimulate exports, it is imperative to free the foreign-exchange market from restrictions that artificially keep the exchange rate down. We shall first consider a unified official exchange rate and next a multiple-rate system.

Payments restrictions under a unified exchange rate

All too often, a currency is overvalued in the sense that without restrictions even on current account payments its value cannot be maintained. If authorities fix the rate at OB, excess demand is CG and foreign exchange has to be rationed one way or another (see Figure 3.4). Beneficiaries earn a rent of ABCE and it is a society with unusually high ethical standards indeed in which no waste of resources through rent-seeking, nepotism or outright bribery will occur. But even in a society of saints, the burden of rationing on the economy is bound to be high. Usually, people have to wait for considerable periods of time before foreign exchange is allotted to them. If the foreign exchange is needed for the import of spare parts, replacement of worn-out machinery or simply for raw materials, production can be seriously affected. Also, the costs of running the system in terms of personnel can be considerable. Finally, people will do their

40 The Exchange Rate as an Export-Stimulation Mechanism

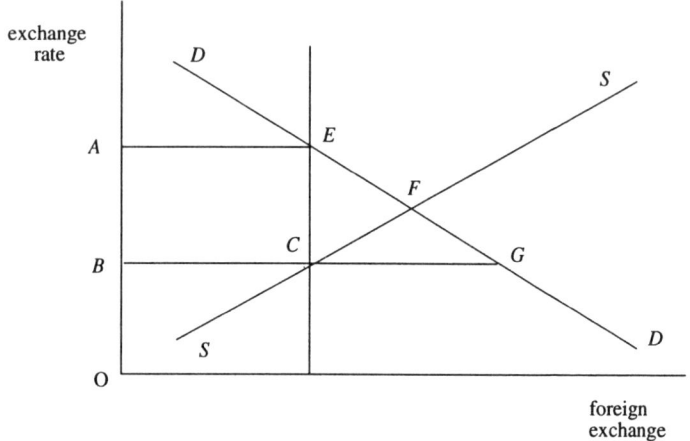

Figure 3.4 The foreign-exchange market with an overvalued currency

utmost to circumvent regulations and resort to over-invoicing in the case of importers and under-invoicing in the case of exporters. (For empirical estimates see Gupta, 1984, and Dornbusch and Tellez Kuenzler, 1993, p. 115, citing figures by J. Cuddington.) Foreign exchange is siphoned off to a black market and the amount available to the authorities shrinks.

When the foreign-exchange market is liberalised, overshooting of the exchange rate may occur. First, the exchange rate may rise to OA. As imports and exports react, the system will move in the direction of F. (For the lags between devaluations and export increases, see Donovan, 1981, Krueger, 1978, p. 176 and Denoon, 1986, p. 5.) If a black market had been flourishing, the black market rate would not have been too much above F and the exchange rate paid by those who had no access to the official market would consequently react less vehemently.

If liberalisation of the foreign-exchange market induces substantial capital inflow – for example, due to foreign loans or a return of flight capital – continued restrictions on capital flows may be needed in order to prevent an appreciation of the currency that would price the country's products out of the market. In principle, though, liberalisation of the capital account has much going for it, even if liberalisation of the current account should take precedence. First, international capital flows are increasingly more difficult to monitor, which means that the smart will be able to get around controls and that controls are costly in terms of administrative capacity absorbed. Second, capital controls may deprive a country of much-needed foreign investment and its concomitant access to foreign technology, managerial skills and sales networks. Third, capital controls make it difficult for domestic firms to expand abroad and for domestic investors, including institutional investors such as pension funds, to diversify their portfolios.

This analysis suggests that not all devaluations are aimed at improving the current account in the first place. Some at least are put into effect as part of a liberalisation effort (Corden, 1993, p. 203). The aim of increasing exports still stands in that case, however, as liberalisation means an increased participation in the international division of labour. Empirical research has shown that devaluations that form part of a liberalisation package give a large impetus to exports, much larger than devaluations that do not (Donovan, 1981, p. 714). This suggests that inputs for export production indeed suffer seriously from import restrictions. Support is provided by Michaely *et al.*, who found that exports grow rapidly after a relaxation of import restrictions and a rise in the RER (Michaely *et al.*, 1991, p. 194, quoted by Falvey and Kim, 1992, p. 916). They even found that exports responded without any appreciable lag.

Dual and multiple exchange rates

International capital flows may cause substantial erratic shocks in the real exchange rate. The authorities may decide to control capital flows or, alternatively, not to intervene but to leave the capital account to its own devices and fix a rate for current account transactions. This is an excellent principle, though one with much often lost in the execution. The monetary authorities would have to screen each and every individual foreign-exchange transaction, so administrative costs would be very high, and there would be strong incentives to cheat. Moreover, it might be difficult to define the boundary between current account and capital account transactions: for example, depending on the various rates, shifts between short-term loans and trade credit will occur. These problems are compounded if instead of a dual exchange rate a system of multiple rates applies.

Just like payment restrictions in a unified exchange-rate system, multiple rates lend themselves easily to abuse for political purposes. The allegiance of powerful groups can be bought by giving them access to cheap foreign exchange. More respectable ends can also be pursued by such a system. A government may, for instance, try to further economic development by applying a low exchange rate for traditional exports and essential imports and a high rate of exchange for non-traditional exports and non-essential imports, in order to stimulate non-traditional exports and curb non-essential imports. In this way, the exchange rate is deployed as an instrument of trade policy and industrial policy. However, such a policy obviously is not first-best, since import duties and export rebates are superior trade policy instruments whereas taxes and subsidies are superior industrial policy instruments (see Fleming, 1974). It is, for instance, hardly commendable to try to hinder imports of luxury goods and thus protect inefficient domestic production of such goods – it is much better to levy an excise which burdens both domestic and foreign produce – and, moreover, this opens the way to abuse once again.

In conclusion, payment restrictions and dual and multiple exchange rates pose a serious threat to welfare. They involve static welfare losses in terms of consumer rent and obstruct the smooth flow of production. Furthermore, they are costly to run and offer only too much opportunity for dubious activities. Also, it appears that trade and payments restrictions often include restrictions on the purchase of foreign know-how (Corbo and de Melo, 1985, Preface). Still, a case can be made for restrictions on capital transactions in order to insulate the real exchange rate from damaging shocks or for a dual exchange rate, for the same purpose, provided the system can be run efficiently by the authorities. Real exchange-rate stability obviously may only come at a price.

3.4 HOW TO GO ABOUT LIBERALISATION

If it is decided that international payments are to be liberalised as part of an overall liberalisation process, the question arises as to which sequence would be best. Several combinations present themselves:

(i) Liberalisation of the current account first, followed by liberalisation of the capital account;
(ii) Liberalisation of the capital account first, followed by liberalisation of the current account;
(iii) Liberalisation of the current account and the capital account simultaneously.

If a liberalisation policy, coupled with a stabilisation policy – suppression of inflation and cutting the government budget deficit – is seen as credible by the public, there is a high probability of substantial net capital import. It will become relatively easy for domestic agents to borrow abroad and in addition flight capital will return. Such net capital import may play havoc with attempts to stimulate exports (see McKinnon, 1973, ch. 11). In a fixed-rate system, capital import, if sizeable, leads to money creation which will make it very difficult to fight inflation. Non-tradable prices will rise relative to tradable prices and the production of tradables becomes less profitable. In a floating-rate system, the currency will appreciate, with similar results. Net capital import may of course subside after some time, but if the production structure has been distorted by the capital import, a restructuring will be painful; forestalling such shocks is preferable. Also, the establishment of distribution networks abroad may be costly and time-consuming and it would be better not to frustrate such efforts at the outset. All this suggests that liberalisation efforts that aim at greater participation of a country in international trade may be seriously undermined by simultaneously liberalising the capital and current account or by liberalising the capital account even before the current account. It would probably be wise, though, to ease restrictions on capital import a little at the time the current account is liberalised. It takes time to build up export capability, whereas liberalised imports may surge at once. In a fixed-rate system, the current account will tend to show a deficit at first, which could put quite a strain on the central bank's currency reserves if capital imports are not allowed to finance the current-account deficit. In a flexible-rate system the domestic currency would tend to depreciate strongly, only to appreciate later when export growth gets under steam. Relative prices, in particular those between tradables and non-tradables, would move first in one direction, then in another, which of course is not very conducive to investment in hardware and in sales networks by exporters.

Of course, one cannot be sure that a liberalisation of the capital account induces net capital inflows. The experiences of the 1970s – when after the 1973 oil crisis bankers seemed to have thrown caution to the winds when selling loans – should not be generalised. Too much capital inflow is undesirable, but no net capital inflow at all might jeopardise the liberalisation effort as well. In order to ensure at least the availability of a modest volume of foreign credit or direct investments, it would be helpful if foreign governments and/or official financial institutions made stand-by credits available. Besides, capital may well flow out of the country, if a government has not yet earned itself a fair degree of credibility or if the domestic capital market has not yet been liberalised and interest rates are still subject to ceilings (Edwards, 1984a, p. 3). A wish on the part of domestic wealth holders for portfolio diversification after liberalisation of the capital account may play a role as well (see for further discussion Mathieson and Rojas Suárez, 1993). Whichever way capital flows, it may be wise for authorities to retain some grip on it. A practical way may be to ease or tighten regulations on capital exports, such as limits on the funds invested abroad by pension funds, or to manipulate reserve requirements on short-term foreign borrowings.

Apart from abolishing payments restrictions, other import and indeed export restrictions can also be reduced. Liberalisation of trade can take different forms: for instance, one could opt for the 'cold turkey' method and sweep aside all import restrictions in one fell swoop, replacing them by a low (uniform) tariff. It is also possible to go about it more cautiously. Liberalisation really implies two different things: removing price distortions and opening up the domestic market to foreign trade. Of course, import and export restrictions in themselves create price distortions, but it is possible to reduce price distortions without opening up the domestic market. As Dornbusch (1991, p. 34) has argued, it is possible, and indeed in some circumstances advisable, to carry liberalisation through in two rounds. First, after payments have been liberalised, quotas and licences can be abolished and a uniform high tariff can be introduced. This goes a long way to reduce price distortions and in addition exposes the domestic tradables sector to the fresh winds of competition, or rather a fresh breeze. Second, tariffs can be lowered gradually. If foreign capital is not available in sufficient amounts and a strong temporary real depreciation is not considered advisable for fear of price instability and possibly also of inflation, this may be an attractive option. In either case, government gets some breathing space before income from trade taxes drops.

It should be obvious from this analysis that no hard-and-fast rule can be given. The measures to be taken depend on expected net capital flows and the expected responses of the tradables sector to a reduction of protection. (For some more refined welfare theoretic points based on second-best considerations, see Falvey and Kim, 1992.)

3.5 OBSTACLES TO LIBERALISATION AND DEVALUATION

Several forces work against liberalisation and the devaluation it implies. First of all, devaluation and liberalisation may be beneficial for exporting industries, but the benefits must be worked for and can only be reaped in the future, whereas the losers, first of all producers of importables, feel their loss at once. The losers therefore will tend to fight harder for maintaining their privileges, that is, their sheltered position in the market, than the beneficiaries fight for liberalisation.

Next, if government has pledged to fight inflation and to maintain a fixed exchange rate, devaluation is tantamount to admitting defeat. If subsequently a crisis develops in which devaluation can no longer be avoided, the political life of the minister of finance or even the cabinet as a whole is in danger (see Cooper, 1973, pp. 193–4 for empirical findings). One should not, though, jump to the conclusion that devaluation is risky for one's political life. Rather, it seems better both for one's political life and for the economy to devalue before a crisis develops than to make promises and be forced to renege on them.

At first sight, there may also be respectable economic arguments against devaluation. Residents who have borrowed abroad or in foreign currency and have failed to cover their position suffer a loss if devaluation takes place – which need not be so if the devaluation was expected at the time the loans were concluded and consequently the risk of devaluation has been reflected in the interest rate difference between domestic currency and foreign currency loans. It may even result in serious bouts of business failures, as was the case in the early 1980s in Chile, Argentina and Uruguay. However, to a large extent this was due to high real interest rates following from attempts to defend the rate of exchange and of distress borrowing by firms in the tradables sector that were trying to survive in the face of a low RER (World Bank, 1990, p. 101 and Corbo and de Melo, 1987, p. 133). Better then, again, to devalue at an earlier stage.

Another concern has been that devaluations hardly help boost export proceeds in a world with low price elasticities. Such fears can be justified in the case of countries that export mostly commodities that have low (short-run) price elasticity of supply. In Latin America (including the Caribbean) manufactured products amounted to only 7 per cent of merchandise export in 1965, but in 1990 comprised 32 per cent of merchandise exports (World Bank, *World Development Report*, 1992, p. 249), so this objection has lost much of its force. Moreover, supply elasticities of primary commodities will be higher in the long run than in the short run.

Devaluation makes the domestic price level rise. If, however, domestic monetary and fiscal policies are sufficiently restrictive, the price level rises less than the exchange rate and real depreciation takes place. (For empirical evidence, see Cooper, 1973, Connolly and Taylor, 1976 and Kamin, 1988.) If, however, macroeconomic policies are insufficiently restrictive, inflation will nullify real depreciation – for such cases, see Bautista, 1982 and Edwards, 1989b.[2] Furthermore, if devaluation is coupled with foreign trade and payments liberalisation, the disappearance of rents, the lowering of import duties and the increased availability of imported inputs will dampen any tendency of prices to increase. If price controls were in force before devaluation, black markets are likely to have been developed and actual prices will have been higher than official prices. In such circumstances, price increases as recorded in official statistics overstate actual price increases. Finally, more exports and a generally higher degree of participation in international trade mean more division of labour, involving the closing down of inefficient industries and the expansion of efficient firms that will enable them to reap economies of scale.

Another problem can be the loss of government income after a liberalisation involving the lowering of import duties. As was mentioned in the preceding section, a shift from non-tariff restrictions to tariffs enables a government to reduce the general level of trade restrictions (expressed in tariff equivalents) and still increase government revenue.[3]

Finally, small countries striving for flexible exchange-rate policies may face collusive behaviour by foreign-exchange traders. The answer is to increase the number of market participants, for example, by granting hotels and other business firms direct access to the foreign-exchange market. Also, publicity on the prices paid by commercial banks for foreign exchange, revealing their margins, may help (see Quirk *et al.*, 1987).

3.6 COFFEE AND OTHER DRUGS AS GERMS OF DUTCH DISEASE

Fajnzylber (1988, p. 18) notes that there is a surprising positive correlation on a world scale between a lack of natural resources and the level of competitiveness in the industrial sector. This is perhaps less surprising than it looks at first sight. Obviously, if a country is able to earn foreign exchange by exporting primary commodities, there is less need to concentrate on exports of manufactures. Indeed, there will be less opportunity to do so. Exports of primary commodities exert such downward pressure on the exchange rate that relatively few manufacturing industries are able to face competition in world markets. In fixed-but-adjustable peg systems export surpluses develop which create inflation or induce a revaluation, in either case effecting a real appreciation.

If, from a given situation, exports of primary commodities start to grow, the manufacturing sector is prone to suffer. We then have a case of Dutch disease (see Corden, 1984). What happens in terms of the dependent-economy model, is the following. We distinguish the tradables sectors of primary commodities T1 and the manufacturing sector T2. T1 produces mainly for export. Let T1 prices rise and T1 exporters earn more dollars. They spend part of it domestically. As a result, non-tradables N become more expensive in terms of T2 and import of T2 increases. Furthermore, factors of production move from T2 to T1 and N. T2 production declines and net import of T2 rises sharply. Thus, there is de-industrialisation.

This effect will be strengthened if export of T1 generates such amounts of money that a nominal appreciation is called for or takes place automatically.

In this way the development of manufacturing industry was hampered in countries such as Chile, with its copper exports, and Colombia, with its exports of coffee, coal and oil. The description by Edwards (1984b) of Colombia during the 1975–9 coffee boom exactly follows the scenario just sketched. Illegal drugs exports are also likely to have contributed to Dutch disease de-industrialisation, to the extent that proceeds from drugs exports have not been spent abroad. Apart from illegal activities, if a country has a comparative advantage for primary commodities, allocational efficiency demands that primary commodities rather than manufactured products are produced and exported. The development policy of many countries has been aimed, however, at supporting manufacturing industry. This policy has been based on the assumption that manufacturing industry is the epitome of modernity or, in a more sophisticated form, on the assumption that industrialisation is associated with increasing returns and external economies and therefore is a prerequisite for continued growth. (For a harsh criticism of forced industrialisation see Lal, 1983, ch. 4.) There is, however, empirical evidence that labour productivity in the agrarian sector need not grow at a lower rate than in the industrial sector.[4] Nevertheless, high productivity growth inevitably leads to an expulsion of labour from the agrarian sector. Wages have to be sufficiently low to make at least some T2 industries competitive and to enable the N sector to absorb sufficient numbers of workers. A sudden expansion of primary commodity exports may lead to real appreciations that hamper such adjustments. Given that money wages are sticky downward, an upsurge in unemployment is bound to result. This is the more harmful for the economy if such a boom is temporary and capital markets imperfections preclude T2 industries from bridging a temporary bad situation. A boom in coffee or drugs exports can thus quite seriously hinder the development of manufacturing industry, at the cost of high unemployment.

3.7 CASE STUDIES

In this section, a brief review will be presented of the exchange-rate regimes of three countries: Chile, Colombia and Uruguay. Figures 3.5–3.9 show the relationship between the openness of the economy, as measured by the ratio between exports and GDP, and RER. It should be noted that price fluctuations of commodities that dominate the export sector may thwart the relationship. If the world market price of such a commodity increases, then – all things being equal – export proceeds as a percentage of GDP of the exporting country will rise too, whereas RER will decline. Given world demand for the commodity, a devaluation of the currency of the exporting economy will also increase openness as measured by the ratio of exports to GDP. However, this time around, RER has increased. The increase in the openness may only be a statistical artefact, resulting from the domestic price increase of such a so-called Tradable II commodity in McKinnon's terminology.[5] For other products, so-called Tradables I, there will generally be a more unequivocally positive relationship between RER and export performance, given sufficiently high elasticities. For that reason figures will be presented for Chile and Colombia including and excluding exports of copper and coffee, respectively. By doing so, at least the direct effect of relative price changes of Tradables II on the ratio of exports to GDP has been reduced.

Chile

After the overthrow of the *Unidad Popular* government in September 1973, the Pinochet government turned in 1975 to Chicago-educated technocrats to run the economy. The so-called Chicago boys or Chicago kids resolved on an unprecedented opening-up of the economy in quite a short period of time. NTBs were abolished and tariffs were reduced from a weighted average of 105 per cent and a maximum of 750 per cent in September 1973 to a 10 per cent flat rate in June 1979, with the exception of tariffs on cars over 850cc capacity (see Corbo and de Melo, 1985, p. 8).

In order to reverse the extremely high inflation that resulted from the policies pursued by the *Unidad Popular* government, an orthodox deflation was engineered. Nevertheless, inflation remained high and devaluations were inescapable. A floating exchange-rate regime was introduced and in 1975 the currency devalued nearly 25 per cent in real terms. The dismantling of the system of import protection was one of the main causes. Moreover, exports were hit by a decline of copper prices and a quadrupling of oil prices. In 1976 the multiple exchange-rate system was replaced by a unified exchange rate and the exchange rate became the main policy instrument in the fight against inflation (Edwards, 1986b, p. 247). In both 1976 and 1977 the currency was revalued by 10 per cent and in early 1978 the *tablita* was introduced. Figures 3.5 and 3.6 show the decline of RER. In true textbook fashion, the capital account was not liberalised in step with the current account of the balance of payments.

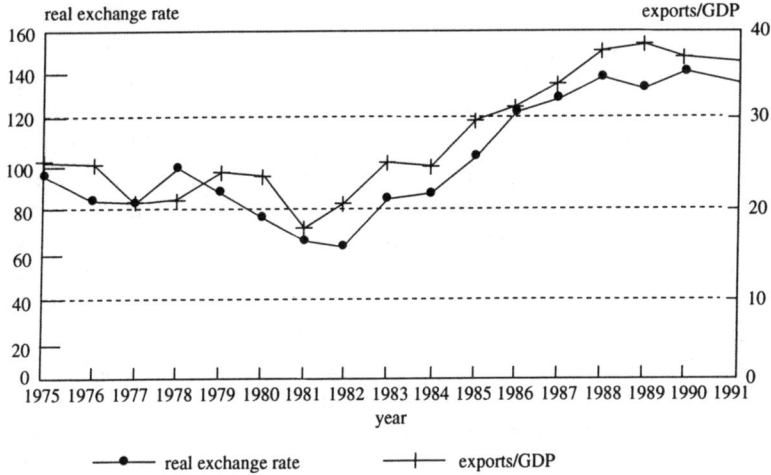

Figure 3.5 RER and openness of the Chilean economy, 1975–91

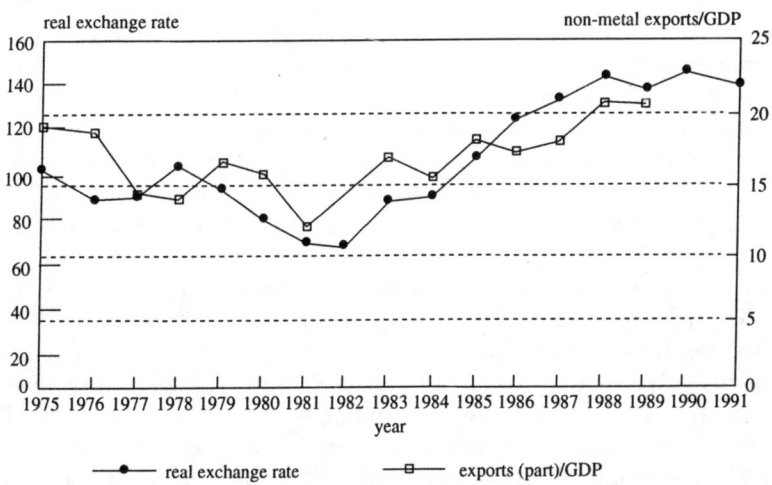

Figure 3.6 RER and openness of the Chilean economy, metals and ores excluded, 1975–91

Restrictions on medium-term capital flows were not lifted until April 1980, but even at that time restrictions remained in place to control inflows of capital with less than two years maturity.

Interviews with entrepreneurs conducted by a team from The World Bank (Corbo and de Melo, 1985, p. 8) show a high credibility of the policy to dismantle trade restrictions, which implies that firms did not hesitate to adjust to the new environment.[6] The virtual abolition of protection resulted in drastic changes in relative prices, not only between tradables and non-tradables, but also among tradables, which was due to the wide variation in rates of import tariffs. To re-allocate factors of production, increased labour mobility was essential. Internal re-allocations of labour between jobs and lay-offs were made easier. Firms responded to the opening-up of the economy by streamlining production in order to reduce costs significantly (Corbo and Sanchez, 1985, pp. 108–9, and Edwards, 1986b, p. 254). Typically, import-competing firms responded also by increasing the quality of their products (Corbo and Sanchez, 1985, p. 111). Inevitably, unemployment increased as a consequence of the depression of 1975 which was the result not only of deflationary policies and the liberalisation policies that induced industrial restructuring, but also of external developments.

Notwithstanding the measures taken, inflation remained at a high level. To squeeze inflation out of the economy, the government decided to increase reliance on the exchange rate as an anti-inflationary weapon. This policy was based on an explicitly professed belief in the applicability of the dependent-economy model. The *tablita* introduced in 1978 was replaced in June 1979 by a fixed dollar rate. The objective of the *tablita* and the fixed dollar rate was to reduce the rate of inflation and the expected rate of inflation. The government was successful in this respect, but it took until 1981 before inflation converged to the average world rate of inflation of 9.5 per cent. This was partly due to wage indexation. During the adjustment period the Chilean price level had risen *vis-à-vis* the world price level. In other words, RER declined, as reflected in Figures 3.5 and 3.6.

The real appreciation of the Chilean peso hit the tradables sector more than was the case a few years earlier. At that time, it was relatively easy to improve efficiency (Corbo and Sanchez, 1985, p. 114, and Galvez and Tybout, 1985). The current account of the balance of payments lurched heavily into a deficit amounting to 13.7 per cent of GDP in 1981 (Corbo, 1985, p. 906), capital inflows soared and the non-tradables sector – such as construction, commerce and other services – boomed, which is in line with the two-sector dependent economy model (Corbo and Sanchez, 1985, p. 51). Capital inflow had contributed substantially to the fast increase in the money supply. Notwithstanding restrictions on capital inflow, the monetary expansion only subsided at the time that the debt crisis of 1981–2 caused a stagnation in international capital flows to Latin America (Corbo and Sanchez, 1985, p. 89).

The experience can easily be analysed in terms of the dependent-economy model. Capital inflow had financed a boom in the non-tradables sector and an excess demand for tradables, resulting in a current-account deficit. RER declined until capital inflow came to an abrupt halt (see Figure 3.5). Projects in the non-tradables sector remained unfinished and RER had to increase steeply to move the current account towards equilibrium. For the same reason, domestic absorption had to decrease. A rise in RER implied either a decrease in prices of non-tradables or an increase in prices of tradables. The first option would have taken time and implied even more unemployment than was actually the case. Consequently, the peso had to be devalued sharply in nominal terms.

A collapse of the financial sector put the entire government policy in jeopardy. Real interest rates remained disconcertingly high since the liberalisation of the capital market. This may have been due to strong demand for loans by firms desperate for funds to avoid bankruptcy, and to devaluation expectations. The squeezing of the tradables sector that resulted from the decline of RER may also have played a role, as it forced firms to seek loans at all cost (Edwards, 1990, pp. 8 and 9). From 1974–5 onwards, banks seem to have been used by businessmen to finance the acquisition and growth of firms within the conglomerates they controlled, accumulating bad loans in the process. Prudential supervision was virtually non-existent. The combination of these bad debts and high dollar liabilities caused the crisis in the banking sector after the fall of the peso in 1982. The government had to step in and take over a number of privatised banks. The privatisation programme suffered a serious setback and re-privatisation of banks started in 1985.

In 1982 the economy was hit by a recession that was triggered by world depression and stagnation of capital inflow, which had amounted to about 15 per cent of GDP in 1981 (Harberger, 1986, p. 235). A low RER, high real interest rates and downward inflexibility of real wages exacerbated the crisis. In June 1982 the peso was devalued by 18 per cent and wage indexation was suspended. More devaluations and changes in exchange-rate policy followed and altogether the peso devalued between June 1982 and June 1983 by 99 per cent – that is, the dollar price of the peso rose by nearly 100 per cent, which resulted in the real depreciation that was needed. In 1984 the Chicago boys were out and import tariffs were raised to 35 per cent. The raising of import tariffs and other measures to stimulate the economy resulted in rapidly increasing inflation. In 1985 Corbo wrote: 'Today it appears that the reforms failed', but the same year a new start was made with policies that relied on market forces and aimed at macro-economic stability (Corbo, 1985, p. 909).

Economic policy aimed firmly at increasing the real exchange rate, that is, at a real depreciation. Thanks to sufficiently restrictive monetary and fiscal policies, the rate of inflation was below the nominal rate of depreciation (Edwards and Edwards, 1992, p. 209). RER increased sharply over a number of years and the openness of the economy increased at about the same rate. New products were offered on export markets. It is noteworthy in this respect that products such as canned fish and canned fruits were not as successful as, for example, apples and grapes, the latter requiring less marketing effort. Government did not provide a clear export promotion strategy (Arriagada, 1985, p. 122) which is in marked contrast to Asian countries such as Taiwan and South Korea (Lin, 1988, p. 157, supplement).

The recent export successes, combined with capital inflow generated by foreign investment and project financing, have put an end to the rise in RER. A further increase does not seem necessary, given the marked improvement in the current account of the balance of payments and the substantial reduction in debt-service payments. As a counter measure, in June 1991 import tariffs were reduced to 11 per cent and capital export was facilitated (Bianchi, 1993).

Colombia

Colombia's policy in the 1950s and early 1960s was based on import substitution but a continuation of this policy was not viable (The World Bank, 1992a, p. 109). Nevertheless, no significant reforms were implemented. The balance of payments was highly dependent on coffee exports and the near-doubling of coffee prices in 1976, for instance, resulted in an external payments surplus, followed by higher inflation in the next year (Dornbusch and Fischer, 1993, p. 20). Expansionary macro-economic policies combined with declining coffee prices and a fall in RER in 1981 deteriorated the external situation. Moreover, loans to conglomerates had resulted in the bankruptcy of a number of banks and government was forced to nationalise them, as was the case in Chile (Supelano, 1992, p. 853). The trade liberalisation efforts that had been under way were put to an end and import licensing became a prominent feature of the trade regime. In 1984 an orthodox adjustment programme was introduced which included a sizeable depreciation in 1985 (Corden, 1991, p. 70 and Liuksila, 1992, p. 40). This programme made RER increase steeply as illustrated in Figure 3.7. The government also liberalised foreign trade by reducing import-licensing requirements and lowering import duties (Schloss and Thomas, 1986 and Hommes, 1990). In 1986 the current account of the balance of payments improved as a result both of restrictive

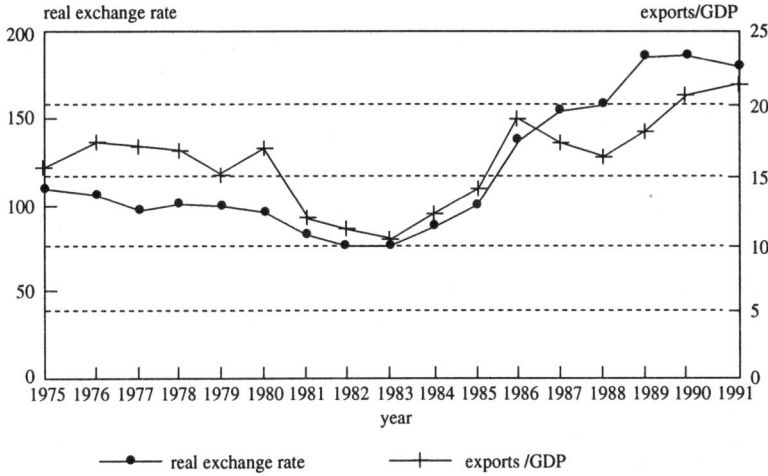

Figure 3.7 RER and openness of the Colombian economy, 1975–91

macroeconomic policies that reduced the budget deficit and of the rise in coffee prices. After 1986, the $US value of coffee exports declined to about half its 1986 value but RER increased and non-coffee exports increased sharply. At the time the new government took office in 1990, measures were introduced to intensify the efforts made by the previous administration in its final days, to liberalise the Colombian economy further (Supelano, 1992, p. 854).

Colombia has to cope with an influx of money from drugs trafficking. At the central bank there is a special window, the *ventanilla siniestra*, where no questions are asked about the provenance of money (EIU, 1989, p. 14). In the period 1987–91 the estimated revenues from cocaine sales were $US 2–3 bn on an annual basis, as compared with $US 1.4–1.7 bn from coffee exports and total export revenues ranging from $US 4.6 bn in 1987 to $US 7.2 bn in 1991 (IMF, various years). On top of the cocaine dollars there was an inflow from illegal exports of marijuana, gold and emeralds (Vaessen, 1990, p. 9). However, according to other sources the estimated dollar values of illegal trade are much higher. Crawley estimates that export revenues of cocaine from Colombia may have amounted to somewhere between $US 11.5 bn and nearly $US 24 bn. An amount between $US 1.8 bn and $US 3.7 bn may have been required to finance the import of raw material for the production of these illegal exports (quoted by Fonseca, 1992, p. 504). It is not clear what share of these export earnings was channelled abroad, but at least some of it was

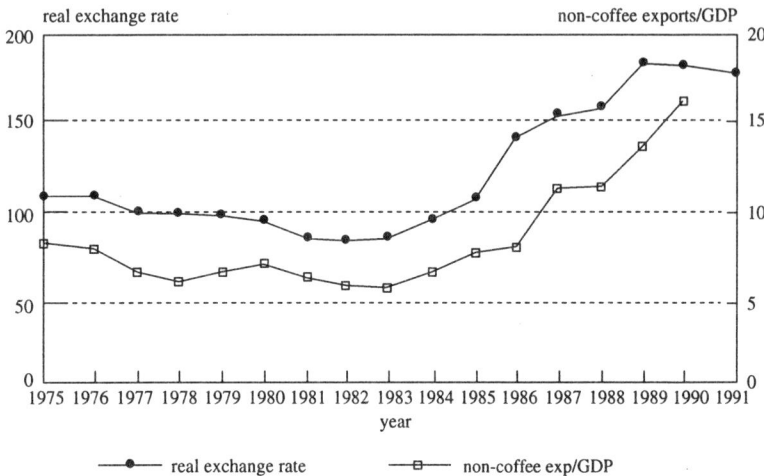

Figure 3.8 RER and openness of the Colombian economy, coffee excluded, 1975–91

invested in land and company shares (Supelano, 1992, p. 853), driving up asset prices and probably the relative price of nontradables.

Figure 3.8 shows that non-coffee exports as a percentage of GDP are closely related to RER. The fall in coffee export proceeds after 1986 was more than compensated for by the increase in non-coffee exports. Non-coffee exports never exceeded 54 per cent of total exports during the period 1975–86, but in more recent years they increased steadily from 63.6 per cent in 1987 to 80.7 per cent in 1991 (IMF, various years). RER and non-coffee exports as a percentage of GDP would most probably have been on a higher level, though, but for drugs exports. That would probably also have had a positive impact on employment, assuming that production of drugs is less labour-intensive than production of alternative non-traditional exports.

Uruguay

In 1959 a dual exchange-rate system was introduced that replaced the multiple-rate system which was in force until that time. The dual system included a fixed commercial rate, which was devalued three times in the year of its introduction, and a floating financial rate. Inflation soared, and during the period 1963–8 the value of the peso declined from 11 to 250 pesos per $US. From 1968 to March 1972 the exchange rate was fixed, but prices continued to rise. The imposition in 1971 of a tax of 50 per cent on all foreign transactions implied a *de facto* devaluation. Early in 1972 the currency was devalued to 500 pesos per $US and a crawling-peg system was introduced. During the period 1974–8 the economic policies of Minister of Economic Affairs Vegh were orientated towards liberalisation and stabilisation. In 1974 the capital account was liberalised, in 1975 import quotas and licensing requirements were abolished and in 1977 controls on capital goods imports were lifted. However, import restrictions were maintained which were connected with extensive rent-seeking activities (de Melo and Dhar, 1992, p. 31). Liberalisation of the capital account came first and was soon accompanied by domestic financial reform (Edwards, 1990, p. 7). During the period 1979–81 the policies of Vegh's successor Arismendi shifted away from stimulation of growth towards reduction of inflation. The authorities firmly believed that the law of one price held true for tradables and, in addition, that capital markets were perfect – that is, that the law of one price held true for the interest rate as well (Mezzera and de Melo, 1985, p. 160). In January 1979 a *tablita* system was introduced and in January 1980 a programme of tariff reductions was announced that aimed at attaining a flat rate of 35 per cent in December 1985. The liberalisation programme was combined with the reduction of export subsidies. The law of one price was proved to be wrong and RER declined, as shown in Figure 3.9. However, exports to Argentina held up for some time because of the real appreciation of the

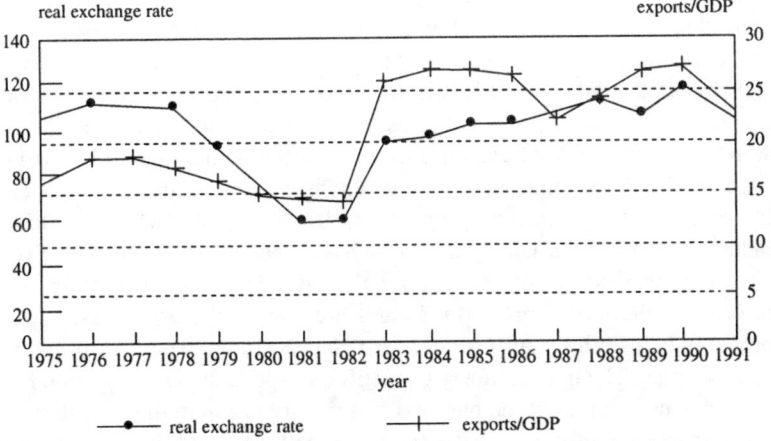

Figure 3.9 RER and openness of the Uruguay economy, 1975–91[a]
[a] The figure of exports:GDP for 1982 is lacking, which gives the probably wrong impression that the curve already starts rising sharply after 1981.

Argentine peso. In line with the theoretical model, demand pressure financed by capital import induced at the same time a boom in the non-tradables sector, especially in residential construction. Private investment in construction increased in 1979 by 45.5 per cent and in 1980 by 12.2 per cent (Mezzera and de Melo, 1985, p. 162). The Uruguay peso became seriously overvalued due to the devaluation of the Argentine currency in March 1981, high energy prices and the international recession. By November 1982 floating of the peso could no longer be averted. Also in this case, a financial crisis developed as banks had taken up $US loans at high interest rates and borrowers were unable to pay off their debts.

The stabilisation experiment ended in failure. Since November 1982, when the peso started to float, its value had declined from 11.59 peso per $US to 2489 pesos per $US by the end of 1991, whereas inflation usually exceeded 60 per cent. The relationship between RER and the openness of the economy is less clearcut in Uruguay than was the case in Chile and Colombia. This may have been due to the preponderance of commodities in exports, but it may also have been caused by the effect rampant which inflation has on the functioning of the price system.

3.8 CONCLUSIONS

Devaluations are an inescapable feature of liberalisation programmes. They help to raise the real exchange rate, provided macro-economic policy is used to support the devaluation effort. Empirical research also suggests that the current account reacts favourably to devaluations in such circumstances and that a rise in RER is instrumental in increasing the openness of the economy. More openness means more competition and a better division of labour and what evidence there is indeed points to an increase in efficiency and better product quality (Thomas, Nash et al., 1991, ch. 5). However, a change in policy implies restructuring between and within industries, which can hardly fail to increase unemployment temporarily. This is a sacrifice in the short term that may be expected to bring in rewards in the long term. All the signs are that orthodoxy works, but it probably helps if a country is not overly dependent on exports of primary commodities. The impact of a rise in RER on exports could be increased if governments supported the business community in improving its international marketing efforts as discussed in some of the country studies in this volume. Openness need not go so far as to imply complete liberalisation of the capital account. Governments may need a handle on capital flows in order to prevent large swings in RER or a very high or low level of RER.

The experience so far has shown that a liberalisation process can be seriously jeopardised by crises in the financial sector. Prudential supervision is apparently a weak spot in a number of countries. In particular, there seems to be a need for stringent supervision on intra-conglomerate loans.

In opening up the economy, Chile's *laissez-faire* approach is not the only option available. Within ECLAC the idea seems to have taken hold that the Latin American countries have to restructure their economies to become competitive and, at the same time, safeguard social equity. This calls for interaction between the government, business firms and non-profit institutions. It is not believed that simply opening up the economy and relying on export growth to dynamise the economy will do (Bitar and Bradford, 1992). The Asian examples of South Korea, Taiwan and Singapore indeed suggest that active government involvement is, at the least, not incompatible with bringing about growth combined with equity, whereas the Hong Kong government has been following a more hands-off type of policy (Morawetz, 1977, p. 39 and OECD, 1988). The idea of liberalising foreign trade itself does not seem to meet with much opposition any longer, and rightly so.

Notes

1. According to IMF figures net capital inflows into non-oil developing countries in the Western Hemisphere declined from $US 40.1 bn. in 1981 to $US 4.1 bn. in 1982 (IMF, 1983).
2. In a fixed-rate regime after liberalisation of the capital account, the emphasis should be on fiscal policy, depending on the interest elasticity of capital flows. For example, attempts to reduce the money supply will force the interest rate upward. This induces capital inflows, which nullify to a larger or smaller degree the reduction in the money supply.
3. According to Dornbusch and Tellez Kuenzler (1993, p. 113) 12 per cent of total government revenue in Latin America derives from taxes on international trade. For more detailed figures on Colombia, Jamaica and Mexico, see Thomas Nash *et al.*, 1991, pp. 123–5.
4. For instance, from 1950 to 1978 labour productivity in Dutch agriculture increased in step with labour productivity in Dutch manufacturing industry. From 1978 onwards the former increased much faster than the latter (Stolwijk, 1992, p. 14).
5. Tradables I are goods 'in which producing firms can control (set) the market price for their own particular products' and 'tradables II are more homogeneous commodities where one firm's output may be graded and precisely compared to that of others' (McKinnon, 1979, pp. 74 and 75).
6. This was not reflected by the investment ratio (for figures see Zahler, 1980, p. 148 and Edwards, 1986b, p. 257). Whereas public investment decreased, allocation of investment will have been improved considerably.

4 Structural Adjustment in the 1980s: Stimulus or Setback for Private Investment in the Industrialisation Process?

Valpy FitzGerald

4.1 INDUSTRY UNDER STRUCTURAL ADJUSTMENT

The experience of policy-driven structural adjustment – whether in response to major external shocks or as a means of overcoming systemic obstacles to growth – is an integral part of Latin American economic history. Indeed, the origins of the present industrial system in the region can be found in the domestic response to exogenous shifts in world trading and financial patterns during the 1929–49 period. However, during the past ten years, a particular form of structural adjustment has been adopted – albeit with variations as to depth and timing – throughout the region both as a response to the 1982 debt crisis and as an attempt to construct a new model of capital accumulation and growth to replace the post-war strategy which, it is felt, can no longer provide sustainable growth.

The objectives of the established structural adjustment model go far beyond the stabilisation of the domestic macro-economy and restoration of access to international capital markets, even though these were the immediate problems created by the debt crisis. It is argued that the model creates the conditions in which manufacturing industry can become technically efficient and internationally competitive, and thus overcome the shortcomings of the previous industrialisation strategy, based on tariff protection and state intervention.

The aim of this chapter is to explore the plausibility of this argument from the viewpoint of the effect of economic policy measures on the investment decisions of manufacturing firms, in terms of both theory and the limited aggregate data at our disposal. In this context the term 'small economy' can be understood to refer not to absolute size as such but rather to dependent status as a price-taker on international commodity markets on the one hand, and to a domestic market insufficient in size to realise significant scale economies in manufacturing, on the other. In other words, a 'dependent economy' in the strict sense of economic theory as defined by Dornbusch (1980) rather than in the sense of *dependencia*. To these 'stylised facts' can be added two more: (i) these small economies are unlikely to be the sites of major technological innovation, and consequently the capability to absorb, diffuse and adapt foreign technology is important; and (ii) access to international capital markets is at exogenous interest rates with implicit rationing based on external assessment of sovereign risk. Broadly, this definition would include all Latin American economies except Mexico and Brazil. These two economies account for two-thirds of all manufactured exports from Latin America, and each has roughly 1 per cent of world trade. The rest of the region shares the remaining 1 per cent of world trade in manufactures from Latin America.

It is perhaps worth recalling that the so-called *desarrollo hacia adentro* industrialisation model was not originally the result of a consciously autarkic strategy. In the period immediately after the Second World War, Latin America had expected to consolidate its wartime position and gain preferential access to the markets of the USA as an exporter of manufactures and farm goods; it was only after this possibility had been denied by the USA at Havana in 1947 and the decline of commodity prices after the Korean War that Latin American governments saw no alternative to import-substitution as an industrialisation policy. Moreover, in this new project they were supported by multilateral organisations and foreign investors. That this stage would eventually be followed by manufactured exports was always proposed, and indeed the state-led heavy industrialisation projects were designed to give Latin America the technological capability to compete in world markets, and the regional common markets were designed to stimulate industrial export experience (FitzGerald, 1994a).

However, the nature of the debt crisis was such that financial exigencies and the conditionality of the Bretton Woods institutions forced an effective change of industrial policy as the result of reduced public expenditure, financial reform and import liberalisation. This new policy was clearly not the result of demands from national industries[1] nor to any overwhelming extent from consumer groups; interestingly, the international commercial banks never pressed for radical changes in industrial policy. The social pressure to reduce inflation and currency convertibility could be met by fiscal reform, whereas debt servicing might have been better achieved by aggressive export promotion including real devaluation and import constraints, both along the lines of the East Asian model.[2] But this was not to be the case.

The central proposition of this chapter is that standard structural adjustment programmes (SAPs) have not adequately taken into account the nature of the private investment decisions and the behaviour of the firms which make them, and that to do so would require a somewhat different approach to macro-economic policy design. The argument is organised as follows. First, the intended effects of the SAPs are outlined in terms of their expected effect on the expansion of efficient manufacturing firms. Second, the available evidence on outcomes is reviewed to assess whether the relevant economic variables have in fact shifted in the way intended, and what the consequences have been for industry in the region. Third, alternative explanations of the observed divergence are discussed, and the respective implications for policy compared. Finally, some tentative suggestions are made as to how policy research might be better designed in order to support a coherent industrialisation strategy for the region.

4.2 INTENDED CONSEQUENCES OF STRUCTURAL ADJUSTMENT FOR INDUSTRY

There is no direct connection between the SAP and the expected industrial restructuring. In a sense there is no new industrialisation strategy as such – any activity that is profitable at world prices should expand and vice versa, so the emerging pattern of production will be efficient by survival rather than by design. Clearly resources do not move by themselves from one sector to another in immediate response to a shift in relative prices: between the macroeconomic policy package and the industrial restructuring targets there lie strong assumptions as to the behaviour of private firms. Here three key elements of structural adjustment will be discussed in order to elucidate these assumptions: (i) real devaluation, (ii) fiscal and financial reform, and (iii) trade liberalisation.[3]

The unification of nominal exchange rates and a permanent downward shift in the real exchange rate involves a structural shift in relative prices in favour of tradables. This is expected to shift resources towards sectors of tradables and thus release the external constraint on growth. The expected effect on industry derives from assumptions about branch-level profitability, labour market flexibility and inter-sectoral capital mobility.

(i) The shift in the price ratio between tradables and non-tradables, and the matching of prices of tradables to world relatives, will increase the profitability of firms in the tradables sector in both absolute and relative terms. This logically implies that real wages will fall,[4]

although to what extent depends upon whether profitability of firms in the non-tradables sector is maintained by mark-up pricing. The overall effect on industrial profits depends upon the distribution of firms between the sectors of tradables and non-tradables.
(ii) Firms in newly profitable branches are expected to take on more labour, and others to shed labour; the net effect on employment should be positive as the labour-intensive activities should display greater comparative advantage and the implicit decline in the real wage should encourage factor substitution. Nevertheless, specific measures (for example, deregulation) may be necessary to increase labour-market flexibility and support the unemployed during the transition.
(iii) 'Resource re-allocation' ideally implies the smooth movement of capital from one branch of production to another branch in response to differential profit rates ('arbitrage'). For fixed capital this is not literally possible, although to the extent that a well-functioning market in used assets (second-hand machinery, land, and so on) exists, the re-allocation can be eased. Otherwise, the process can only take place dynamically through new investment.

The positive consequences for industry expected from fiscal and financial reform mainly arise through the impact on corporate profitability, credit availability and foreign investment.

(i) The reduction in the fiscal deficit will be based on reduced administrative expenditure, resulting in less bureaucratic regulation of markets and firms. Tax restructuring, such as the reduction of customs tariffs and the move towards value-added taxation, will reduce industrial costs and market distortions, while privatisation should increase business confidence.
(ii) The reduced requirement of the public sector to borrow will in turn release more of the available national savings for private investment in industry, and the deregulation of capital markets themselves should allow companies better access to risk capital, particularly through the expansion of stock exchanges. Even though real interests rates may rise, this will stimulate further savings and ensure that firms themselves only undertake efficient investment.
(iii) The lower sovereign risk brought about by the control and reduction of public debt will stimulate direct investment inflows from abroad. Financial deregulation and expanding securities market will attract foreign portfolio investment to the benefit of industrial firms in terms of capital funding and technology transfer.

The expected positive effect of trade liberalisation on industrial competitiveness arises from cheaper inputs, increased competition and direct access to export markets.

(i) The availability of imported inputs enables all firms to produce at the lowest costs and to take advantage immediately of technological advances worldwide.
(ii) Firms in the sectors of tradables are forced to increase the efficiency with which they use resources, or to invest to acquire new technology, in order to compete with imported goods – or else lose markets and go bankrupt.
(iii) The dismantling of official export authorities and exchange controls establishes a direct link between world prices and revenues of exporters, increasing their net profitability and bringing domestic relative prices into line with their international equivalents.

In other words, for the deregulation of domestic markets and exposure to world trade to generate industrial efficiency, firms must be induced to expand production in competitive sectors and shut down plant in uncompetitive sectors, or else to reorganise inefficient activities in some radical fashion. That this should happen as planned depends on a large number of assumptions about institutional behaviour, and a particular neo-classical vision of the firm itself (FitzGerald, 1992).

However, as Table 4.1 indicates, the record of private investment in the 1980s does not reflect at all a rapid recovery under structural adjustment in which firms and households respond to the new market incentives.

Table 4.1 Shares of private investment in GDP in selected countries, 1970–90 (%)

	Argentina	Chile	Colombia	Peru	Venezuela
1970–79	12.6	7.0	12.5	14.8	22.1
1980–81	12.7	16.6	11.7	21.5	11.7
1985	7.6	6.8	9.4	12.6	10.6
1990	4.5	15.6	7.4	12.0	4.9

Source: Pfefferman and Madrassy, 1992.

4.3 THE APPARENT CONSEQUENCES OF ADJUSTMENT POLICY FOR LATIN AMERICAN INDUSTRY

It is of course very difficult – if not foolhardy – to make generalisations about the experience of fifteen economies over as many years. None the less, some general points do seem to emerge from the data which indicate that the experience of structural adjustment has been rather different from what might be expected from the standard model summarised above.

As far as relative prices are concerned, the key variable – the real exchange rate – appears to have been more difficult to adjust and keep stable than had been expected.[5] In part this is due to the fact that the real exchange rate itself is not a policy variable at all, because it cannot be directly controlled. One empirical definition would see it as the ratio between the nominal exchange rate and the domestic rate of inflation. However, the nominal exchange rate itself is no longer under direct central bank administrative control in most countries of the region, and even open-market operations are constrained by the need to maintain minimal reserve levels so as to retain private sector confidence, or in some cases are limited by specific legislation. The domestic rate of inflation has thus become the main target in most cases, to be reduced by monetary policy – that is, by high interest rates and cuts in public expenditures. As a consequence, it is through control of inflation rather than export promotion that macroeconomic policy has affected industry – with inconsistent effects on profitability and investment incentives. On the one hand, reduced domestic demand and high interest rates are widely observed to have reduced profit margins. On the other hand, improved real exchange rates and real wage reductions induced by unemployment have probably improved them in some instances.

Another policy-related empirical definition of the real exchange rate would see this as essentially determined by the ratio of nominal exchange rate to the nominal wage rate.[6] The nominal exchange rate itself is highly sensitive to exogenous shocks in the form of fluctuations in the external terms of trade, the generally downward trend of which during the period has tended to favour export industry. However, the recent return of flight capital to the region, attracted by high real interest rates and the privatisation of public enterprises, has tended to force up nominal exchange rates. Schadler (1992) stresses the need to sterilise these inflows in order to avoid overvaluation, but from the point of view of industrial modernisation it would seem that programmed imports of capital goods and technology would seem to be more helpful – as well as placing downward pressure on the real exchange rate itself. The nominal wage rate, in turn, has been held down at least below the rate of inflation by a variety of mechanisms. In some cases, direct wage controls or means of social repression have been applied, which have often been successful in retaining costs inflation but have also affected productivity negatively and have been difficult to sustain. In particular, social unrest has tended to disturb investor confidence. In other cases, some sort of mutual linkage of the growth of prices (that is, profits) and wages has been negotiated as an implicit real-exchange-rate policy, although this has proved very difficult to sustain for prolonged periods of time and has not enjoyed the same support from the Bretton Woods institutions as the standard shock therapy has. The two 'large' regional economies that are outside the scope of this study, Mexico and Brazil, provide good examples of social 'pacts' which do seem to be effective in achieving macro-economic stabilisation, despite their heterodox origins. In addition, the changing nature of capital inflows has generally had a negative effect on employment generation.[7]

In all cases, the real exchange rate appears to have exhibited wide fluctuations from one year to the next, as well as a general tendency for the real devaluations of the mid 1980s to have been 'lost' by the early 1990s, as Table 4.2 indicates. In other words, not only has the expected structural shift in relative prices proved difficult to attain, but there is

Table 4.2 Relative prices and public investment in selected countries

	Argentina	Chile	Colombia	Peru	Venezuela
Real exchange rate (1980 = 100)					
1988–9	279	190	170	82	179
1992–3	121	178	171	43	193
Real wage rate (1980 = 100)					
1988–9	90	101	122	60	48
1992	78	114	135	40	41
Real interest rate (RIR) (%)					
CPI inflation (1991–2)	17.8	14.1	25.0	60.8	34.5
Bank loan rate (1991)	15.1	23.9	37.3	173.8	33.9
Implicit RIR	–14.3	64.9	47.3	182.8	–1.6
Public investment (% of GDP)					
1981	8.6	5.2	8.6	7.3	12.8
1990	3.0	4.6	7.6	2.3	10.3

Sources: IDB, *Economic and Social Progress in Latin America* (various years) as quoted in Felix (1994); The World Bank, *World Development Report 1994*; Pfefferman and Madrassy (1992).

every reason to believe that the corresponding profit rates have fluctuated too, thus making the expected return on new industrial investments in the tradables sectors uncertain. In the sector of tradables – or at least that part remaining after import liberalisation – unit profit rates may have been more stable, but levels of demand have remained depressed in many cases, while recovery in others has been only sporadic.

Throughout the region there has been a sharp decline in the share of public investment in GDP, closely linked to attempts to resolve the debt crisis.[8] On the one hand, strenuous efforts have been made to reduce the public sector borrowing requirement as a whole. On the other hand, close limits have been placed on overseas borrowing by state enterprises by both central governments and international agencies. This decline has been exacerbated by the 'transfer problem', where the current-account surplus required to repay debt can only be obtained by a cut in public investment inversely proportionate to its traded goods content.[9] This sacrifice did not lead to reduced public sector borrowing requirements in the 1980s, due to the rising world interest rates on external debt, although the burden has eased in the 1990s as prime rates in the USA have declined. However, this collapse of public investment in Latin America has been accompanied by a fall in the private investment rate in most countries in the region. The recovery, where present, is found only after prolonged periods of decline (Cardoso, 1993; Greene and Villanueva, 1993).

High real interest rates are widely observed to have affected private investment negatively in a number of countries, and as the origins of these rates are to be found in financial market liberalisation and the defence of exchange-rate 'anchors', they have not declined with falling fiscal deficits. High real interest rates have undoubtedly reduced industrial profitability as well as reducing the relative attraction of industrial shareholding. What is more, the liberalisation of interest rates where goods and factor markets do not freely clear, and where inadequate supervision of banks leads to adverse selection and moral hazard, is hardly likely to stimulate investment in tradables sectors.[10] Much faith has been placed in emerging stock markets as a means of channelling resources into industry, but in practice it would appear that this has not happened, probably for three reasons. First, these markets have been dominated by speculative funds, attracted by high-yield government bonds, bank paper and privatisation issues. Second, these markets only quote a few large industrial groups, which do not permit a sufficient proportion of voting stock to be traded to make a takeover possible and thus force management to become more efficient. Third, companies rely on retained profits and long-term bank credit to finance fixed investment. The net effect of privatisation on industrial investment is hard to assess. On the one hand, such measures have undoubtedly increased investor confidence as a whole and are widely regarded as 'locking in' governments to a more market-orientated strategy and to future fiscal prudence. On the other hand, a great deal of investible private funds, particularly returning flight capital, is being used to purchase government assets in the non-traded utilities sectors.[11]

The converse case for 'crowding in' – that is, that declining public investment has caused private investment to fall – is difficult to confirm empirically, largely because the effect could only be expected in the long run.[12] None the less, partial evidence would suggest that three effects are widespread in the region. First, the lack of public investment in transport, telecommunications and urban infrastructure has left small and medium Latin American economies behind in the worldwide competition for direct foreign investment. Second, the reduction of state expenditure on technological research, and the training and education of the workforce has sharply reduced the capability of domestic corporations to compete internationally. Third, the elimination of specific credit and technical assistance programmes for small firms has reduced their ability to enter the industrial sector.

The evidence on the international competitiveness of Latin American industry over the past decade[13] is somewhat ambiguous. In terms of RCAs advances have often been made in resource-based sectors, and there is no evidence that labour-intensive industries have been made more competitive by declining real wage costs. However, it is difficult to conclude that a major shift in the competitive structure of Latin American industry, which was to be expected from the exposure to world prices, has taken place during the 1980s. In terms of firm size, there are numerous indications that small and medium enterprises in particular have been negatively affected by import liberalisation.

4.4 ALTERNATIVE EXPLANATIONS OF THE APPARENT GAP BETWEEN THE MODEL AND EXPERIENCE

There is clearly a general agreement among policy-makers of all persuasions that a strong real exchange rate, fiscal solvency and a competitive traded-goods sector are desirable goals both for the economy as a whole and for industry in particular. However, as we have seen, the first two objectives are difficult to sustain and the third objective requires massive private investment which has yet to take place.

One widely held explanation of this gap between the structural adjustment model and the reality as experienced in Latin America is that the policies themselves, while correct in design, have not been properly implemented. This approach, which is properly associated with The World Bank and the IMF, runs the obvious danger of being tautologically true and thus unverifiable: if a particular industry has failed to recover, then this can only be because the government did not pursue the right policies. This approach has three distinct variants.

(i) The SAP was not implemented in the right sequence so that, for example, the failure to close the budget deficit while liberalising capital markets forces up real interest rates and penalises industrial investment;[14]

(ii) The SAP was not implemented for long enough, so that, for example, the private sector remained uncertain as to whether the real exchange rate would be maintained in the future. This is also a good reason why recent programmes cannot be properly evaluated;[15]

(iii) The SAP was hampered by populist measures such as wage indexing, employment creation or food subsidies which, though well-intentioned, distort the market and have a greater social cost than that which they were intended to avoid.[16]

This stress on implementation is reinforced by the critique of the limited administrative capability of Latin American governments – the problem of governance – due not so much to a shortage of skilled state managers as to the lack of clear legislation and social accountability. It should also be remembered that authorities such as The World Bank do point out that, although the reforming Latin American economies have undertaken the correct trade policies, particularly the abandonment of import controls and the reduction of tariffs to GATT levels, their OECD partners have maintained protective barriers which prevent the potential for manufactures exports being realised.

Finally, if all else fails, there remains a reductionist solution: only sectors which are efficient survive structural adjustment. So, if and where particular industrial sectors fail to prosper, this merely indicates that they have no comparative advantage and it would be better from the point of view of both stakeholders in that sector and society as a whole if they were to be closed down and the resources used elsewhere. There is also, of course, a methodological difficulty here of the *post hoc propter hoc* variety: if the survival of a sector after adjustment is accepted as proof of its efficiency, then by definition adjustment makes industry more efficient unless it is eliminated completely – and even in this case, the economy as a whole has become more efficient by dispensing with industry.[17]

The other main explanation of the gap – notably associated with ECLAC and more generally regarded as a 'heterodox view' – is that the design itself is at fault.[18] Indeed, it is argued that the implementation of SAPs has had a series of negative effects on industrial advance in the region and the view held by many Latin American economists is that the fault lies in the policy design itself.

(i) Stabilisation based on monetary policies has resulted in excessive domestic demand contraction, which leads to industry working at low capacity-utilisation and high direct production costs, while high real interest rates on working capital increase total unit costs still further, both reducing industrial output unnecessarily and making it less competitive internationally;
(ii) Wholesale import liberalisation has undermined domestic firms – particularly small and medium enterprises – putting many out of business or reducing their domestic market share before they have had time to react to favourable real exchange rates and move into export production on the basis of economies of scale or scope;
(iii) SAPs have involved a sudden reduction of public investment in infrastructure and support functions ranging from transport and power to research and training, and have reduced the technological capability of Latin American manufacturing to respond to new opportunities in world markets.

In addition, as in the orthodox critique, much is made of the failure of the OECD countries to liberalise access to their own markets, although ECLAC would emphasise the barriers to more advanced industrial exports including production services, as opposed to The World Bank, which would stress access to markets in more labour-intensive products where comparative advantage is held to be stronger.

There is, of course, some truth in both explanations, and the second in particular has the merit of focusing upon specific industrial bottlenecks. They both assume, however, that what happens to the macro-economy – and by extension industry – is the result of government policy, either good policy poorly applied or poor policy rigorously applied. This assumption probably underestimates the influence of events in the world economy or within the private sector itself, which may have as great an effect on industrial investment as macro-economic policy.

However, both lines of explanation seem to miss the central issue: just what has happened to industrial firms under adjustment *as firms*. Research on this topic is only at an initial stage, but four aspects of firm behaviour seem to merit particular attention.

(i) Recent econometric work on private investment behaviour in LDCs,[19] as well as the central tradition of macro-economic modelling, would tend to indicate that sustained demand growth is the main factor explaining gross fixed capital formation – which can be regarded either as reflecting long-run profit expectations or a process of capital stock adjustment with an extended lag structure. Other significant explanatory factors appear to be public investment and external debt levels, both of which can be seen as reflecting profit expectations, and not the real exchange rate or real interest rates. Clearly it is the expectation of profitability, rather than relative prices or domestic debt, which is of key importance in investment decisions;

(ii) The expansion of a firm, particularly in the case of small and medium enterprises, requires a stable long-term relationship with financial intermediaries.[20] The illiquidity generated by large industrial projects and the non-marketable nature of technology as an asset both require a long-term bank support even though most investment is financed by retained profits. Many Latin American banks were undermined in the 1980s by bad debts from their industrial clients, and financial liberalisation itself has deliberately dismantled the regulatory mechanisms which forced banks to support industry.[21] This phenomenon of 'disintermediation' affects small firms rather than larger firms, which can count upon the support of a bank in their *grupo* or even upon international banks;

(iii) Industrial investment decisions are made by managers who must balance acquisition of fixed assets in manufacturing against possible returns and risk of alternative assets. This trade-off is not expressed through stock markets or even alternative uses of bank credit, rather it is a strategic decision by family ownership consortia or multifirm *grupos* where alternatives are likely to be more liquid trading opportunities, particularly imports, or foreign assets.[22] Consequently, the relative degree of risk may be more important to the investor than immediate profitability, and in this context the attraction of the recent reflux of capital to public debt, privatised parastatal utilities and short-term deposits is of considerable relevance;

(iv) Uncertainty is a serious constraint on private investment in projects of long maturation,[23] and in the case of the smaller Latin American economies the uncertainty about both external shocks transmitted from the world economy and the continuity of the policy regime has undoubtedly increased over the past decade. In addition, political uncertainty clearly affects private investment uncertainty.[24]

4.5 IMPLICATIONS FOR FUTURE INDUSTRIALISATION STRATEGY

The implications of the two canonical positions defined above for future industrialisation policy are quite different. On the one hand, the orthodox school would argue that the same policies must be pursued, but more consistently and over a longer period, so that private sector expectations are permanently changed and both capital and labour shift in response to market signals. In particular, overvaluation of exchange rates by capital inflows should be avoided by appropriate sterilisation measures and social expenditure to combat unemployment should be targeted to the very poor so as not to impede labour-market clearing. Above all, free-market policies should be 'locked in' by credible institutional commitments such as central bank autonomy and privatisation of state enterprises, and moral hazard should be avoided by the authorities' refusing to bail out bankrupt firms or banks.

The heterodox alternative is not to deny the need for macro-economic stability or favourable real exchange rates, but rather to suggest that specific government interventions are needed in addition to allow new competitive industrial branches to emerge where there are scale economies and extended learning periods. Such interventions, rather than relying on tariff protection as in the past, would focus on the provision of specific industrial infrastructure, upgrading the labour force and subsidising R&D as a means of strengthening technological capability.

There seem to be elements of good sense in both positions, and it could even be argued that they are not incompatible. However, the argument presented in this chapter would seem to imply a somewhat different approach to policy, based on effective domestic support for internationally competitive firms. This is, of course, the policy practice in the 'miracle economies' of East Asia (Felix, 1994). This in turn would have implications for finance and trade policy. The importance of the institutional setting for the deregulation of interest rates and credit allocation is crucial here, because goods markets that reflect world prices will not be enough to ensure the private investment necessary to restructure production. In particular, adequate supervision over banks to limit the incidence of adverse selection and moral hazard is clearly crucial. However, probably even more important is an ownership and control structure in industry that combines financial discipline over management with a capability to provide a conditional financial shield for corporate restructuring.

To stimulate industrial investment itself, stable market expectations, tax conditions favouring re-investment of profits and long-term credit are probably the most important factors under government control. Technological and infrastructure support are probably more important to allow medium-sized firms to grow than to ensure investment in either large or small firms. Foreign direct investment in manufacturing appears to be attracted by much the same factors, logically enough. Pfefferman and Madrassy (1992) and The World Bank (1994) suggest that country characteristics such as infrastructure and skills are determinant in attracting foreign direct investment.

To this would have to be added a more coherent approach to small and medium firms, which still tend to be regarded by policy-makers in the region as a means of soaking up industrial unemployment. Experience in both the European Union and east Asia, however, indicates that small and medium firms play a crucial role as subcontractors to large competitive firms – although this relationship has to be stimulated by specific institutional arrangements and long-term support from banks.

Finally, as far as international trading relations are concerned, apart from the obvious need for negotiated market access – having lost the opportunity to demand this as the counterpart to reduced import tariffs within the Uruguay Round – there is a real need for a more rigorous competition policy on an international scale so that Latin American firms can survive on world markets.[25] Similarly, special regulatory arrangements may be required in order that corporate stock can achieve appropriate investment grades on international capital markets in its own right – rather than simply as depository receipts. International corporate finance of this kind is required to provide the working capital for exporters, because fixed investment will be funded primarily by retained profits.

The central point in the somewhat speculative argument put forward in this chapter is that successful structural adjustment requires a high rate of private investment in internationally competitive traded production and supportive non-traded public investment and that the macro-economic stabilisation policies implemented in practice have not been such as to promote this outcome. The chapter suggests that the market provides on its own neither the stable expectations nor the long-term access to markets and finance that successful structural adjustment requires.

Notes

1. Indeed, they are castigated by The World Bank (1993) as 'rent-seekers' who conspire with governments in order to shelter behind tariff barriers.
2. Felix (1994) suggests that in addition the wrong 'lessons' are being learned from the east Asian 'miracle'.
3. This section is drawn from Summers and Pritchett (1993), Mills and Nallari (1993) and Khan and Knight (1985).
4. Define the relevant variables as follows: e = nominal exchange rate; e' = real exchange rate; p_t = prices of tradables; p_{nt} = prices of non-tradables; p = average prices; w = nominal wage rate; w' = real wage rate; a = share of traded goods in output; r = profit margin ('mark-up'); l = unit labour input to non-traded output, that is, the inverse of productivity. Then Dornbusch (1980) defines the real exchange rate as:

    $$e' = p_t/p_{nt}$$

    and

    $$w' = w/p$$

    where

    $$p = ap_t + (1-a)p_{nt}$$

    so that

    $$w' = w/[\{ae' + (1-a)\}p_{nt}]$$

    Defining prices of non-tradables, for simplicity, as:

    $$p_{nt} = (1+r)wl$$

    then

    $$w' = [\{ae' + (1-a)\}(1+r)l]^{-1}$$

5. This problem is discussed exhaustively in IDB (1993) and The World Bank (1993, 1994). There appears to be a real conflict within these two institutions (and with the IMF) as to the relative merits of monetary stabilisation based on a nominal exchange rate 'anchor' (which implies overvaluation of the exchange rate in practice) and real devaluation to force structural adjustment with inevitable – albeit hopefully temporary – inflationary consequences.

6. Dornbusch and Helmers (1988) use this concept empirically. In the notation of no. 21, we have

$$e' = \frac{e}{w} \cdot \frac{p'}{(1+r)1}$$

7. A macro-economic model which demonstrates this process is set out in FitzGerald and Mavrotas (1994).
8. This seems to be a world-wide phenomenon (Greene and Villanueva, 1993).
9. Bacha (1990) provides a model of this, and points out that the effect on private investment depends on which constraint (fiscal, foreign exchange or savings) on GDP growth binds at any one time.
10. The ambiguous effect of financial liberalisation on private investment is demonstrated by Morisset (1993).
11. The World Bank (1994) indicates that this is a world-wide phenomenon.
12. Both Cardoso (1993) and Leff and Sato (1988) provide econometric evidence for this phenomenon.
13. See IDB (1993) for a comprehensive study.
14. This seems to be the general conclusion of Corbo *et al.* (1992).
15. Serven and Solimano (1992a) conclude that this is a general problem beyond Latin America as well.
16. Along with the previous two points, this 'institutional' point is stressed in The World Bank (1993).
17. This ignores, of course, questions of dynamic efficiency – where short-term market forces can lead to reduced rates of industrial investment (Lucas Jr, 1988; Romer, 1986).
18. This, of course, is the longstanding *cepalino* argument in the structuralist tradition (ECLAC, 1990a).
19. FitzGerald and Mavrotas (1994) discuss this in depth, and offer an adapted form of the standard accelerator model that takes into account exogenous shocks transmitted from the world economy.
20. Gibson and Tsakalotos (1992) show how financial disintermediation, by breaking the long-term link between industrial firms and their bankers, has led to declining manufacturing investment in Southern Europe.
21. Morriset (1993) suggests that this might be so for sound theoretical reasons, in sharp contrast to the simplistic model of capital markets that informed the influential 'financial repression' model (Vogel and Buser, 1976).
22. See FitzGerald (1992) for a discussion of the implications of this phenomenon (which seems to characterise all semi-industrialised economies) for firm behaviour.
23. Risk depresses investment to the extent that this is 'irreversible' (Bertola and Caballero, 1994); *a fortiori* uncertainty reduces investment as it arises from lack of information about future risks.
24. Although a case can be made for democracy having a positive effect (Pastor and Hilt, 1993).
25. The NAFTA is a very special case of territorial integration based on a high degree of prior intra-industry integration, and is not at all likely to be extended to the rest of Latin America (FitzGerald, 1994b).

5 The Scope for Industrial Policy in a Free-Trade Environment

José Tavares de Araujo Jr

5.1 INTRODUCTION

In his book *The Work of Nations*, Reich highlights one of the most compelling characteristics of our times, the survival of national states within the framework of a global economy:

> Each nation's primary political task will be to cope with the centrifugal forces of the global economy which tear at the ties binding citizens together – bestowing ever greater wealth on the most skilled and insightful, while consigning the less skilled to a declining standard of living. As borders become ever more meaningless in economic terms, those citizens best positioned to thrive in the world market are tempted to slip the bonds of national allegiance, and by so doing disengage themselves from their less favored fellows. (Reich, 1991, p. 3)

This tension is present at several ongoing processes in the world economy, such as the trend towards regional economic integration, the multilateral negotiations in the GATT, and the constant mutations in the time-honoured battle between free traders and protectionists. From the perspective of industrial organisation, it appears under the format of an intricate challenge for policy-makers. During the last twenty years, technical progress has allowed a dramatic reduction in the costs of information and data processing, through innovations such as personal computers, modems, and fax machines. These technologies form the core of the present trend towards globalisation that signifies, among other things, a standardisation of business practices and expectations. Until recently, only TNCs were able to maintain weekly contacts with their clients and partners in different countries. Today, small firms have on-line access to international data banks, and can watch the daily behaviour of their foreign competitors. In this context, several conventional instruments of industrial policy such as tariffs, quotas, and capital controls become anachronisms that are incompatible with the material base of contemporary society. They are either worthless or unnecessary sources of commercial complaints at home and abroad.

However, the continual re-creation of uneven conditions of competition is intrinsic to technical progress, and this characteristic has been particularly intense in the recent past. This generates two sources of protectionist pressures. On the one hand, innovating firms lobby for regulations that will allow them to extend the period during which they can extract Schumpeterian rents from their new technologies. Such regulations seldom imply explicit barriers to merchandise trade, but to the knowledge embodied in the innovations, – that is, legislation on patents, trade marks, licensing, and other instruments to preserve intellectual property. On the other hand, industries that suddenly became obsolete push for temporary relief, in order to restructure and regain international competitiveness.

Thus, while the gains from global competition become more appealing, domestic industries press their governments for privileges in order to enter into that game. This is the contemporary dilemma of industrial policy: how to create special conditions for capital accumulation at home, without establishing direct constraints on the international movements of citizens, goods, and financial resources.

The objective of this chapter is to discuss the industrial policy dilemma in three steps. The first step, presented in Section 5.2, is a brief inquiry into the analytical instruments that explain the process of competition in a global economy. It will be argued that Coase's classical paper 'The Nature of the Firm' provides a basic tool to deal with corporation strategies, namely, the interplay between the costs of production and transaction. As Coase's approach is complementary to the theories on contestable markets and Schumpeterian competition, his contribution can be integrated into a general framework that covers the two relevant themes of any study on international competitiveness: the firm and the industry structure. The second and third steps, presented in Sections 5.3 and 5.4, refer, respectively, to the domestic and the international dimensions of the industrial policy dilemma. The essence of the argument to be made is that, nowadays, every country – whatever its size or stage of development – must carry out its public policies under constraints imposed by global competition. What varies among nations is their ability to draw a clear cut border-line between homework and international bargaining. The main conclusions are summarised in Section 5.5.

5.2 INTELLIGENT FIRMS, SUSTAINABLE CONFIGURATIONS AND SCHUMPETERIAN COMPETITION

A convincing explanation of the managerial innovations that have been changing the competition patterns of the world economy since the mid 1980s was provided, although indirectly, by Coase in 1937. His paper 'The Nature of the Firm' contains an insightful answer to three basic questions for the theory of industrial organisation: why firms exist, what determines the number of firms and what determines firms' activities. His answer is well known: it all depends on the relation between production costs and transaction costs. Transaction costs, in Dahlman's neat definition, are 'search and information costs, bargaining and decision costs, policing and enforcement costs' (Dahlman, 1979, p. 148). Thus, as Coase restated recently:

> Although production could be carried out in a completely decentralized way by means of contracts between individuals, the fact that it costs something to enter into these transactions means that firms will emerge to organize what would otherwise be market transactions whenever their costs were less than the costs of carrying out the transactions through the market. The limit to the size of the firm is set where its costs of organizing a transaction become equal to the cost of carrying it out through the market. This determines what the firm buys, produces and sells. (Coase, 1988, p. 7)

The ratio between production costs and transaction costs is a direct function of existing technologies. Whenever technical progress reduces more intensively the former than the latter type of costs, the likely trend will be towards larger firms, vertical integration, and economic concentration; and vice versa. In the recent past, as the rate of innovations has been similar in both directions, a rather peculiar situation is emerging. On the one hand, new economies of scale are pushing towards a greater internationalisation of production lines. On the other, diminishing information costs are generating new economies of scope, – that is, new opportunities for re-arranging production vectors. Thus, as Reich pointed out:

> while competition among high-volume producers continues to compress profits on everything that is uniform, routine, and standard – that is, on anything that can be made, reproduced, or extracted in volume almost anywhere on the globe – successful businesses in advanced nations are

moving to a higher ground based on specially tailored products and services. The new barrier to entry is not volume or price; it is skill in finding the right fit between particular technologies and particular markets. Core corporations no longer focus on products as such; their business strategies increasingly center upon specialised knowledge. (Reich, 1991, p. 84)

These changes have been crystallised under the concept of intelligent enterprises, created by Quinn (1992): those firms that are able to define narrowly their core capabilities, and concentrate their output exclusively on those activities they can perform according to the best international practice. Every item included in the firm's output vector that cannot be produced under this rule must be subcontracted or bought from external suppliers. 'Intelligent' firms are very often small or medium-sized, have a 'flat' organisational lay-out, and their main strategic weapon is human capital. They constitute a contemporary illustration of Coase's approach.

Although no general survey has been published yet, there is a flourishing literature on the diffusion of managerial innovations inspired by the notion of 'intelligent' enterprises, and on the new roles for small and medium firms in the world economy. However, it is interesting to notice that this literature also registers the revitalisation of large corporations, and the corresponding trend towards economic concentration in several branches of industries. The theories on contestable markets and on Schumpeterian competition may explain these mixed trends.

The contestable markets theory addresses the same questions raised by Coase, but from a slightly different perspective. Instead of focusing on activities of firms, it is more concerned with the determination of industry structure. According to this theory, an industry configuration, that is, its number of incumbent firms, their respective output vectors, market shares, and price vectors, results from the interaction of three variables: the nature of available productive techniques, market size, and potential competition.

> One fundamental concept in this theory is that of sustainable configuration. It is: a price vector and a set of output vectors, one for each of the firms in the configuration, with the following properties. First, the quantities demanded by the market at the prices in question must equal the sum of the output of all the firms in the configuration. Second, the prices must yield to each active firm revenues that are no less than the cost of producing its outputs. And, last, there must be no opportuni-

ties for entry that appear profitable to potential entrants who regard the prices of the incumbent firms as fixed. (Baumol *et al.,* 1982, p. 5)

In other words, a sustainable configuration:

> must minimize the total cost to the industry of producing the total industry output. That is, no different number, size distribution, output quantities, or productive techniques for the industry's firms can provide the industry's output at a lower total cost than that incurred by the firms in a sustainable configuration. (p. 26)

In contrast with conventional wisdom, the contestable markets theory shows that monopolies and oligopolies are, in many cases, sustainable configurations. In principle, they can be highly transient, since technical progress, economic growth and public policies are constantly redefining the sustainability parameters. Yet, in practice, they frequently are long-lived, as aircraft, automotive, flat glass, electrical equipment, and several other manufacturing industries illustrate. The normative consequences of these features will be discussed in the next section. But, before that, let us consider other forces that are affecting concentration in the world economy.

Two outstanding aspects of the current patterns of global competition are the internationalisation of small and medium firms, and the partition of old TNCs into semi-independent business networks. Coase's approach provides, as we have seen, an interpretation for these institutional innovations: due to the sharp decline of transaction costs, large firms became superfluous entities for many industries. There are, of course, countervailing forces in this process, and the theory on Schumpeterian competition indicates one of them: firms have memory. As Nelson and Winter (1982) show, when confronted by similar market signals, firms may react differently, according to their own history of achievements and failures. The knowledge acquired from these experiences is stored in the firm's routines, which do not change easily. Managerial strategies that warranted leading positions for decades will not be abandoned without second thoughts, and the same innovation, assessed as a new technological paradigm by one firm, may be treated as a passing fashion by its competitor. IBM, GM, and other symbols of the American production system in this century are now immersed in this type of doubt. Their resistance to adopting new competition policies may either delay the ongoing decentralisation trends, or generate hybrid forms of industrial organisation, wherein, for instance, old administrative lay-outs would be combined with updated decision-making procedures.

5.3 INDUSTRIAL POLICY INSTRUMENTS: CONSISTENCY AND EFFICACY

According to the contestable markets theory, every government should have one permanent industrial policy target, namely, to ensure conditions of sustainability for all sectors of the economy. An alternative statement for this target would be to maximise the aggregate competitiveness of the industrial system, which is a direct function of the number of sustainable configurations operating therein. When a local industry has such a configuration, the incumbent firms do not need tariffs, subsidies, administrative controls, or any other form of governmental support in order to face foreign competition in the home economy. Thus, sustainability is a form of structural protection of the domestic market, which is more efficient than conventional protectionism, since it does not absorb public resources, generate rent-seeking, or distort prices.

Evidently, sustainability is the best answer to the industrial policy dilemma commented upon in Section 5.1. Although just a theoretical possibility, that will be realised only rarely, it has two fundamental merits. The first merit is that it provides a non-ideological reasoning for industrial policy, avoiding tiresome debates on 'market failure versus bureaucratic action' and 'invisible hands versus special interests' and, incidentally, showing that Reich was wrong in his caustic assertion that 'industrial policy is one of those rare ideas that has moved swiftly from obscurity to meaninglessness without any intervening period of coherence' (Reich, 1984, p. 32). The second merit is that of setting a clear policy target that can be used as a conceptual framework to evaluate governmental conduct.

In practice, there is a need for industrial policy in two circumstances: (i) to confer sustainability on an infant industry that may be running under a feasible configuration only because of protection;[1] and (ii) to return to a sustainable configuration that had lost its status due to technical progress in the rest of the world, or any other type of external shock. The former case is more frequent in LDCs, whereas the latter is the case for industrial restructuring that is typical in OECD countries. But, in every economy, and in either circumstance, there is a minimum set of conditions to be provided by the government. Although non-controversial, this set is not easily attained and is composed of three permanent requirements.

The first requirement is exchange rate equilibrium, within a context of macro-economic stability. This chapter does not aim to discuss the international monetary system and related issues, such as the harmonisation of macro-economic policies. However, it is necessary to remember that the economy's structure of effective protection becomes rather uncertain when the RER is volatile. Local production can be either overprotected, or exposed to unfair competition from abroad, depending upon RER swings. Among other harmful effects, this instability inhibits long-term contracts between local firms and independent foreign counterparts, due to the high risks involved in such types of operation. Together with intra-firm trade, these contracts form the core of intra-industry trade, which is a basic source of dynamism of contemporary world trade. In other words, RER instability raises transaction costs and precludes the realisation of the benefits generated by technical progress in the computer and telecommunication industries.

The second requirement is symmetry between the demand upon public resources and the capability of government to tax. The size and composition of public investment may vary according to the peculiarities of each economy, but the headings are similar everywhere: defence, education, infrastructure, science and technology, social security, and welfare. These expenditures play two strategic roles as industrial policy instruments. The first is Keynesian, by preserving a foreseeable demand source that equips local producers with better conditions to face market oscillations. This means lower levels of planned idle capacity, and, consequently, smaller unit costs. The second is Schumpeterian, through the public support to R&D activities, the ultimate growth source of industrial capitalism.

In an open economy, the maintenance of an adequate and non-inflationary level of public investment requires a fiscal system that is able to reconcile international competitiveness and social fairness with a heavy tax burden. This implies a long-run fiscal policy systematically committed to reducing tax rates and to enlarging the tax base, objectives that only become feasible when education and income distribution are permanent national top priorities. The capability to meet this challenge is, nowadays, a fundamental attribution that differentiates advanced from developing countries. On an average, between 1981 and 1988, the tax burden jumped from 41.3 to 44.4 per cent of GDP in the European Community, and remained around 36 per cent in the OECD countries (OECD, 1990). In contrast, among the six largest Latin American economies, only Chile has been able to keep a performance similar to the OECD pattern, albeit far from the European levels (ECLAC, 1992a).

The third requirement to be attained within an industrial strategy is the provision of an institutional framework to regulate the competition process. Recently, the Industry Development Division at The World Bank presented a comprehensive approach on this subject, covering the whole set of policy and institutional measures that would ensure a competitive environment to modern economies (Atiyas *et al.,* 1992). Three types of measures are proposed therein: those that strengthen discipline, enhance mobility and improve the availability of resources. One basic assumption is that these measures are strictly complementary to each other. Emphasis on one set of measures to the neglect of the others is likely to be ineffective, or at worst, counter-productive. Hence when resources are not available and mobility is restricted, increased discipline may aggravate financial distress, which, in turn, may force the government to relax discipline once again. In such an environment, the government's intentions to strengthen discipline may in fact not be credible *ex ante*. Similarly, an environment with ample resources but insufficient discipline is likely to result in their inefficient allocation and use (Atiyas *et al.,* 1992, p. 3).

The discussion in Section 5.2 suggests an additional assumption, that those measures should be convergent with the natural trends prevailing in the industrial system. Hence, industry decentralisation should be stimulated whenever the ratio of production costs to transaction costs is raising, and, consequently, the competitiveness of the 'intelligent' enterprises is improving; but the restructuring of sustainable monopolies or oligopolies should never be forced. As Baumol observed, 'a history of absence of entry in an industry and a high concentration index may be signs of virtue, not of vice' (Baumol, 1982, p. 14).

When an industry has a contestable configuration, no governmental intervention is necessary, since the discipline imposed by potential competitors is sufficient to preserve the public interest.[2] However, non-contestable but sustainable configurations need careful monitoring. This is the case where incumbent firms control a new technology that is not accessible to potential entrants.

5.4 CONCLUSION

This chapter's argument can be summarised by recalling a comment made by Mill some 150 years ago:

> There are some things with which governments ought not to meddle, and other things with which they ought; but whether right or wrong in

itself, the interference must work for ill, if government, not understanding the subject which it meddles with, meddles to bring about a result which would be mischievous. (Mill, 1848, p. 277)

Within the context framed by the contemporary dilemma of industrial policy, governments ought to meddle with four things: the first is to achieve exchange-rate steady equilibrium, which may demand some supra-national efforts regarding the harmonisation of national macro-economic policies, as argued elsewhere (Tavares de Araujo, 1992). The second is to maintain a tax system that is compatible with the levels of public investment required by the current international patterns of technical progress and welfare. The third is to monitor the conduct of the business community, but under the normative parameters indicated by the structural characteristics of each industry, that is the ratio of production costs to transaction costs, the nature of entry barriers, and the interplay between the existing technologies and the market size. The fourth is to pursue an international negotiating strategy that, on the one hand, would avoid injuring the performance of other economies, but, on the other hand, would ensure reciprocity from the rest of the world.

Notes

1. An industry configuration is feasible when all incumbent firms can serve the market without runnning into losses. Feasibility is a weaker requirement than sustainability, since a feasible configuration need not be the most efficient configuration. See Baumol, *et al.*, 1982, pp. 24 and 25.
2. Baumol, *et al.* (1982, p. 5) define a perfectly contestable market as one that is accessible to potential entrants and has the following two properties:

    > First, the potential entrants can, without restriction, serve the same market demands and use the same productive techniques as those available to the incumbent firms. Thus, there are no entry barriers in the sense of the term used by Stigler. Second, the potential entrants evaluate the profitability of entry at the incumbent firm's pre-entry prices. That is, although the potential entrants recognize that an expansion of industry output leads to lower prices – in accord with the market demand curves – the entrants nevertheless assume that if they undercut incumbents' prices they can sell as much of the corresponding good as the quantity demanded by the market at their own prices.

6 Export Processing Free Zones as an Export Strategy for Central America and the Caribbean

Teresa S. Weersma-Haworth

6.1 INTRODUCTION

The growth of EPFZs – also known as special economic zones, foreign trade zones or free economic zones – is probably one of the most significant institutional innovations to have spread on the world economic scene in the past twenty years. Two areas of concern come to mind when considering EPFZs as an alternative option to the export development strategy for countries in the region of Central America and the Caribbean. The first can best be expressed in terms of the characteristics and the past experience with EPFZs in developing countries with respect to their contribution to export and/or industrial development; the second in terms of the ways EPFZs are being used as instruments of export development in countries of the region within a changing international environment, and their potential for growth.

6.2 CHARACTERISTICS OF EXPORT PROCESSING ZONES

For the purpose of this chapter the concept of an EPFZ used is that of an industrial estate which forms an enclave within the national customs territory, usually situated near an international port or airport. The entire production of such a zone is normally intended for export. Imports of raw materials, intermediate products, equipment and machinery required for export production are not subject to the payment of customs duty. Other facilities usually offered include a tailor-made physical and communication infrastructure including essential industrial services, special financial and fiscal incentives ranging from tax holidays to guarantees for profit repatriation and, in most cases, exemptions from labour laws prevailing in the host country. Time-consuming customs procedures on importation into the zones and exportation from the zones are kept to a minimum. At the broadest level, EPFZs are created by LDCs for the purpose of promoting the development of export-oriented manufacturing industries with foreign investment expected to provide the main impetus.

The role played by EPFZs in promoting industrialisation has always been a controversial topic. Experience in many countries, in particular in east and south-east Asia, has shown that such zones can contribute substantially to the generation and promotion of manufactured exports and to the provision of employment opportunities. However, they have more often than not been characterised by a concentration on only a few industrial branches, by the use of simple and fragmented production technologies, and by the lack of backward linkages with the domestic economy (Fröbel et al., 1980). Below I shall discuss some characteristics of EPFZs that are critical to a proper assessment of their contribution to industrial development.

One observation on EPFZs is that they attract non-complex industries which are usually vertically integrated into TNCs. The foreign firms have moved labour-intensive stages of their production processes to EPFZs, mainly in response to labour-costs differentials between developed and developing countries. Major sectors of production in EPFZs are electronics, clothing, footwear, leather products, electrical products, optical goods, plastic, toys, sporting goods, car parts and minor transport equipment. The pre-assembly stages which may require advanced technology usually remain located in the industrialised countries.

EPFZs have by and large maintained their enclave character and have not established substantive linkages with the industrial sector of the host economies. Also, except within a limited number of EPFZs which have been operating for some time, where some instance of full manufacturing can be found, there has been no marked diversification in the structure of production and only slight increases in levels of complexity.

Although production processes in EPFZs are customarily outwardly integrated into globally organised production systems, in most cases they have few, if any, linkages with adjacent processes within the export enclaves. In general, foreign-owned plants in export zones exhibit a low level of production linkage to existing or proposed 'indigenous' plants. Where marginal and occasional recourse is made to local suppliers and sub-contractors, this imposes a form of specialisation on local producers which does not favour a more developed form of integration.

Another observation on EPFZs when considering them as an option for industrial development is that the zones rarely if ever develop according to their original plan. This is illustrated by the development of a number of zones into industrial monocultures, rather than into well-balanced and diversified enclaves, as often envisaged by the planners. So, though on the one hand EPFZs may assist a country to diversity its exports, there is the danger that EPFZs can become too specialised and dependent on the vicissitudes of the international market.

This evolution, found to varying degrees in practically all EPFZs, appears to have little to do with the host country's factor endowments or with the marketing strategy of the zone's authorities. It seems to be linked largely to the nature of the first investors in the zone: if the first investors are electronics firms, for instance, the subsequent investors will almost automatically tend to belong to the same industry, thus leading to an electronic monoculture in the zone and, indeed, in all zones of the country. And if the first investors belong to the textile and garment industry, this will most likely lead to a textile and garment monoculture. Thus, textiles and garments account for 89.9 per cent of employment in Sri Lanka's EPFZs (1981), 61.3 per cent in the Dominican Republic's zones (1985), and 54 per cent in Egypt's zones. Electronics accounted for 74.5 per cent of employment in Malaysia (1979) and 54.3 per cent in Mexico (1984).

This phenomenon is due to a number of complex sociological and economic reasons which suggest that an EPFZ, like any other complex social organisation, has a life of its own and an internal dynamism that the planning process cannot anticipate or control.

A further observation on the structural benefits of EPFZs is their track record and impact on employment in the host countries. Employment in all EPFZs located in LDCs is currently estimated to be slightly less than 3 per cent of the officially registered work force in manufacturing industries in these countries. This observation, although requiring substantiation from case studies by country, does indicate the potential EPFZs could have in increasing employment in manufacturing and specifically in the registration of the work force in manufacturing. At present it can be stated that EPFZs create substantial new employment opportunities, but usually have no positive effect on the unemployment rate of the host countries. The reason for this is that the zones' industries tend to attract large numbers of young women who, in other circumstances, would not have sought or found a job. In other words, the employment effects stem from an increase in the participation rate in the labour force and not from providing jobs to unemployed workers. The main reason for this is that EPFZs' production sites offer employment predominantly to low-skilled manpower performing simple manual operations which can be learned in comparatively short periods of time. It should however be noted that in virtually all countries, as industrial production for export becomes more significant, the demand for technically qualified personnel for the maintenance, operation, supervision and repair of manufacturing equipment increases. At some EPFZ sites the increasing automation of existing production is likely to bring about a gradual change in skill requirements. Some of the longer established sites are beginning to exhibit types of production which go far beyond mere assembly. For example, integrated production lines for the full manufacture of quite sophisticated products such as motorcycles, engines, cameras and TV sets can be found in EPFZs in Brazil, Mexico, Singapore and South Korea. This more complex structure of production naturally requires a much greater depth and diversity of occupational skills.

The contributions of EPFZs to exports, value added, capital accumulation and foreign-exchange earnings have been subject of empirical analysis. A review by UNCTAD (1983) showed that the contribution of EPFZs to total manufactured and semi-manufactured exports in many developing countries was less than 5 per cent. However, at sectoral levels, EPFZs may account for more sizeable contributions.

The same review identified that the share of domestic value added in EPFZ exports does not normally exceed 25 per cent. Wages paid to production workers account for at least 70 per cent of domestic value added in EPFZs. The balance is accounted for mainly by charges paid for local public and private services, including the lease of land and the rent of factory buildings to EPFZ enterprises. Income from local supplies of tradable production inputs to companies in EPFZs is in most cases insignificant.

The contribution of foreign investment in EPFZs to the capital stock of the host economies was comparatively unimportant during the 1970s, as EPFZ plants were normally simple production units carrying out labour-intensive operations. On the other hand, public investment expenditure on the development of an EPFZ estate may include the costs of public utilities and other infrastructure, constructed especially to meet the requirements of the free zones.

Perhaps the most difficult characteristic of EPFZs to ascertain is their contribution to net foreign-exchange earnings for the host country. The net foreign-exchange earnings are the amount earned on domestic value added which is essentially limited to the wage bill and some additional expenditure on local services, as discussed above. The amount of gross export sales less the foreign-exchange outlays on imported inputs would overstate the foreign exchange retained by host countries. Most of the profits of foreign investors are repatriated and not reinvested. Similarly, reserves set aside for depreciation purposes are not necessarily kept in the host economy. Tax revenues from EPFZ enterprises, which would represent foreign-exchange earnings for the host country, do not accrue in the case of a country offering tax holidays for a protracted period. When taxes are paid, manipulation of transfer prices can reduce taxable profits of subsidiaries in EPFZs.

An observation is in place pertaining to the mobility of foreign companies operating in EPFZs. The preference for relatively small plants in EPFZs, the low investment costs per workplace, the use of relatively inexpensive and simple equipment, the lack of backward linkages and the availability of standard factory buildings in nearly all EPFZs enable companies to relocate production from one country to another comparatively quickly. The footloose character of industries in EPFZs is, nevertheless, sometimes overestimated. Enterprises will undertake a move only if the present value of the difference between profits in alternative locations exceeds the costs of relocation, and in the case of joint-ventures, the costs of establishing a new partnership. Moreover, a threat of political unrest and economic upheaval may limit the options. Finally, fierce competition among countries to attract foreign investors forces host countries to provide increasingly attractive fiscal and financial incentives in order to prevent established firms from relocation.

Finally, the rapid growth of manufactured exports from LDCs during the late 1980s has gone hand in hand with significant changes in the behaviour of foreign investors, notably growing preference for non-traditional forms of industrial collaboration with enterprises of the host country, as well as in the strategies of local firms. There has been a clear shift towards more export-orientated and diversified forms of collaboration such as joint ventures, new forms of technical co-operation, licensing agreements and sub-contracting arrangements, and even direct participation of local firms in EPFZs.

6.3 EPFZs IN CENTRAL AMERICA AND THE CARIBBEAN

EPFZs are not a new phenomenon in Central America and the Caribbean but the way they operate has been changing significantly in five ways.

(i) Many zones are becoming quite specialised, with some operations moving away from the low-tech, foot-loose activities typical of the past, to more skill-intensive undertakings. For instance, two zones in the Dominican Republic, San Isidoro and Las Americas, are strictly reserved for high-tech and service industries such as data entry, data processing, computer graphics and telemarketing. In an investment which is typical of this trend, Teleport International, a USA-Japanese joint venture, set up the regions' first system for processing data from satellite transmissions in Jamaica's Montego Bay zone.

(ii) Another important change has been the introduction of private ownership and management of the zones. In the Dominican Republic, for instance, the trend has been accompanied by a proliferation of key support services provided by the zone developers, including legal and engineering consulting, manager and worker recruitment, and worker training.

(iii) Foreign direct investment in EPFZs in the Dominican Republic used to be dominated by US firms. Today there are investors from Taiwan and South Korea, who seek easy access to the market of the European Union, as well as a growing tendency of Dominicans to own companies in EPFZs, which encourages links with local suppliers. The San Cristobal Zone was set up by two local business groups and the local subsidiary of GTE. For the subsidiary, Codetel, part-ownership was a way to diversify operations and raise foreign-exchange earnings to finance expansion plants for its telephone business.

(iv) Both EPFZ developers and producers have been looking into alternative ways of financing. For instance, Costa Rica and the Dominican Republic considered plans to convert some foreign commercial debt in equity investment in their EPFZs. Another alternative source of financing is the SEC.936 funds that Puerto Rico is offering as low-costs loans for production-sharing arrangements between Puerto Rico and neighbouring Caribbean countries.

(v) The proliferation of EPFZs in the region has resulted in fierce competition to attract foreign investors. Countries have developed a wide array of incentives as shown in Table 6.1.

The countries in the region designed incentives based primarily on the critical resource they had to offer: cheap labour. To this have been added fiscal and other incentives such as the freedom to repatriate profits and exemption from tariffs and customs duties. Moreover, a variety of support services has been made available including advanced telecommunications and information processing facilities. Whereas previously a basic infrastructure sufficed, such as transport facilities, energy and water supply, nowadays more sophisticated technological infrastructure is required.

Table 6.1 Incentives offered in EPFZs

	Zones	Taxes	Tariffs	Market access	Other incentives
Costa Rica	(1) Limon (2) Santa Rosa (3) Cartago (4) Coto Sur	Six-year income tax exemption, then 50% for four years	No import/export quotas Import/export duty exemption, but 0.6% service charge on imported goods and raw materials and on c.i.f. value added of exports	CBI, GSP, TSUS 806/807 Cartago: Limited and controlled access to domestic market and CACM	Free repatriation of profits
Dominican Republic	(1) Puerto Plata (2) La Romana (3) San Pedro de Macoris (5) San Cristobal (6) Bani (7) San Isidro (January 1987) (8) Las Americas (mid-1987)	15-year exemption on all taxes	Duty-free import of capital goods, raw materials and equipment (but imports must be listed and approved in advance)	CBI, GSP, TSUS 806/807 Limited domestic market access	Free repatriation of profits On-site business support services provided by several zones
El Salvador	San Bartolo	10-year income tax exemption on corporate and personal income	Duty-free import of equipment and materials for 10 years; indefinite if firm exports 100% of production	CBI, GSP, TSUS 806/807 Limited and controlled access to domestic market and CACM	Free repatriation of profits
Guatemala	Santo Tomas de Castilla	12-year income tax exemption	No duties, levies or quotas on imports or exports	CBI, GSP, TSUS 806/807 Limited domestic market access	Free repatriation of profits

91

Table 6.1 Continued

	Zones	Taxes	Tariffs	Market access	Other incentives
Haiti	Port-au-Prince	Eight-year exemption on all taxes	Duty-free import of capital goods, machinery and raw materials	CBI, GSP, TSUS 806/807 Lomé Convention	Free repatriation of profits Reduced wages for workers during training period
Honduras	Puerto Cortes	Federal, state, local income sales and corporate tax exemption in perpetuity	Duty-free import/export of all goods	CBI, GSP, TSUS 806/807	Free repatriation of profits Business support services provided on site
Jamaica	(1) Kingston (2) Montego Bay (3) Spanish Fort	Income, profit tax exemption in perpetuity; local sales and property tax exemption	Duty-free import/export of all goods: no quotas or levies on imports/exports	CBI, GSP, TSUS 806/807 Lomé Convention	Free repatriation of profits; no other foreign exchange controls
Panama	Colon	15-year income tax exemption; local sales and property tax exemption	Duty-free import of capital goods, equipment and approved raw materials	CBI, GSP, TSUS 806/807 Limited domestic market access	Free repatriation of profits No licensing of imports/exports; training programs and preferential financing available
Puerto Rico	(1) Mayaguez (2) San Juan (3) Ponce	US federal tax exemption on corporate and personal income	Duty-free import of raw materials and finished goods	Free access to domestic US market	Special incentives offered to service industries Preferential financing for 'twin-plant' projects with other Caribbean Basin countries; US laws apply

Source: US Department of Commerce, Caribbean Basin Division.

In addition to the wide range of fiscal incentives offered, the firms also enjoy special privileges of market access to the USA and in some cases to the market of the EU. The countries listed are all beneficiaries of the Caribbean Basin Initiative (CBI). The centrepiece of the CBI is duty and quota-free access to the USA market through 1995. However, some products such as apparel and textiles have been excluded. Though Puerto Rico is not a CBI beneficiary, operations in that country can benefit indirectly, since value added in Puerto Rico can be combined with that added in other CBI nations to make a product qualify for duty-free entry under the programme.

CBI beneficiaries also qualify for duty-free access to the market of the USA according to the GSP. Benefits of Items 9801 and 9802 of the US Tariff Schedule may also apply. These provisions allow products such as textiles that are processed offshore to re-enter the USA with duties levied only on the amount of value added generated outside the USA.

Haiti and Jamaica enjoy duty-free access to the European market under the Lomé Convention, which benefits former European colonies. Under Lomé there is no exclusion of sensitive products such as apparel, but producers must meet certain value-added criteria, as under the CBI. The English-speaking Caribbean islands also qualify for Canada's duty-free programme, known as Caribcan. It requires a minimum of 60 per cent local value added and excludes numerous products considered sensitive by Canadian industry.

To make an appropriate assessment of the contributions EPFZ may make to industrial development and the new insertion of small countries in world trade, analyses at a more disaggregated level are required. The next chapter provides a detailed study of a small EPFZ with a long history.

7 The Export Processing Free Zone of San Bartolo in El Salvador

Geske Dijkstra and Carlos Rivera Alemán

7.1 INTRODUCTION

The previous chapter by Weersma-Haworth has indicated that EPFZs are not a new phenomenon in Central America and the Caribbean and that an increasing number of zones has been established in the countries in the region. The study shows that nearly all countries in the region have designed packages of instruments to attract foreign investors to the zones within their borders. Moreover, it has been indicated that the way zones operate has been changing in several respects and that zones may differ substantially in terms of management and organisation, sources of investments and types of specialisation. As a consequence, it is hard to generalise about the contribution of EPFZs to industrial development, employment and exports. This chapter reviews the policies pursued in El Salvador to stimulate the establishment of EPFZs and presents a case study of the functioning of the San Bartolo EPFZ.

7.2 INDUSTRIAL POLICY AND THE PROMOTION OF EPFZs

Development of the domestic manufacturing sector in El Salvador was stimulated mainly by import-substitution policies until 1989. Throughout the period, industrial firms were supported by high import tariffs on final goods, and low tariffs on intermediate inputs and capital goods, as well as by tax exemptions and subsidies.

During the 1980s the exchange rate became overvalued due to the inflow of substantial amounts of foreign aid to support the government in the civil war. This 'aid-induced Dutch disease' (Saborio, 1992, p. 298) hampered industrial development and exports of manufactures.

As of 1989, the country started to open the economy. Overall protection of the manufacturing sector was reduced, tariffs on imports of final goods were lowered and tariffs on intermediate goods were increased. Export-promotion schemes were extended and plans were developed to expand the number of EPFZs in the country.

During the 1990s, a rapid trade liberalisation is taking place, the currency has become less overvalued and the bias against exports outside the EPFZ has been reduced significantly. According to the *Plan de Desarrollo Económico y Social* (MIPLAN, 1989), the most important instruments for promoting manufacturing industry are the opening of the economy and incentives for foreign investors. This plan does not include a special section on manufacturing development. As a result, export-promotion policies do not consider the possibly harmful impact that duty-free imports of raw materials and intermediate goods may have on local manufacturing.

Before the overall trade liberalisation was introduced, the country pursued a dualistic industrial policy: the domestic market was protected and at the same time exports were stimulated by means of specific instruments and the establishment of an EPFZ. In 1974 the first Export Promotion Law was introduced. A 'temporary import regime' was introduced which allowed for duty-free imports of intermediate goods used in export production. In particular the law stimulated export-orientated assembly activities.

The first EPFZ in San Bartolo became operational in October 1976 and is located at a distance of about ten kilometres from San Salvador, near Ilopango airport. In line with the dominant approach of the time, San Bartolo was developed as a state-owned, public project. It was financed with a loan of colon 55 million by the Bank for Central American Integration. This loan covered all construction expenses. The management of San Bartolo has been in the hands of different government institutions. At the moment, it is under the General Directory of Free Zones of the Ministry of the Economy.

The original project implied the construction of 120 000 m^2 of manufacturing space. The zone currently has a factory space of 66 000 m^2 and 22 business premises. It has a well-developed infrastructure, including water, electricity, telephone, fax, industrial waste service, security service and even sport facilities. Firms enjoy duty-free imports, and exemptions from income and property tax.

The Export Promotion Law of 1986 introduced the possibility of EPFZs being privately owned or administered by Salvadoreans and foreigners. This law also broadened the group of firms that qualify for establishment in an EPFZ to international trading companies, assembly firms and firms carrying out related or supplementary activities. Firms located in an EPFZ may also transfer duty-free imported inputs for assembly to other persons or firms in the country and outside the EPFZ, without paying import duties.

In 1990, the new government proclaimed a new Free Zone and Tax Haven Law. The new tax regime implied that all firms that export all of their production, or are exclusively active in international trade, enjoy exemptions from import, income and property taxes. In 1991, these benefits were also granted to firms exporting part of their production, in proportion with the share of output exported. In order to promote the construction of new EPFZs, the export-orientated firms were exempted from import duties on machinery, equipment, and other inputs necessary for constructing and operating the zone, and from income tax, property tax, and value added tax. By 1992, 106 firms had registered as tax havens, many of which were already established in El Salvador. One of the consequences is that these firms now have an incentive to import their raw materials and intermediate goods from abroad instead of purchasing them locally.

The new Export Promotion Law is related to the policies of the US Agency for International Development (AID). At the end of the 1980s, the AID demonstrated renewed interest in EPFZs. It made a fund available of $US 26m for the promotion of EPFZs in El Salvador, to be spent exclusively by the private sector. With AID funding, the central reserve bank of El Salvador finances up to 75 per cent of the total cost of developing or expanding an EPFZ, including construction of buildings, machinery and equipment, and promotion activities. The AID identified 17 regions suitable for establishing an EPFZ. By October 1992, three new zones were being constructed. The total planned area of the 17 EPFZs is 918 200 m^2 and the zones are expected to generate 115 000 new jobs. This would imply that 230 firms of the scale of San Bartolo firms must establish in these new EPFZs.

According to FUSADES (Salvadorean Development Foundation and a think-tank for the government financed by AID) the aims of the EPFZ project in El Salvador are:

(i) promotion of foreign investment by offering physical infrastructure, basic services and labour;
(ii) development of regions with limited natural-resource availability and development potential;
(iii) promotion of non-traditional exports;
(iv) creation of employment and stimulation of technology transfer to the local economy.(FUSADES, 1991a)

Since the introduction of a trade-liberalisation policy at the end of the 1980s, the special advantages of investing in an EPFZ have been reduced, the more so since firms willing to invest in El Salvador can also apply to the Tax Haven Regime. For these reasons, EPFZs seem to have become less important. Moreover, regional competition for foreign investment is strong. In spite of the generous incentives, it seems unlikely that all seventeen new EPFZs planned will be constructed.

7.3 THE SAN BARTOLO EXPORT PROCESSING FREE ZONE

The first firm that started operations in the zone was the Japanese firm AVX (electronic components) and it is still continuing export production. The 14 firms currently established in San Bartolo represent a wide range of products: textiles and clothing (7), shoes and other leather products (2), paper bags (2), cardboard boxes (1), electronic components (1), and jewellery (1).

Table 7.1 presents some indicators for the functioning of the San Bartolo zone in the period 1976–92. There was much variability in the numbers of firms and in employment. The number of firms reached a maximum in 1979 and 1980, but declined thereafter as a result of the civil war. It started to expand again at the end of the decade. However, the maximum of 4170 workers in San Bartolo in 1979 has not been reached in the 1980s.

In general, preferential market access has been an important factor for the development of EPFZs (Alter, 1991). Access of firms in El Salvador to the US market increased significantly in the 1980s because of the CBI. Many non-traditional exports from the region were admitted duty-free. CBI also provided a stimulus for US firms to invest in the region by giving them tax incentives in their home country. In 1991, Salvadorean exports under the CBI included sugar cane, dielectrical conductors, yellow ochre, paper bags and cardboard boxes. Other countries in the region seem to have benefited from CBI by increasing the number of EPFZs in the 1980s. In El Salvador the number of EPFZs did not expand due to the civil war.

Table 7.2 compares some indicators for the functioning of the San Bartolo zone with zones in four countries in the region. Measured in absolute terms, the contributions of EPFZs to employment and exports are most sizeable in the Dominican Republic and least significant in El Salvador. In 1991, San Bartolo was the only zone in operation in El Salvador. However, in more recent years the number of zones in El Salvador has increased rapidly. As shown, only 13 firms were established in the zone in 1991, creating no more than 7000 jobs. Firms in El Salvador were large as compared to firms operating in other zones in terms of employment and exports. Moreover, it is noteworthy that overall labour intensity of production in the zone was significantly higher than was the case in zones operating in Honduras and the Dominican Republic.

Table 7.1 Some indicators of EPFZ San Bartolo, 1976–92

Year	No. of Firms	No. of employees	Wages ($US 000s)	Rents ($US 000s)	Investment[a] ($US 000s)	Investment[a]: employee ($US 000s)	Wage: employee ($US 000s)
1976	2	456	820	42	600	1.3	1.8
1977	4	1 503	2 705	127	8 128	5.4	1.8
1978	7	2 956	5 323	286	12 348	4.2	1.8
1979	14	4 170	7 506	406	13 178	3.2	1.8
1980	14	2 231	4 016	247	8 634	3.9	1.8
1981	8	1 028	1 850	272	5 461	5.3	1.8
1982	4	795	2 146	196	7 222	9.1	2.7
1983	5	1 478	2 236	118	7 583	5.1	1.5
1984	5	1 479	2 804	261	9 462	6.4	1.9
1985	5	1 800	2 723	367	10 554	5.9	1.5
1986	8	2 100	2 438	475	7 474	3.6	1.2
1987	8	2 955	2 660	475	10 751	3.6	0.9
1988	10	3 410	3 069	530	15 091	4.4	0.9
1989	9	3 556	3 475	478	18 777	5.3	1.0
1990	12	2 878	n.a.	n.a.	19 343	6.7	n.a.
1991	n.a.	n.a.	n.a.	n.a.	n.a.	n.a.	n.a.
1992	14	6 500	n.a.	n.a.	n.a.	n.a.	n.a.

[a] stock of investment.
Source: Based on data from the General Directory of Free Zones, Ministry of Economics.

100 The Export Processing Free Zone of San Bartolo in El Salvador

Table 7.2 Some indicators of EPFZs in selected countries, 1991

	Costa Rica	Honduras	Dominican Republic	El Salvador
Number of EPFZs	8	9	25	1
Business area (thousands m^2)	140	149	1079	66
Number of firms	80	49	426	13
Employment (thousands of workers)	10	19	116	7
Exports 1991 ($USm)	150	95	825	85
Number of employees per firm	125	378	272	500
Exports per employee ($US 000s)	15.0	5.1	7.1	13.1
Exports per firm ($USm)	1.9	1.9	1.9	6.5

Source: Based on FUSADES (1991b), *Boletín Económico y Sosial* (San Salvador: FUSADES).

Exports and value added

Table 7.3 shows the contribution of the San Bartolo zone to El Salvador's non-traditional and total exports in the period 1977–91. Exports from San Bartolo increased until 1978, declined sharply in the beginning of the 1980s and started growing significantly only by the end of the 1980s. In the course of the 1980s and early 1990s the zone started to make a significant contribution to the development of non-traditional exports, but its share in overall export revenues is still rather modest. The rapid growth of exports from the zone has increased the interest of AID in expanding EPFZs in El Salvador. To assess the contribution to foreign-exchange earnings, export revenues have to be compared with imports by firms in the zone, but such data are not available.

Table 7.4 shows the component of domestic value added in exports and the contribution of the zone to overall value added in the manufacturing sector in the period 1976–90. Value added has been estimated by adding the $US values of wages and rents presented in Table 7.1. Clearly, wages are by far the major component of value added in these labour-intensive activities. As shown, the share of value added in exports was rather large in the 1970s but declined to rather low levels in the course of the 1980s.

Forward and backward linkages

Generally, spread effects – forward and backward linkages – of EPFZs are limited and zones tend to remain a sort of enclave in the economy

Geske Dijkstra and Carlos Rivera Alemán 101

Table 7.3 Exports from EPFZ San Bartolo, 1977–91

Year	EPFZ ($USm)	In % of non-traditional exports	In % of total exports
1977	7	n.a.	1
1978	21	n.a.	3
1979	20	n.a.	2
1980	13	n.a.	1
1981	12	5	1
1982	20	9	3
1983	29	14	4
1984	32	15	4
1985	30	18	4
1986	25	15	3
1987	26	13	4
1988	53	24	9
1989	73	30	15
1990	69	24	12
1991	85	27	n.a.

Source: Banco Central de Reserva de El Salvador (1992).

Table 7.4 EPFZ San Bartolo, value added and exports, 1976–90

	Value added ($USm)	Exports ($USm)	Value added: exports (%)	Value added: manufacturing value added
1976	0.9	n.a.	n.a.	0.2
1977	2.8	7.3	38	0.7
1978	5.6	21.1	27	1.2
1979	7.9	20.4	39	1.5
1980	4.2	13.1	32	0.8
1981	2.1	11.8	18	0.4
1982	2.3	20.2	11	0.4
1983	2.3	28.9	8	0.4
1984	3.0	32.4	9	0.4
1985	3.1	29.9	10	0.3
1986	2.9	24.5	12	0.5
1987	3.1	25.8	12	0.4
1988	3.6	52.7	7	0.4
1989	4.0	73.1	6	0.4
1990	n.a.	68.9	n.a.	n.a.

Source: Based on data from the Banco Central de Reserva de El Salvador (1992).

(Verbruggen, 1985; Warr, 1989; Alter, 1991; and Rondinelli, 1987). If government regulations require firms to export all production, forward linkages are precluded. In San Bartolo, all firms export, or produce intermediate goods for exporting firms in the zone.

Fiscal incentives stimulate firms in the zone to use imports instead of local raw materials or intermediate goods. Locally produced intermediate goods tend to be more expensive than imported products due to protection of manufacturing production (Rondinelli, 1987). There are two more factors that may limit the use of local raw materials (Warr, 1989):

(i) the corporate strategies of TNCs that have a preference for imports from their own subsidiaries;
(ii) the inadequate quality of local inputs.

These additional reasons for importing rather than purchasing locally produced goods probably also hold true in El Salvador. There are indications that some sectors in EPFZs are more likely to generate backward linkages than other sectors do: textiles and clothing offer good opportunities for use of local materials, but in electronics, opportunities to use local inputs are limited (Verbruggen 1985, p. 293 and Warr, 1987, p. 35). In San Bartolo, seven out of fourteen firms produce textiles and clothing and consequently there may be ample opportunities for linkages with domestic industries. Nevertheless, the indirect production and employment effects of the zone (excluding the tax haven regime firms) seem to be limited and the indirect employment opportunities involve temporary work in construction and services, jobs in the packing industry, small restaurants, bars and *pupuserías* and in the administration and custody of the zone itself.

Employment effects

Most studies indicate that employment in EPFZs is not stable, due to the footloose character of the export operations (Rondinelli, 1987). Also, the skill-intensity of production and assembly activities is low, and possibilities for diffusion of technological know-how are few (Verbruggen, 1985, p. 294). Moreover, costs of employment creation are high in terms of government expenses on infrastructure (Rondinelli, 1987 and Alter, 1991).

In El Salvador, employment in San Bartolo decreased significantly in the 1980s due to the civil war. Relatively, employment in the San Bartolo zone decreased more than total manufacturing employment did. This reflects the footloose character of EPFZ investment: it was relatively easy to withdraw from San Bartolo.

In more recent years the political situation has become more stable and employment in the San Bartolo zone increased to 6500 in 1992, which is a significant contribution to overall employment in the manufacturing sector, as shown in Table 7.5.

Employment in the zone has the following characteristics.

(i) It is seasonal labour, for two reasons:

- many firms fire workers at the end of the year, to hire them again a few weeks later in order to avoid payment of the thirteenth month and ancienty benefits;
- when stocks are reduced, firms also fire part of their workers.

The following example illustrates the seasonal character of work. In May 1992, two firms in San Bartolo fired 3 and 12 per cent of their average numbers of workers during the first trimester, respectively. Another firm fired 21 per cent of its average semestral workforce between March and June (Arriola *et al.*, Alemán and Rivera, 1993). In addition, workers are generally hired on the basis of three-month or six-month renewable labour contracts. The precariousness of the workplace is one of the essential aspects of the so-called new pro-

Table 7.5 Employment in EPFZ San Bartolo, 1976–90

Year	No. of employees	Employees: manufacturing employment (%)
1976	456	1.1
1977	1503	3.3
1978	2957	6.4
1979	4170	7.1
1980	2231	4.1
1981	1028	2.0
1982	795	2.1
1983	1478	2.4
1984	1479	3.0
1985	1800	3.6
1986	2100	5.1
1987	2955	6.3
1988	3410	7.7
1989	3556	7.6
1990	2878	6.1

Source: Based on data from Banco Central de Reserva de El Salvador.

duction forms and the flexibility of work processes. Not only the footloose character of investments but also flexible production strategies make employment in EPFZs unstable.

(ii) About 85 per cent of all work done in the zones is unskilled or low-skilled work. Most workers are young females between 16 and 24 years of age. Out of fourteen firms in the zone, six employ fewer than five white-collar workers for each 100 blue-collar workers. In only two firms does the number of white-collar workers exceed one in three.

(iii) Work schedules are heavy and working conditions are beyond legal regulations. In some firms, just-in-time production planning is used. This implies that many employees work more than the legal maximum of 44 hours a week. Although labour unions are not formally prohibited, labour contracts make it difficult to unionise. There are no unions active in the San Bartolo zone.

(iv) The costs of creating employment in San Bartolo are high. In 1974, investment costs were colon 55 million, the equivalent of $US 22 m by that time. Assume the government has to pay back the loan: the only revenues the government receives from the firms in the zone are rents; adding up rents received between 1976 and 1989 (see Table 7.1) this amounts to $US 4.3 m – it so follows that employment in San Bartolo was subsidised by the government by about $US 18 m, even excluding repair and maintenance costs, interest payments on the loan and, moreover, possible subsidies on energy, water, custody and other services provided by the government.

As noted earlier, the tax haven law of 1990 liberalised significantly the trade and production regime for export-orientated industries in Costa Rica. At the same time, new EPFZs have been promoted in selected regions. Recently, the number of such zones has increased and so has the number of firms established in such zones. The experience of the San Bartolo zone shows that foreign investors are particularly attracted to the zones by the availability of an adequate infrastructure, the possibility to organise production in a flexible way and limited labour regulations. From the perspective of overall economic development such an export strategies raises critical questions.

8 The Historical Experience: Growth Accounting[1]
André A. Hofman

8.1 INTRODUCTION

The objective of this chapter is to identify and measure the main factors that account for overall economic growth in some small Latin American countries during the post-war period. Growth accounting analysis provides insight into the contribution of factor accumulation and the overall efficiency of the economy to economic growth. We shall follow the approach put forward by Maddison (1991), whose analysis of economic performance is conducted basically at two levels: 'ultimate' and 'proximate' causes of growth. 'Ultimate' causes of economic growth refer to institutions, ideologies, pressure groups, historical accidents and economic policy at the national level. At the same time, positive and negative influences from outside the country are involved. It is rather difficult to quantify these 'ultimate' features and legitimate scope for disagreement on what is important remains.

'Proximate' causes of economic performance have been quantified in all kinds of models developed by economists and statisticians. Macroeconomic growth accounts attempt to 'explain' GDP growth (per caput) and productivity by measuring inputs of labour and capital, availability of natural resources and influences affecting the efficiency with which resources are combined.

This chapter focuses on 'proximate' causes of growth by applying quantitative supply-side analysis; the 'ultimate' causes of growth such as national and international policies and institutions are dealt with in other chapters of this volume.

The group of small Latin American countries in this study includes Chile, Colombia, Ecuador and Venezuela. These countries have been selected on the basis of data availability. Capital stock estimates require data that are not available for many countries.

The performance of these four small Latin American countries is compared with the performance of four other groups of countries:

The Historical Experience: Growth Accounting

(i) three large Latin American countries – Argentina, Brazil and Mexico;
(ii) three Asian developing countries with a remarkably high growth performance during some decades – South Korea, Taiwan and Thailand;
(iii) Portugal and Spain, which have an institutional heritage that has a good deal in common with Latin America; and
(iv) six advanced countries – France, Germany, Japan, The Netherlands, UK and USA, which have levels of income per caput and productivity that are amongst the highest in the world.

A growth accounting framework is presented, using data analysis for the period 1950–89. This period has been subdivided into 1950–73, 1973–80 and 1980–89, according to the common practice of scholars in the field. The period 1950–73 was a Golden Age and several interrelated factors may explain this performance. The new world order which was created after the Second World War had many more elements of stability than the order created after the First World War, which had built-in elements of instability. This new order affected the options of most countries in a positive way, offering greatly enlarged opportunities for trade and specialisation and improved access to foreign capital and technology. Domestic policies were directed towards promoting high levels of demand and employment in the advanced countries and orientated to development objectives in other regions of the world. Finally, there was a large increase in investment ratios and capital stocks, an accelerated educational effort and improvements in international trade and specialisation (Maddison, 1989, p. 65). In Latin America the change in policy attitudes and instruments was smaller, since the region had fared relatively well in the previous period. There was a general tendency in the region towards more inward-looking policies.

The period 1973–89 cannot be characterised as clearly as the previous periods. OECD countries experienced a slowdown after 1973, but in the other countries of our sample this slowdown was not as straightforward. Latin America continued to grow until the beginning of the 1980s, with the substantial support of increased capital inflow at low interest rates. However, inflation increased and my results show clearly that productivity indices started to fall in most Latin American countries as early as 1973. Since the beginning of the 1980s Latin America has experienced a crisis that can only be compared with the Great Depression.

The Asian countries also experienced some problems: Japan's growth rate fell dramatically, but the developing Asian countries have continued to grow at a high rate, in some cases even higher than during the Golden Age.

8.2 THE POST-WAR PERIOD

The post-war period will be analysed from two angles. First I shall give a brief review of economic policy and performance during this period. Next I shall present a growth accounting exercise for the period 1950–89.

Policy and performance

In 1950 there began a period of unparalleled expansion of the world economy which continued without interruption until 1973, when the first petroleum price shock erupted. Growth of world output during this period was the highest ever recorded.

During this quarter century Latin America also achieved an expansion which probably outstripped regional growth in any previous twenty-five year period. Furthermore, the rate of growth of regional output between 1950 and 1973 exceeded the rate of growth of world GDP as well as the rate of growth of output of the industrialised countries as a whole.

However, there was a fundamental contrast between the growth performance of Latin America and the rest of the world. Expansion of world trade, and especially the trade of developed countries, exceeded the growth of world output by far, but in Latin America this was not the case: growth rates of Latin America's exports were significantly below the rate of growth of GDP in the region. Moreover, whereas the unprecedented expansion of the industrialised countries was accompanied by an exceptional degree of price stability, the acceleration of growth in many countries in Latin America was accompanied by inflation.

From the Great Depression onwards, mildly expansionary monetary and fiscal policies combined with large devaluations promoted the strong recuperation of the economies of Latin American, and such expansionary monetary and fiscal policies were continued or even intensified during the 1950s and 1960s – that is, a long time after output had returned to its potential level. Moreover, in a number of countries the growth of the money supply exceeded by far the potential rate of growth of output. Thus, during this era macro-economic disequilibria were progressively built up (Bianchi and Nohara, 1988).

Growth of income resulting from the expansion of primary exports led the rise in demand for manufactured consumer goods and their inputs in Latin America. This demand was satisfied to an increasing degree by domestic production that enjoyed 'natural protection' provided by transportation costs, complemented in some cases by tariff protection prior to the Second World War. Foreign-exchange shortages created by the fall in primary exports during the Great Depression and limited access to foreign goods during the Second World War subsequently boosted import substitution. Only after the war, however, did import substitution become a doctrine, guiding policy-making in much of Latin America.

Structural problems still concealed (1973–80)

During the period 1973–80 the group of OECD countries as a whole experienced a sharp slowdown of their growth performance: the growth rate of GDP per caput was less than half the rate in the previous period. However, the countries in Latin America and Asia continued to grow. During this period GDP per caput in Latin America continued to grow faster than in the USA and reached a comparative level of 32 per cent in 1980, the highest level of the entire twentieth century until now. However, the Asian developing countries more than doubled their level, and the other OECD countries also markedly improved their relative stance *vis-à-vis* the USA.

The dramatic changes that occurred in the world system at the beginning of the 1970s, such as the breakdown of the Bretton Woods system of fixed exchange rates in 1971 and the action of the OPEC price cartel, did not have the same effect on policy-making in Latin America as in developed countries that changed their economic policy significantly. The new disturbance was simply conceived as a new variation on a familiar theme, and was not regarded as a razor's edge situation, calling for drastic policy change (Maddison, 1989).

The combination of biased macro-economic policies and compensatory sectoral subsidies with unlimited access to international capital markets was accompanied by economic growth in the 1973–80 period. Eventually it created pervasive imbalances, including stagnation of exports and imports other than manufactured products, overproduction of non-traded goods and services, uncommonly large resource gaps, unparalleled excess external debt and rampant domestic price instability, all of which contributed to the unusual severity of the 1980s crisis (Bianchi and Nohara, 1988).

During this period several countries experimented with neo-conservative economic policies – that is, with the marriage of monetarist views concerning economic stabilisation with radical conservative approaches.

The lost decade (1980–89)

During the period 1980–89 the world economy recuperated somewhat from the low growth rates in the previous period, with the exception of

Latin America. In developed countries GDP grew on average at 2.5 per cent a year compared to around 2 per cent in the period 1973–80. Developing countries in Asia continued to grow at the same rates or at even higher rates. The growth performance of Latin America was abysmal and the 1980s may be considered a lost decade for the continent in this respect.

In 1989, GDP per caput in Latin America had fallen, on an average, to the lowest relative levels of the twentieth century. From a comparative level of 32 per cent of the USA in 1980 it declined to 24 per cent in 1989. Between 1980 and 1989 Latin America experienced its deepest and longest economic crisis since the ill-fated years of the Great Depression. The average level of GDP per caput as measured in constant $US declined from $US 4392 in 1980 to $US 3727 in 1989. The decline of per caput income was particularly dramatic in Argentina and Venezuela and to a lesser degree in Mexico.

Another disturbing characteristic of the economic crisis of the 1980s was the generalised and simultaneous deterioration of nearly all economic indicators. Many countries experienced not only a declining growth rate of output, but also a deterioration in the employment situation and decreases in real wages as substantiated in the contribution by Van der Hoeven and Stewart in this volume (Chapter 9). Moreover, inflationary processes intensified enormously and became widespread.

Growth accounts

The growth accounts presented here cover the 1950–89 period, with 1973 and 1980 as benchmark years. Growth accounting exercises may serve different purposes, such as explaining differences in growth rates between countries, illuminating processes of convergence and divergence, assessing the role of technical progress and calculating potential output losses. Here we shall present the results for our sample of sixteen countries with respect to the most traditional explanatory factors – that is, changes in the quantity and quality of inputs of labour and capital. Natural resources have been included as an additional explanatory factor because of the abundant natural resource endowment of Latin America as compared to other countries in our sample. The decomposition of economic growth gives an insight into the costs of increasing the growth rate. However, growth accounting can only explain part of the process of economic growth, since it does not take into account factors such as economic policy, the national and international environment and non-economical factors such as natural disasters and war.

Labour

Labour input is computed in terms of total annual hours worked and not in terms of employment, since the average number of hours worked per employee on an annual basis varies enormously between countries. We have elaborated a consistent set of estimates with respect to annual hours worked per employee for Latin America and the other countries in our sample.

An important aspect of the labour input is the change in the quality of labour as represented by the change in the level of education.

Table 8.1 summarises the main trends in labour quantity and quality. Note the significant differences in average annual growth rates of the quantity of labour between developed and developing countries. In Asia and Latin America these growth rates are much higher than in developed countries. In the period 1973–89 the growth rate of the quantity of labour inputs was even slightly negative in the latter groups of countries.

In the Asian countries the two factors that determine the growth of the quantity of labour input – that is, employment and hours worked per year – show very high growth rates. In 1989 employment is between two and three times as high as it was in 1950, and during the period 1950–89 the estimated number of hours worked per year increased by about 10 per cent. Latin American employment also grew fast, but annual hours worked declined steadily throughout the whole period.

The average number of years of formal educational experience of the population has been used as an indicator of the quality of labour. Due to lack of data it has not been possible to estimate the attained educational level of the labour force. Without corrections for educational achievements and differences in the efficiency of education between countries, the quality of labour in Latin America is probably overestimated as compared to Asia and the developed countries.

The quality of labour as reflected by the level of education shows a steady increase over the whole period in all sample countries. In this respect the Asian countries outperform all other countries with a rather wide margin. Latin America and the Iberian countries show rather high growth rates as well. The level of education increased at a much lower rate in the developed countries that had already achieved fairly high educational levels in 1950.

Without taking into consideration capital and output growth (that is, assuming equal growth rates and constant capital:output ratios) one can infer some elements about labour and total productivity growth. The clear tendency in Asian countries is towards faster labour productivity growth,

Table 8.1 Labour inputs 1950–89 (average annual compound growth rates)

	Labour quantity			Labour quality			Augmented labour input		
	1950–73	1973–80	1980–89	1950–73	1973–80	1980–89	1950–73	1973–80	1980–89
Chile	0.53	1.88	2.93	0.59	0.94	0.96	0.67	1.69	2.33
Colombia	1.90	2.13	2.56	0.65	0.79	0.83	1.53	1.75	2.03
Ecuador	2.36	2.43	1.72	0.65	0.79	0.83	1.80	1.94	1.53
Venezuela	2.87	5.10	2.79	0.94	1.11	1.16	2.29	3.73	2.37
Arithmetic average	1.92	2.89	2.50	0.71	0.91	0.95	1.57	2.28	2.07
Arithmetic average:									
Latin America	2.15	2.66	2.40	1.23	1.14	1.87	2.03	2.28	2.56
Asian countries	3.35	3.21	1.72	1.55	2.01	2.61	2.94	3.14	2.60
Iberic countries	0.06	−0.65	0.39	1.14	1.14	1.94	0.72	0.29	1.40
Developed countries	0.50	−0.22	0.50	0.41	0.40	0.63	0.55	0.11	0.68

Source: See Appendix 8.1, pp. 119–21.

whereas in Latin America rates of productivity growth are lower for two reasons. First, the growth rate of the quantity of labour in Latin America was high and increasing until 1980 and remained high afterwards while it was decreasing in Asia. Second, in Asian countries the growth rate of the quality of labour increased steadily and this had a positive effect on productivity growth, but in Latin America this growth rate was much lower.

The augmented labour input estimates presented in Table 8.1 reflect changes in the quantity and quality of labour inputs. These estimates are the weighted sum (with an assumed factor share of labour in GDP of 0.6)[2] of the growth rates of the quantity and quality of labour input and in that way reflect the contribution of labour to the growth of GDP. Growth rates of augmented labour inputs are distinctly different between developed and developing countries and within the group of developing countries the Asian countries show by far the highest rates of growth.

Within the group of small Latin American countries a similar pattern is discernable with respect to the growth of the quality of labour input but the development of the quantity of labour inputs is different. Compared to the sample of Latin American countries, Chile shows extremely low growth rates of the quantity of labour input in the periods 1950–73 and 1973–80 but in the period 1980–89 this growth rate was higher than the average of all groups of sample countries. The opposite is the case in Ecuador, where labour absorption declined in the period 1950–89.

Capital

One of the major impediments to growth accounting in developing countries is the lack of data required to estimate the capital stock.[3] Gross and net capital stocks have been estimated according to the 'Permanent Inventory Method' developed by Goldsmith (1951). The capital stock has been disaggregated into machinery and equipment, non-residential and residential structures, with respective service lives of 15, 40 and 50 years.

In the augmented version of the capital contribution to growth we have included technical progress in the form of a qualitative improvement of successive vintages of capital, as suggested by Solow (1993). The basic argument is that physical investment is the prime vehicle for technical progress. This capital embodiment effect is not a 'catch-all' effect of technical progress, as suggested initially by Solow, since part of technical progress is embodied in the labour force and in organisational and other improvements. As data on embodiment of technical progress in capital are almost non-existent in Latin America, we have used a growth rate of 1 per cent for non-residential construction and of 2 per cent for machinery and equipment. This has resulted in the growth rates of the quality of capital presented in Table 8.3.

The factor share for capital was 0.3 for all countries. This may in fact be a rather crude assumption, as we know that in some cases the capital share has been higher in Latin America and probably also in some countries in Asia.

Table 8.2 presents rates of growth of capital inputs (gross non-residential capital stock) in the period 1950–89. The period 1950–73 shows a world of great homogeneity, with annual average growth rates of capital stock around 6 per cent for our complete sample. However, Chile and Colombia were outliers with only some 4 per cent growth.

During the period 1973–80 the growth rate of capital stock showed two markedly different tendencies. In developed countries this growth decelerated markedly, except for France and the USA, while it accelerated in LDCs and the Iberian countries, particularly in South Korea and Taiwan. Again, Chile and Colombia showed extremely low rates of capital accumulation.

In the period 1980–89 the growth of capital stock decelerated drastically in all countries, with the exception of Colombia. The decline in the growth rate of the capital stock in Latin America was the largest of all regions. The deceleration of the growth rate in Chile and Colombia was below the average of all other countries, but in Chile capital accumulation was already at an extremely low level. Growth rates of capital stock in Asia were double the rates in Latin American in the period 1980–89.

Table 8.2 shows a uniform growth rate of the quality of the capital stock of about 1.6 per cent for all sample countries during the period 1950–73. In the period 1973–80 only the Asian countries had higher growth rates and in the period 1980–89 all countries except for Germany and Japan experienced a drastic decline in the growth rate of the quality of the capital stock.

In the augmented capital input the quality and quantity effects are combined and weighted by 0.3, which is the assumed factor share of capital, and reflect the tendencies described above.

Land

The availability of land has a significant impact on patterns of specialisation and the type of economic growth. As compared to other regions, land has been abundantly available in Latin America.[4] Land has been included as a proxy for natural resource endowment of countries, and natural resources have been measured as the amount of land in use. To allow for

Table 8.2 Capital inputs 1950–89 (average annual compound growth rates)

	Capital quantity			Capital quality			Augmented capital input		
	1950–73	1973–80	1980–89	1950–73	1973–80	1980–89	1950–73	1973–80	1980–89
Chile	4.21	2.34	1.58	1.26	0.99	1.04	1.64	1.00	0.88
Colombia	3.79	5.14	4.80	1.19	1.32	1.26	1.49	1.94	1.82
Ecuador	6.29	7.54	5.05	1.27	1.42	0.96	2.27	2.69	1.18
Venezuela	7.59	5.78	3.74	1.25	1.36	1.08	2.02	2.14	1.45
Arithmetic average	5.47	5.78	3.74	1.25	1.36	1.08	2.20	2.14	1.45
Arithmetic average:									
Latin America	7.04	7.68	3.52	1.38	1.45	0.99	2.53	2.74	1.50
Asian countries	5.52	10.79	8.33	1.57	1.72	1.43	2.13	3.75	2.93
Iberic countries	5.91	6.09	4.20	1.63	1.58	1.7	2.26	2.30	1.64
Developed countries	5.94	4.81	3.54	1.65	1.41	1.11	2.28	1.87	1.39

Source: See Appendix 8.1, pp. 119–21.

differences in quality of land, the following weights have been used: arable and permanent crop land 1, permanent pasture 0.3 and forest land 0.1. It has not been possible to include more sophisticated measures of natural endowment. The factor share for land was 0.1 in all countries.

Levels of explanation

Tables 8.3 and 8.4 summarise the results of the growth accounts. Table 8.3 presents the growth rates of JFP and DAJFP. JFP results from the difference between the growth rate of GDP and the growth rates of the quantities of capital and labour weighted by the factor shares of labour and capital, as presented in Tables 8.1 and 8.2.[5] DAJFP also includes capital and labour quality in the joint productivity measure.

In Table 8.4 the residual JFP or DAJFP is presented as a percentage of GDP. The remaining residual is a kind of 'catch all' term including the effect of disembodied technical progress on long-term growth and statistical and other errors. It is clear that the value of the residual depends strongly on the methodology used. Many studies presents JFP without quality augmentation.

Table 8.4 shows that on average 48 per cent of GDP growth in the sample of small Latin American countries during the period 1950–73 cannot be explained by increases in factor inputs. In the large Latin American countries this share is 38 per cent.

The unexplained residual in Chile, Colombia and Ecuador in the period 1950–73 was about the same as in the Asian countries and about 10 percentage points higher than the average unexplained residual in Latin America. In the period 1973–80 the residual in the three small Latin American countries was even higher than in the Asian countries. The levels of overexplanation in Latin America become substantial during the 1980–89 crisis. These negative residuals reflect the economic losses in this decade in Latin America and the declining productivity of capital and labour. The performance of Chile, Colombia and Ecuador, was not as abysmal as in the rest of Latin America in this regard, although in the period 1980–89 also residuals were very small or even negative.

A comparative analysis of the residuals reveals two striking developments. First, differences between the values of the residuals in the smaller Latin American countries and the Asian countries in the period 1950–80 are relatively small. During the period 1950–73 residuals are the same. However, residuals in the large Latin American countries are 15 percentage points lower. In the period 1973–80 Latin American countries have a 5 per cent lower residual than the Asian countries.

Table 8.3 GDP and JFP, 1950–89 (average annual compound growth rates)

	GDP			JFP[a]			DAJFP[a]		
	1950–73	1973–80	1980–89	1950–73	1973–80	1980–89	1950–73	1973–80	1980–89
Chile	3.42	3.39	2.90	1.75	1.48	0.74	1.02	0.62	−0.15
Colombia	5.12	4.97	3.26	2.85	2.16	0.15	2.10	1.29	−0.73
Ecuador	6.07	6.36	2.03	2.78	2.59	−0.57	2.01	1.94	−1.36
Venezuela	6.56	4.10	0.37	2.49	−1.38	−2.28	1.55	−2.56	−3.29
Arithmetic average	5.29	4.71	2.14	2.47	1.21	−0.49	1.67	0.32	−1.38
Arithmetic average:									
Latin America	5.67	5.25	0.79	2.16	1.27	−1.69	1.01	0.14	−3.11
Asian countries	7.73	7.51	7.64	3.93	2.31	4.09	2.53	0.59	2.10
Iberic countries	5.81	2.65	2.70	4.03	1.26	1.22	2.86	0.10	−0.32
Developed countries	5.34	2.23	2.56	3.26	0.93	1.20	2.52	0.26	0.49

[a] Land has been included in the calculation of JFP and DAJFP. The effect of this variable is negligible.
Source: See Appendix 8.1, pp. 119–21.

Table 8.4 Explaining economic growth 1950–89

	Growth of GDP[a]			Unexplained residual (JFP·GDP)[b]			Unexplained residual (DAJFP·GDP)[b]		
	1950–73	1973–80	1980–89	1950–73	1973–80	1980–89	1950–73	1973–80	1980–89
Chile	3.42	3.39	2.90	51	44	26	30	18	(5)[c]
Colombia	5.12	4.97	3.26	56	43	5	41	26	(22)
Ecuador	6.07	6.36	2.03	46	41	(28)	33	31	(67)
Venezuela	6.56	4.10	0.37	38	(34)	(616)	24	(62)	(889)
Arithmetic average	5.29	4.71	2.14	48	24	(154)	32	3	(246)
Arithmetic average:									
Latin America	5.67	5.25	0.79	38	24	(214)	18	3	(394)
Asian countries	7.73	7.51	7.64	51	31	54	33	8	27
Iberic countries	5.81	2.65	2.70	69	47	45	49	4	(12)
Developed countries	5.34	2.23	2.56	61	42	47	47	12	19

[a] Average annual compound growth rates
[b] Percentage shares
[c] Values in parenthesis indicate overexplanation.
Source: See Appendix 8.1, pp. 119–21.

118   *The Historical Experience: Growth Accounting*

Second, during the period 1980–89 the crisis in Latin America caused the residual to become very negative, indicating negative total factor productivity growth. This contrasts with developments in Asia and the OECD countries, where JFP remained positive, although with declining growth rates.

8.3 CONCLUSIONS

In this chapter I have shown the significant differences between countries with respect to the contributions of factor accumulation and total factor productivity to overall economic growth. The contribution of JFP was rather small in the large countries of Latin America and more significant in the smaller countries, especially in Chile, Colombia and Ecuador.

No attempt has been made to disaggregate the residual factor labelled 'technical progress'. In the Asian countries the role of technical progress was somewhat more important than in Latin America. During the period 1973–80 these countries increased their joint factor input and especially capital, and the contribution of technical progress fell somewhat, even causing overexplanation in South Korea. During the 1980s the Asian countries continued to grow at a high rate and technical progress contributed about 20 per cent to growth.

The role of total factor productivity was more important in developed than in developing countries, is mainly due to different factor inputs. The growth of labour input was in particular much smaller in developed countries than it was in developing countries. This may also suggest that the strains of fast development and high resource mobilisation tended to decrease the efficiency of resource allocation. Total factor productivity growth slowed down or even became dramatically negative in Latin America during the 1980s. Levels of productivity in Latin America are still much lower than in developed countries, but if Latin America is able to resolve its major macro-economic problems and improve the allocation of resources, it has the potential for a return to accelerated growth of productivity based on the acquisition of foreign technology.

The poor performance of the smaller countries in Latin America can be attributed in particular to low levels of factor accumulation, and not as much to allocative inefficiency as was the case in the large countries of Latin America.

The contribution of labour to growth differed significantly between the regions during the period 1950–89. First, the quantity of labour inputs increased rapidly in developing countries, although not fast enough compared to demographic trends. In developed countries growth virtually came to a halt. Second, annual hours worked per employee show markedly different trends in Latin America and Asia during the period 1950–80. In Latin America there is a clear downward trend, but in the Asian countries in the sample annual hours worked per person increased substantially. However, since 1980 annual hours worked per employee have tended to decline in the Asian countries as well. With respect to the quality of labour, it may be noted that education grew by far the fastest in Asia, at twice the rate that was achieved in Latin America and the Iberian countries.

During the period 1973–80 growth of the capital stock increased markedly in the groups of developing countries and Iberian countries, particularly so in South Korea and Taiwan, while it decelerated in the developed countries, except for France and the USA. In 1980–89 growth rates decelerated drastically in all Latin American countries, with the exception of Colombia. Asian capital quantity growth rates were double those of Latin America in 1980–89.

The quality of the capital stock improved at a uniform rate of about 1.6 per cent per year in all countries in our sample during the period 1950–73. In the period 1973–80 only the Asian countries experienced higher growth rates than in the previous period. During the period 1980–89 all countries in the sample, except Germany and Japan, experienced a dramatic decline in the growth rate of the quality of capital.

APPENDIX 8.1: SOURCES OF DATA

GDP and capital

GDP and capital stock estimates for Latin America, South Korea and Spain have been based upon sources described in Hofman (1991) and (1992). GDP estimates for France, Germany, Japan, The Netherlands, Portugal, Taiwan, Thailand, UK and the USA have been taken from Maddison (1989). An update for OECD countries to 1989 has been taken from OECD, *National Accounts* (Paris: OECD, various issues). An update for Taiwan and Thailand to 1989 has been made on the basis of Council for Economic Planning and Development, *Taiwan Statistical Data Book 1990*. Capital estimates for France, Germany, Japan, The Netherlands, UK and the USA have been taken from the worksheets of Maddison (1991): the benchmark year has been changed from 1985 to 1980 and different assumptions have been made pertaining to the economic lifetime of assets. For Taiwan the perpetual inventory methodology has been used as described in Hofman (1991) and (1992) on the basis of investment data for 1900–38 from M. Mizoguchi and

M. Umemura (1988), *Basic Economic Statistics of Former Japanese Colonies 1895–1938* (Tokyo:Toyo Keizai Shinposha). For the period 1939–51 the ratio of total capital formation to GDP was estimated as follows: 15 per cent for the period 1939–42, 10 per cent for the year 1943, 5 per cent for the period 1944–9 and 8.3 per cent for the period 1950–1. Capital formation has been disaggregated as follows: 30 per cent machinery and equipment, 60 per cent non-residential construction and 10 per cent residential construction. Data on total and disaggregated capital formation for the period 1952–89 have been taken from the Council for Economic Planning and Development (1990). For Portugal no disaggregated data were available. The short-cut method has been applied as described in Hofman (1991) to estimate the capital stock on the basis of data from sources described in Maddison (1989).

Population

Data on Latin American countries have been taken from CELADE, *Boletín Demográfico*, vol. 23, no. 45 (Santiago de Chile: CELADE). Data for other countries have been taken from Maddison (1989) and have been updated to 1989 on the basis of OECD (1991), *Main Economic Indicators* (Paris: OECD). Data on South Korea have been updated to 1989 on the basis of the Council for Economic Planning and Development (1990). For the period 1950–85, five-yearly estimates by CELADE have been interpolated. For the period 1986–9, yearly estimates by CELADE have been used.

Employment

Employment data for Latin America have been taken from ECLAC (1990a). Estimates for OECD countries have been taken from OECD, *Labour Force Statistics* (Paris: OECD, various issues). Estimates for other countries have been taken from Maddison (1989) and have been updated to 1989 by applying growth rates for the period 1980–86. Estimates on hours worked for Latin America have been taken from Hofman (1990), *Note on Hours Worked* (Santiago de Chile: ECLAC, mimeo). For other countries estimates have been taken from Maddison (1989) and have been updated to 1989 by applying growth rates for the period 1980–86.

Land in use

Data on land in use have been taken from *Production Yearbook* (Rome: ECLAC: FAO, various issues). The following weights have been used: arable land 1, pasture land 0.3 and forest 0.1.

Education

Data on average numbers of years of formal educational experience of population aged 15–64 years have been taken from Maddison (1989). In order to obtain equivalent years of education per person of 15 years and over, the following weights have been used: primary education 1, secondary education 1.4 and higher education 2. Data on Venezuela for the year 1950 have been taken from Ministerio de Fomento (1957), *Octavo Censo General de Población* (Caracas: Ministerio de Fomento). Data for other years have been based on OCEI (1988), *Indicadores de la Fuerza de Trabajo, Segundo Semestre 1987*, (Caracas: OCEI). Data on The Netherlands have been taken from Maddison (1987). Data on Thailand have been estimated as an arithmetic average of South Korea and Taiwan. Data on Portugal and Spain have been estimated on the basis of OECD (1974), *Educational Statistical Yearbook*, vol.I (Paris: OECD). Data for the period 1986–9 have been estimated by extrapolating growth rates for the period 1980–86.

Notes

1. This is a revised version of Hofman (1993).
2. In this study we have used for all countries the same weights for capital, labour and land, since it has not been possible to include country-specific weights. An estimate based on the national accounts of Mexico has shown results close to the estimates in the present study. However, differences may be substantial for other countries.
3. These capital-stock estimates have been generated by the ECLAC project Long Run Economic Growth in Latin America. See Hofman (1991, 1992).
4. This is the case in Chile, where natural resources such as minerals and products from the sea are important. However, due to lack of resource-specific data, it has not been possible to include these resources in the growth-accounting exercise. Consequently, the growth of the natural-resources factor may have been underestimated in this study, and JFP overestimated.
5. Both JFP and DAJFP have also been calculated including land as a separate variable. Results hardly differ, and have not been presented here. Moreover, according to common practice, all data have been transposed to logarithms.

9 Social Development during Periods of Structural Adjustment

Rolph van der Hoeven and
Frances Stewart

9.1 OVERVIEW OF SOCIAL DEVELOPMENT IN THE 1980s

Introduction

In this chapter, we shall focus on social development in Latin America during the period 1980–90, in which most Latin American countries applied adjustment policies. In assessing social development, we shall use so-called social outcome indicators such as poverty, health status, education levels and employment status; process indicators which are the outcome of economic and social policy measures, such as the personal and functional income distribution, the intersectoral distribution of production and employment; and input indicators, which are, in most cases, more closely related to policy variables such as expenditure on social services, and human capital formation.

As described in previous chapters of this volume, the major elements of the adjustment policies are real devaluation, stricter application of monetary policies and fiscal policies, and liberalisation of trade and labour markets. The major aim of the policies is to control inflation and the fiscal deficit, and to increase exports and reduce imports in order to reduce the current account deficit and to accommodate debt repayments.

Real devaluation is achieved through nominal devaluation while bringing inflation down, often by lowering real wages. Monetary policies attempt to contain inflation by higher interest rates and restricted money supply. Fiscal policies aim at reducing the budget deficit mainly by cutting expenditure. Trade liberalisation aims at the reduction of barriers to exports and imports. Finally, deregulation of the labour market aims at increasing the mobility of labour by abolishing minimum wages and reducing real wages.

As the description above makes clear, adjustment policies have a direct bearing on social policies: the real wage level, together with employment, largely determines household income; interest rates affect industrial production and employment levels; public sector expenditure affects the level of public employment and the goods and services for all strata of the population; and deregulation of the labour market can affect minimum income levels and protection measures.

The extent to which the various social classes in a country are affected by adjustment policies depends largely on their initial social situation and factor endowments, on the position of labour in the production process and on the capability of labour to move into higher yielding activities if available. Moreover, it depends on the claims households can make on public services and social expenditure.

There has been much controversy about adjustment policies. It has been argued by Williamson (1990) and others that there is consensus among governments and international financial agencies on the general philosophy of adjustment policy. What is striking, however, is that Williamson's list of policies does not include social policies, with the exception of the allocation of expenditures in the context of fiscal policy.[1]

Latin America suffered from a decline in income per caput which amounted to about 25 per cent in countries such as Bolivia, Argentina, Guyana, Haiti and Nicaragua. Income per caput stagnated in other countries such as Chile, Colombia and Barbados. During the first half of the 1980s all countries experienced a more or less uniformly negative pattern. After 1985, one observes more differentiated developments. Several commentators have ascribed this differentiated development to application of different macro-economic and micro-economic policies (Stewart, 1992; ILO, 1992a).

Employment and wages

The 1980s witnessed some important changes in the nature and status of employment. The crisis manifested itself particularly in the early years of the decade, when all countries in Latin America confronted an acute foreign-exchange crisis, largely due to the debt situation, and subsequently experienced severe recession, in part due to the deflationary policies governments were forced to adopt.

As a consequence, average urban unemployment in Latin America rose to unprecedented levels of over 10 per cent by the mid 1980s. Also, the contribution of manufacturing industry to total employment declined. This was not the manifestation of a post-industrial society as in Western

Europe, but the result of a severe crisis. The crisis in the manufacturing sector is reflected by two other trends. First, employment in large enterprises declined rapidly while employment in small enterprises almost doubled. This trend continued towards the end of the 1980s. Second, there was an increase in employment in the informal sector. This trend did not continue after the mid 1980s and the contribution of the informal sector to non-agricultural employment was more or less stable.

The general crisis and the changing nature of employment also affected wages. Here, several trends are noticeable. All wage indicators were lower in 1990 than at the beginning of the 1980s. Moreover, they declined sharper than did GDP per caput. Until the mid 1980s the minimum wage, the wage in the construction sector, which is often taken as a proxy for wages for unskilled labour, and the agricultural wage all show a decline of about the same magnitude. Wages in the manufacturing sector, which reflect higher skill levels, declined less than the other wages and more or less in proportion to the decline in per caput income. After 1985, this pattern changed. The minimum wage declined much faster and so did the wage in manufacturing industry. The wage in the construction sector was somewhat higher in 1990 than it was in 1985. GDP per caput was in 1990 more or less the same as in 1985. Thus, the system of wage differentials changed significantly: minimum wages declined and so did wages for skilled labour. Wages for unskilled workers were stable.

What these changing wage trends do to poverty and deprivation is difficult to judge. Much depends on whether the cut-off point for the poverty line is situated around a level of income that corresponds to the minimum wage or to the wage of unskilled workers. The number of poor households as a percentage of total population rose considerably in the early 1980s and was more or less stable during the second half of the 1980s, indicating that the decline in minimum wages was already picked up in the increase in the poverty incidence at the beginning of the decade.

Table 9.1 shows that in most countries, with the exceptions of Colombia and Costa Rica, the minimum wage dropped considerably and faster than the wage in the manufacturing sector. In Costa Rica, the minimum wage increased, while the industrial wage declined, which was one of the major factors contributing to the rapid decline of poverty in that country.

The major conclusion from the employment wage trends is that recession and adjustment drove minimum wages down quickly, which had an adverse effect on poverty. However, if special measures were taken, the process was halted, even in recessionary periods, as was the case in Costa Rica and Colombia.

Social Development during Periods of Structural Adjustment

Table 9.1 Urban unemployment and wages in selected countries, 1980–91

	1980	1985	1990	1991
Latin America				
Urban unemployment (%)	6.7	10.1	8.1	8.5
Minimum wage (index)	100.0	86.4	68.3	66.2
Industry wage (index)	100.0	93.1	85.3	n.a.
Intensive adjustment lending countries:				
Bolivia				
Urban unemployment (%)	7.1	5.8	9.5	8.1
Minimum wage (index)	n.a.	33.2	31.2[a]	n.a.
Industry wage (index)	100.0	59.9	n.a.	n.a.
Chile				
Urban unemployment (%)	11.7	17.0	6.5	7.9
Minimum wage (index)	100.0	63.4	73.3	79.9
Industry wage (index)	100.0	90.4	104.4	n.a.
Colombia				
Urban unemployment (%)	9.7	14.4	10.3	10.5
Minimum wage (index)	100.0	108.0	105.7	105.9
Industry wage (index)	100.0	113.5	115.0	n.a.
Costa Rica				
Urban unemployment (%)	6.0	6.7	5.4	5.0
Minimum wage (index)	100.0	112.2	120.8	n.a.
Industry wage (index)	100.0	88.1	86.8	n.a.
Other adjustment lending countries				
Honduras				
Urban unemployment (%)	8.8	12.1	6.9[b]	n.a.
Minimum wage (index)	100.0	90.7	73.9	n.a.
Industry wage (index)	100.0	98.9	n.a.	n.a.
Panama				
Urban unemployment (%)	10.4	15.7	20.0	19.0
Minimum wage (index)	100.0	100.8	99.0	n.a.
Industry wage (index)	100.0	113.0	n.a.	n.a.
Uruguay				
Urban unemployment (%)	7.4	13.1	9.3	9.2
Minimum wage (index)	100.0	91.1	69.0	61.9
Industry wage (index)	100.0	97.7	111.1	n.a.
Other countries				
Guatemala				
Urban unemployment (%)	2.2	12.0	6.0	n.a.
Minimum wage (index)	100.0	94.0	n.a.	n.a.
Industry wage (index)	100.0	127.4	n.a.	n.a.

Table 9.1 Continued

	1980	1985	1990	1991
Paraguay				
Urban unemployment (%)	3.9	5.1	6.6	n.a.
Minimum wage (index)	100.0	99.4	130.0	124.8
Industry wage (index)	100.0	89.4	102.4	n.a.
Peru				
Urban unemployment (%)	7.1	10.1	8.3	n.a.
Minimum wage (index)	100.0	54.2	21.4	15.5
Industry wage (index)	100.0	53.3	25.0	n.a.
Venezuela				
Urban unemployment (%)	6.6	14.3	10.5	10.9
Minimum wage (index)	100.0	95.3	65.2	61.0
Industry wage (index)	n.a.	n.a.	n.a.	n.a.

[a] 1983 = 100
[b] 1989
Source: ILO, 1992, based on PREALC household surveys and official data.

Exports and labour intensity

One of the principal aims of adjustment policies is to increase exports. A real depreciation of the exchange rate is one of the appropriate instruments for this. In order to achieve a real depreciation of the exchange rate, a nominal depreciation of the exchange rate is applied, which must be accompanied by a controlled inflation rate, in order to bring about a real depreciation. The inflation rate can be controlled by several means: a reduction of the fiscal deficit to reduce the monetary overhang or to free savings; a large increase in the real interest rate, to make money more expensive; and a repression of real wages in order to reduce production costs. The effects on the poor of a traditional stabilisation and adjustment programme is thus ambiguous, depending on production and consumption patterns of tradables and non-tradables.

The poor will benefit if employment is created in the labour-intensive export sectors. To what extent did this happen? Given the importance of this possible effect (since it is always used in discussions), it is astonishing to find so little analysis on labour intensity and exports. As a proxy, one can look at an increase of exports of products which are typically produced in a labour-intensive manner, such as textiles and footwear. In some countries (for example, Colombia, Costa Rica, Dominican Republic, Jamaica and Panama) textiles and clothing increased their shares in exports, which may have been beneficial for poor people, but in most countries the shares did not change significantly. Another indicator is the large increase in the export of footwear, where Latin America increased its world market share from 0.9 per cent in 1970 to 4.4 per cent in 1980 and 7.5 per cent in 1990. Hence, there is some evidence that adjustment policies resulted in an expansion of opportunities for poor workers in export industries. However, at the same time employment opportunities were reduced in other manufacturing sectors and in the public sector.

Income distribution and poverty

Income distribution in Latin America has always been more uneven than in other regions of the world. A joint study by the ILO and The World Bank on income distribution, based on data for the 1960s and 1970s, reported a Gini ratio of 0.52 for countries in Latin America and a Gini ratio of 0.39 for developing countries in other regions (van Ginneken and Park, 1984). The income share of the bottom 20 per cent in Latin America was less than half compared to the other group: 3.1 per cent as compared to 6.5 per cent. Some authors even argue that the frequent recourse to stabilisation and adjustment policies, which started in most Latin American countries much earlier than the 1980s, is in effect a consequence of deep-seated internal conflict about the distribution of national income which fuels inflation time and again (Hirschman, 1981; Sachs, 1987b).

A recent study by The World Bank observes that the unequal character of most Latin American countries has not been diminished and may even have increased (Psacharopoulos *et al.* 1992). Continuation of an unequal income distribution combined with a decline or stagnation of income per caput, as occurred in many countries in the region, inevitably leads to increased poverty. In Latin America, the total number of persons living in poverty has increased by 45 per cent during the 1980s. For every newborn child, the chance of being poor was well over 50 per cent.

Over the decade, we have thus noticed a rather worrying trend of increased poverty caused by persistent income inequality and low or stagnant levels of production. Some may ask to what extent the low levels of production and the persistent income inequality are the consequences of adjustment policies. Prima facie, one can argue that with so many adjustment policies adopted in Latin America and considering the policies were carried out for a decade in most cases, adjustment policies could be held accountable for the increase in poverty and deterioration of living conditions. Others argue, however, that the adjustment policies prevented a further fall in production and income and that without the adjustment policies, the situation and, as a consequence, poverty would have been much worse. In our mind, this often-held debate is somewhat fruitless, although given the large adjustment applied and given the fact that there appears to be now a full Washington consensus, we tend to think that the first argument, that adjustment was at fault, is correct.

Social indicators

The social situation changed drastically in the 1980s. In many countries primary enrolment ratios declined or progressed at a rate insufficient for countries that need to improve their human resource base. Various country examples – for example, Sri Lanka – have shown that even at modest levels of per caput GDP, universal primary education can be achieved. Given the relatively high income levels in most countries in Latin America, universal primary education should easily be attainable. However, in seven out of the fourteen countries for which data are available, primary enrolment declined or remained unchanged over the period 1980–85. No data are available for more recent years. This is an extremely worrying trend, since education is an investment. In cross-country analyses, increased levels of education are among the most important variables 'explaining' economic growth (Birdsall, 1993).

The lack of progress towards universal primary education and towards significant increases in secondary education is also a source of continued income inequality. Tinbergen (1975) explained reduced income equality in industrialised countries by the increased supply of education. More recently, Psacharopoulos et. al. (1992) found that educational attainment was the single strongest factor in explaining inequality among workers' income and could explain 25 per cent of the variation in income.

It is worrying that in three out of four countries in which income inequality declined, primary school enrolment declined as well. This indicates that concern for income and income policy, such as a minimum wage policy, does not necessarily imply that there is sufficient concern for human capital formation.

Regarding the health situation, statistics are often unreliable or lacking, and that is certainly the case for mortality figures. Figures reported are frequently extrapolations of complicated life tables, reflecting past trends rather than the actual situation (see Albañez et al., 1989). Changes in the rate of decline of infant mortality should therefore be interpreted cautiously. This rate declined only a little in countries such as Brazil and

Panama, but in other countries it declined significantly. Maternal mortality rates also showed variation and are surprisingly high in some countries. Contrary to previous trends, maternal mortality increased in Costa Rica (where it was very low before), Guatemala and, according to some statistics, Mexico.

9.2 MEASURES TO DEAL WITH THE SOCIAL CONSEQUENCES OF ADJUSTMENT POLICIES

One can distinguish different phases in dealing with the social consequences of adjustment policies. Until 1985, policy-makers and international financial agencies showed little appreciation of the need to deal with the social consequences. Adjustment policies had a rather uniform character and were mainly designed to deal with the debt problem and to contain the foreign-exchange crisis. Moreover, there was a rather optimistic belief that adjustment policies would lead to a quick turnaround. Some 'belt-tightening' was considered necessary but magnitude and duration were underestimated.

The turnaround in the mid 1980s came as a consequence of two parallel events. By that time, sufficient reports had become available showing that economic and social hardship had increased for many people in the region, and workers' organisations and national and international organisations concerned with the poor and family welfare were raising their voices. At the same time, international financial agencies and many policy-makers in the region came to realise that the adjustment process could not be carried out quickly, but was much more of a long-term process with the aim of putting countries on a different growth path. Stabilisation alone was judged to be insufficient.

As a consequence of the more recent long-term focus of adjustment policies, the variety in adjustment measures increased and the experiences of countries started to become more divergent. The implication of this shift in focus was, however, that the argument of 'short-term suffering for longer-term gains' could no longer be used. Hence, to appease criticism and guided by long-term concern, attention to social deprivation and poverty increased. This was mainly reflected by increased concern for patterns of public expenditure within the limits set by the macro-economic environment. Moreover, compensatory programmes and social investment funds were established (van der Hoeven and Stewart, 1993).

Notwithstanding increased attention to social issues, the underlying philosophy of the adjustment model was not put into question. There still appears to be little feedback from social policies to macro-economic policies.[2]

Restructuring public expenditure

A convenient and practical method to assess how the poor benefit from public sector expenditure is to use a chain of various expenditure ratios (Stewart, 1992) – the ratio of public expenditure to GDP (G:Y); the ratio of social sector expenditure to public expenditure (S:G); and finally the ratio of social expenditure which actually reaches the poor, the priority ratio (P:S).

Consequently, public expenditure may be focused on the poor in different ways: targeting expenditure on the poor (high P:S), diverting an essential part of public expenditure to social expenditure (S:G) and a high level of public expenditure in general (G:Y).

The data on public expenditure presented in Table 9.2 show the wide variety on social expenditure as reflected by expenditure on education and health, and the drastic changes that took place in some countries with regard to social expenditure.

Education and health spending of the central government as a percentage of GDP in 1990 varied greatly from 2.44 per cent and 1.95 per cent in Brazil and Argentina to almost 12 per cent in Costa Rica and Panama. However, some countries in Latin America have a federal structure and consequently data on central government expenditure do not adequately reflect total government expenditure in that area. This distorts international comparisons and consequently it may be more relevant to investigate systematic changes in central government expenditures in the course of time, provided that no changes in responsibilities of central and federal governments took place. It follows that spending on education as a share of public expenditure declined in all countries that were intensively involved in adjustment processes over the decade, except for Brazil. Changes were less significant in the other countries.

Note that in most countries where education and health expenditure as a percentage of GNP decreased, the ratio of health and education expenditure as a percentage of total government expenditure declined as well. This implies that in most countries declining investments in human resources were largely policy-induced and not merely due to the recession.

It is true that the decline of social expenditure in those cases may be compensated by a shift in expenditures in favour of programmes and activities to support the poor. However, data on the distribution of social expenditure on poor and non-poor groups in society are hardly available.

Table 9.2 Allocation ratios in adjusting countries, 1981–90

	Expenditures on health and education: total expenditures (% shares)			Expenditures on health and education: GNP (% shares)			Index of expenditure per caput (1980 = 100)	
	1981	1990	Change	1981	1990	Change	1981	1990
Intensive adjustment lending countries								
Bolivia	31.6	20.3	−11.3	4.01	3.82	−0.2	1.22	0.78
Brazil	11.2	12.5	1.3	2.18	2.44	0.25	1.87	2.09
Chile	20.8	16.0	−4.8	6.45	5.25	−1.2	1.24	1.77
Costa Rica	53.4	44.2	−9.2	12.66	11.98	−0.68	1.23	1.02
Jamaica[a]	21.3	19.8	−1.5	10.33	8.34	−1.99	0.89	0.83
Mexico	20.1	15.8	−4.3	4.18	2.91	−1.27	0.77	0.61
Other adjustment lending countries								
Uruguay	11.5	11.9	0.4	2.86	3.27	0.41	1.05	1.09
Argentina	8.7	11.3	2.6	2.05	1.75	−0.3	0.55	0.71
Ecuador	38.0	29.2	−8.8	6.5	4.56	−1.94	0.87	0.67
Panama	26.0	36.4	10.4	9.39	11.58	2.19	1.00	1.4
Venezuela[b]	25.6	29.6	4.0	7.4	6.84	−0.56	0.64	0.74

Table 9.2 Continued

	Expenditures on health and education: total expenditures (% shares)			Expenditures on health and education: GNP (% shares)			Index of expenditure per caput (1980=100)	
	1981	1990	Change	1981	1990	Change	1981	1990
Other countries								
Dominican Republic	23.6	20.8	−2.8	4.01	3.18	−0.83	0.86	0.76
El Salvador	26.3	24.0	−2.3	4.87	2.38	−2.49	0.51	0.47
Guatemala	n.a.	29.4	n.a.	n.a.	3.53	n.a.	0.61	n.a.
Nicaragua	26.2	24.29	−1.91	7.91	9.89	1.97	0.84	0.78
Paraguay	16.3	17.0	0.7	2.14	1.58	−0.55	0.67	0.7
Peru	16.6	21.3	4.7	3.35	2.13	−1.22	0.35	0.45
Trinidad and Tobago	18.1	23.8	5.7	7.38	8.78	1.4	0.64	0.84

[a] Data for 1989 not 1990.
[b] Data for 1988 not 1990.
All averages are unweighted averages.

There is some evidence that expenditure on education, particularly on primary education, tends to reach the poor better than does expenditure on health, which is often for curative care in larger hospitals to which the poor have little access. Moreover, there is also evidence that in the course of the 1980s expenditure on education became more supportive of the poor. The opposite holds true of expenditures on health (Stewart, 1992).

Public sector revenues

In studies of the social consequences of adjustment policies, most attention is paid to expenditure ratios. However, when assessing the effects of adjustment on the poor, it is also important to analyse the burden of taxes on different income groups and how this has changed since the introduction of adjustment policies. Tax policies are an important part of the meso-policies and may change the nature of traditional adjustment policies, but so far tax policies have received only little attention.

Table 9.3 shows a mixed picture for the region. In some adjusting countries, the share of direct taxes decreased and in other countries the share of indirect taxes decreased. Direct taxes are usually progressive, whereas indirect taxes tend to be more regressive, although this need not always be the case. Among the countries where poverty declined as measured by pre-tax income, the share of indirect taxes decreased in Costa Rica and Uruguay and the share of direct taxes increased in Colombia.

9.3 INTEGRATING SOCIAL POLICIES AND ADJUSTMENT POLICIES AS A NECESSARY PRECONDITION FOR INDUSTRIAL RESTRUCTURING

To what extent has the decline in social conditions affected the possibilities of undertaking a more vigorous process of industrial restructuring in Latin America? Several relationships may be distinguished. Social development does not take place in isolation but is the expression of perceived attitudes and the outcome of a power struggle between various groups in society. Some authors have argued that the large degree of income inequality in most countries in Latin America acts as a hindrance to development. Large income inequalities are a source of discontent. Discontent about the distribution of resources often leads to inflation and provides an unstable climate for industrial activities (Hirschman, 1981). Moreover, high inequality leaves the bottom end of the income scale out of the market for industrial consumer goods and forces industrialists to

Table 9.3 Tax structure, 1981–90

	Direct taxes		Indirect taxes[a]		Social security		Other	
	1981	1990	1981	1990	1981	1990	1981	1990
Intensive adjustment lending countries								
Bolivia[b]	15.2	4.9	67.2	38.9	n.a.	8.8	17.6	47.4
Brazil[b]	13.2	11.5	30.5	15.3	25.7	16.6	30.6	56.6
Chile[b]	16.9	23.3	46.4	46.9	15.3	6.0	21.4	23.8
Colombia[b]	23.1	27.8	43.6	45.5	11.6	12.6	21.7	14.1
Costa Rica[b]	14.6	9.8	53.0	50.4	25.2	28.8	7.2	11.0
Mexico[b]	37.1	36.5	60.9	60.6	14.4	13.6	-12.4	-10.7
Other adjustment lending countries								
Uruguay[b]	7.3	6.7	55.6	45.7	24.6	27.0	12.5	20.6
Argentina	5.5	4.3	54.7	33.8	15.8	43.4	24.0	18.5
Ecuador	43.7	56.9	46.1	35.8	0.0	0.0	10.2	7.3
Panama	24.9	14.7	27.4	26.2	18.9	27.3	28.8	31.8
Venezuela	75.0	57.5	8.6	11.0	3.6	2.7	12.8	28.8

Table 9.3 Continued

	Direct taxes		Indirect taxes[a]		Social security		Other	
	1981	1990	1981	1990	1981	1990	1981	1990
Other countries								
Dominican Republic	19.0	20.9	54.2	60.9	3.7	4.1	23.1	14.1
El Salvador	20.9	18.8	65.0	56.9	0.0	0.0	14.1	24.3
Guatemala	12.0	18.1	49.4	56.0	11.2	0.0	27.4	25.9
Nicaragua[b]	7.8	12.5	62.6	57.0	8.9	12.2	20.7	18.3
Paraguay	16.2	9.3	37.5	39.6	14.6	0.0	31.7	51.1
Peru	15.8	10.0	71.0	70.5	0.0	0.0	13.2	19.5

[a] Includes domestic taxes on goods and international taxes
[b] Data for 1987, not 1990
Unweighted averages have been used.
Source: The World Bank, *World Development Report* (various years).

concentrate on providing products for the more sophisticated upper end of the market and for exports (Sachs, 1987b).

Yet industrial experience in East Asian countries has shown that a more vigorous industrial development is achieved if industry develops itself gradually up the technology ladder, starting with production of basic consumer goods and then moving to more sophisticated goods. Learning by doing has been a powerful catalyst for sustainable industrial development (Lall, 1992).

It is, however, not only the structure of the market but also its stability which provides a better industrial climate, as advanced by FitzGerald in this volume (Chapter 4). High income inequality may not be conducive to political stability and may threaten potential industrialisation. This has been exacerbated in recent years during the stabilisation and adjustment policies, which were often carried out without a clear concept of income policy in mind, as discussed earlier. Yet a good incomes policy often determines the success or failure of a stabilisation and adjustment process (Dornbusch, 1991).

Social policies also have an impact on industrialisation through their effect on the supply of labour. In the 'old' growth theories (Solow, 1993) as well as in the 'new' growth theories (Romer, 1990), education is one of the most powerful explanatory variables of either a high level of growth or an acceleration of the growth rate.

In several countries, including intensive adjusting countries and other countries, primary school enrolment declined and it became increasingly difficult for poor and middle-income families to finance secondary and tertiary education for their children. This setback in human resource development will affect industrial development considerably.

Hence, in general there is not a trade-off between social policies and industrial development. On the contrary, improved social development will support a more vigorous industrial development and restructuring through the various mechanisms described above.

Notes

1. In Williamson (1993) two more items have been added to the list: birth control and targeted social expenditures. Still, this falls short of the whole gamut of social policies, as we shall discuss below.
2. The Managing Director of the IMF, M. Camdessus, stated

   > These [Fund] programs involve, first and foremost, macroeconomic discipline, beginning with the reductions of fiscal deficits and monetary measures aimed at achieving price stability and realistic exchange rates...

Let me say outright: these policies serve the poor, and we must do our utmost to implement them if we are to be efficient in the fight against poverty. (Statement to the UN Social and Economic Council, 11 July 1990)

A review of World Bank policies towards the social dimensions of adjustment concluded that 'Changes in the design of adjustment programmes can promote the longer run interests of the poor, but have received relatively little attention' (Ribe *et al.*, 1990).

10 Trade Policy and Changing Trade Patterns
Cees van Beers

10.1 STRUCTURAL CHANGE AND TRADE POLICY

The basic question for developing countries with respect to their international trade relations is how trade can contribute more to economic growth and industrialisation. There is a certain agreement among economists that international trade and economic growth are interrelated. However, the way in which they are related – trade as an engine or a handmaiden of economic growth – is still a matter of dispute as discussed in the contribution by Linnemann in this volume (Chapter 2). Industrialisation is a complex dynamic process influenced by many factors. Chenery (1960) showed that there are some similar tendencies in the industrialisation processes across countries. In his famous paper 'Patterns of Industrial Growth' he showed a strong positive correlation between an increase in income per caput and the rise of value added per capita in industry (manufacturing and construction). The per capita income elasticity of value added of industry and of manufacturing appeared to be larger than one, indicating that the share of industry and manufacturing in national production increases.

Empirical studies have shown a positive correlation between increases of GDP per caput and the growth of trade flows of countries. Accentuating Chenery's conclusions, there is a positive relation between the degree of industrialisation (as measured by the share of industrial or manufacturing output in total output) and changes in trade flows. A country that industrialises shows a declining share of manufactured final products in total imports as an increasing share of these products is made domestically. This is an import substitution effect. This does not imply that the import flow will decrease, since at the same time imports of intermediate goods and raw materials will increase. The composition of imports changes because of demand factors. On the other hand, determinants on the supply side are responsible for changes in the export structure.[1] Industrialisation leads to a rising potential export of manufactured products and when this materialises the structure of total exports changes – that is, the share of manufactured exports in total exports increases (Michaely, 1984).

The empirical analyses by Chenery provide a clear picture of what happens with industrial production and its composition when a country moves towards a higher level of economic development. However, they do not provide clear policy advice on how to facilitate or stimulate structural change. Besides structural variables, differences in trade policy may be an important explanatory variable for differences between countries in the contribution of foreign trade to economic development or the influence of economic development on international trade. An important observation in this respect is that in many Latin American countries in the 1960s there was already a substantial level of industrialisation which was not reflected in the export structure of these countries. This was true for the small Latin American countries in the 1970s and for some of them even during the 1980s (van Dijck, 1986). Table 10.1 shows that even in 1990 – after all the adjustments of the trade regimes that took place in the 1980s – the share of

Table 10.1 Shares of manufacturing production in GDP (1) and of manufactured exports in total exports (2) in selected countries, 1970, 1980 and 1990

	1970		1980		1990	
	(1)	(2)	(1)	(2)	(1)	(2)
Chile	0.29	0.04	0.24	0.10	0.22[a]	0.10
Uruguay[b]	0.42	0.20	0.45	0.38	0.42[c]	0.39
Venezuela	0.13	0.02	0.16	0.02	0.21	0.11
Argentina[b]	0.49	0.14	0.47	0.23	0.40	0.35
Brazil	0.32	0.14	0.35	0.39	0.29	0.53
Colombia	0.22	0.08	0.24	0.20	0.20	0.25
Ecuador	0.22	0.02	0.21	0.03	0.20	0.03
El Salvador	0.18	0.39	0.18	0.20	0.17[d]	0.23
Honduras	0.13	0.08	0.14	0.13	0.15	0.07
Mexico	0.26	0.33	0.29	0.12	0.31	0.44
Peru	0.26	0.02	0.26	0.17	0.22	0.16
South Korea	0.15	0.77	0.29	0.90	0.36	0.94
Malaysia	0.15	0.07	0.25	0.19	0.30[c]	0.44
Thailand	0.19	0.08	0.26	0.28	0.29	0.64

[a] refers to 1982
[b] For Argentina and Uruguay data on industrial production, not on manufacturing production, have been used.
[c] refers to 1989
[d] refers to 1987
Source: The World Bank, 1992.

manufactures in total exports was significantly lower in the Latin American countries than was the case in south-east Asia.[2]

Apparently, the connection between manufactured exports and the emergence of the manufacturing sector was – and in many cases still is – rather loose in Latin America, whereas in several south-east Asian countries this connection was more direct. An important explanation in this respect is the implementation of import-substitution industrialisation policies in many Latin American countries during the 1950s and 1960s. Consequently the domestic production process was protected from world market competition and the lack of incentives to import and to produce at competitive prices for global markets gave rise to high domestic prices, overvalued exchange rates and consequently poor export performances.

The economic policy environment can roughly be divided in two categories: trade policy and macro-economic policy. The World Development Report 1987 distinguished four trade strategies:

(i)   strongly outward-orientated,
(ii) moderately outward-orientated,
(iii) moderately inward-orientated
(iv) strongly inward-orientated. (The World Bank, 1987, p. 82)

The first two trade strategies concentrate on a reduction of disincentives to exports such as import barriers, whereas governments that pursue the latter two strategies create incentives in favour of production for the domestic market.[3]

With respect to the macro-economic performance, the World Development Report 1987 shows that countries with outward-orientated strategies had lower incremental capital to output ratios in 1973–85 than had inward-orientated countries (The World Bank, 1987, p 84). A lower incremental capital to output ratio means more intensive growth – that is, growth generated by using existing production factors more efficiently. The classification presented in the World Development Report 1987 points out that most countries with outward-orientated trade policies are in southeast Asia, whereas most countries in Latin America pursued more inward-orientated policies.

Two reasons may be distinguished for the switch which several Latin American countries started to make in the 1980s from inward-orientated towards outward-orientated policies: the demonstration effect of the economic successes of countries in south-east Asia, and the international debt crisis which forced many countries in Latin America to implement adjustment programmes. The results of these programmes were rather disappointing in many respects. The international environment of the 1970s and the 1980s was completely different from the stable economic world order of the 1960s when several south-east Asian countries started their macro-economic and trade policy reforms. Consequently, a trade policy that would copy blindly the East Asian success model, may not guarantee success in Latin America. (For a discussion of demand-related reasons why liberalisation policies may not be a guarantee for success, see Cline, 1984.)

As a consequence, a new kind of thinking on economic development emerged in Latin America, the so-called 'new' or 'national competitiveness' paradigm. In this context the phrase 'inside looking outward' has been coined. A significant difference between the 'national competitiveness' paradigm and the 'orthodox' paradigm can be traced to the controversy over the relationship between growth and trade: growth-led exports according to the national competitiveness paradigm versus the orthodox policy approach of export-led growth. In the first paradigm growth is supply-driven and from inside. The 'new' paradigm focuses on trade reform as just one, not the main, element of development in Latin America. Other elements include the strengthening of democratic structures and investment in human resources. This new approach emphasises not adjusting passively to world market conditions but the promotion of internal adaptions to shifts in the international economic context. According to some authors (Fajnzylber, 1992), special attention should be paid to link manufacturing industries in Latin America to the available natural resources. This underlines also the difference from the successful countries of east Asia that are poorly endowed with natural resources.

The contribution of this new approach is the recognition that trade reform in itself is not sufficient to stimulate economic development in the small Latin American countries. In addition, priority for investment in human resources is considered crucial for successful economic and social development. However, the approach includes many different aspects of economic and social policy, and is not specific enough to provide solutions to problems that may occur during the stage of transition. It does not become clear what the consequences are of the simultaneous implementation of different policy reforms for the achievement of a more efficient and flexible domestic economic structure, since they may interact. Theoretical and empirical analyses are required to understand the relationships among these policy areas.

It has become fashionable to classify industries and countries as winners and losers (see, for example, Fajnzylber, 1992). Not only is such an approach incorrect, as Krugman (1994) pointed out, but it also bypasses the question of whether a government is capable of determining whether an industry is competitive or not, even if it knows what competitiveness actually means. It is not clear why a government would be in a better position than the market is to know what winners are. If markets do not function properly, first-best policy is to remove the obstacles that distort the functioning of markets. However, this is not the only problem. Suppose the government has correctly picked a potential winner, but in the course of time market prospects change and the selected industry loses its competitiveness. The question arises whether the government will be prepared to shift incentives from this industry to another industry that may gain competitiveness in the future. It may not be easy to resist pressure groups from the sector initially privileged. If the government proves unable to resist this pressure, new winners will have to compete with losers for scarce government resources. This complicates control of the government budget. Moreover, it renders government policy to promote national competitiveness unclear. As many Latin American countries have a poor reputation in this respect, such a policy may contribute to uncertainty about macro-economic conditions and give the wrong signals for domestic and foreign investments.

It is neither possible nor desirable to escape from the pressures exerted by external market forces and this is especially true of small countries. This implies that the new insertion of Latin America in the world economy can only be achieved by making adjustments to the economic conditions of the world market – that is, to the main conditions that govern the pattern of comparative advantage. Governments may assist this insertion by investing in human capital and by removing all kinds of impediments to the optimal functioning of markets.

10.2 TRADE PATTERNS

The structure of trade changes over time as its determinants and impediments such as factor endowments, technological knowledge and trade policies change continuously. Government policy can only change factor endowments and technological knowledge in the long run. Trade policies can be changed in the short run, but the structure of trade may change only gradually. The structure of trade is an important determinant of future export growth. Below we shall analyse changes in the export structure in some Latin American countries in the 1960s, 1970s and 1980s, and make a comparison with the export structure in three countries in south-east Asia that have successfully penetrated international markets in this period.

144   *Trade Policy and Changing Trade Patterns*

Table 10.1 shows the contribution of manufacturing production to total production and the share of manufactured exports to total exports in fourteen countries in 1970, 1980 and 1990. Two observations may be made. First, it is striking that at the beginning of the period under investigation the level of industrialisation in the Asian countries was low when compared to the Latin American countries in our sample. However, during the 1970s and 1980s the contribution of the manufacturing sector to GDP increased substantially in Asia, while it tended to reduce or stagnate in the Latin American countries, except for Venezuela and Mexico. Second, the contribution of the manufacturing sector to overall export performance of the Asian countries tended to increase significantly during these two decades. Note that the export performance of Malaysia and Thailand was very much dominated by primary products in the 1970s, as was the case in most Latin American countries at that time. However, the contribution of manufactured exports to total exports increased in many Latin American countries in our sample, albeit to a lesser extent than was the case in the Asian NICs.

Table 10.2 shows the contributions of the five most important manufacturing export sectors in five selected countries in Latin America at the end of the 1960s, 1970s and 1980s. Table 10.3 shows such contributions in three selected countries in south-east Asia. Three observations may be made. First, in the selected countries in Latin America as well as in Asia shifts took place regarding the five largest exporting manufacturing sectors during the 1970s and 1980s. Chile is the major exception in this regard. Apparently, the exports of Chile were already in line with the country's comparative advantage for resource-intensive industries at the end of the 1960s, and trade liberalisation in the 1970s did not change the structure of exports.

Second, the contribution of the five largest exporting manufacturing sectors in Latin America was rather unbalanced during the 1960s: over half of manufacturing exports were generated by only one sector. The contribution of sectors became more balanced during the 1970s and particularly during the 1980s as a result of trade liberalisation. In the Asian countries the contribution of sectors was more balanced from the outset, especially in South Korea, which was already pursuing a policy of trade liberalisation in the second half of the 1960s, and which shows a fairly even distribution of its manufactured exports.

Third, in Asia non-traditional, high-technology sectors, such as electrical machinery (ISIC 383) and transport equipment (ISIC 384), that make intensive use of human capital and show a dynamic development pattern have increased their contribution to exports significantly. In the five Latin

Table 10.2 Contributions of the five largest manufacturing export sectors to total manufactured exports in five Latin American countries, 1968–70, 1978–80 and 1988–90

	1968–70		1978–80		1988–90	
	ISIC code	share	ISIC code	share	ISIC code	share
Chile	372	0.90	372	0.70	372	0.64
	341	0.03	311	0.08	311	0.12
	311	0.02	341	0.07	341	0.07
	351	0.01	351	0.04	331	0.04
	331	0.01	331	0.04	351	0.04
Ecuador	311	0.89	353	0.56	353	0.68
	352	0.04	311	0.37	311	0.23
	322	0.03	331	0.02	331	0.03
	331	0.01	382	0.01	322	0.01
	353	0.01	322	0.01	351	0.01
El Salvador	311	0.51	311	0.49	311	0.44
	321	0.14	321	0.13	321	0.13
	352	0.05	352	0.05	352	0.09
	351	0.05	341	0.05	341	0.07
	322	0.14	322	0.04	372	0.04
Uruguay	n.a.	n.a.	311	0.39	311	0.37
	n.a.	n.a.	322	0.16	321	0.22
	n.a.	n.a.	321	0.15	322	0.11
	n.a.	n.a.	323	0.08	323	0.11
	n.a.	n.a.	324	0.03	351	0.06
Venezuela	353	0.97	353	0.95	353	0.70
	311	0.01	372	0.02	372	0.11
	371	0.01	371	0.01	371	0.05
	382	0.00	351	0.01	351	0.03
	372	0.00	354	0.00	381	0.01

American countries the emerging sectors are resource-based – for example, food industries (ISIC 311), wood products (ISIC 331), paper products (ISIC 341) and non-ferrous metals (ISIC 372).

Table 10.4 presents calculations of a measure of the RCA of Latin American and Asian countries. A country has an RCA in a product category when the share of that category in the country's total exports exceeds its share in world trade (Balassa, 1965). Thus, a country has a comparative

146   *Trade Policy and Changing Trade Patterns*

Table 10.3 Contributions of the five largest manufacturing export sectors to total manufactured exports in three Asian countries, 1968–70, 1978–80 and 1983–5

	1968–70		1978–80		1983–5	
	ISIC code	share	ISIC code	share	ISIC code	share
South Korea	322	0.32	322	0.19	384	0.21
	321	0.21	321	0.15	322	0.15
	331	0.16	383	0.12	383	0.14
	390	0.08	384	0.09	321	0.10
	383	0.07	371	0.08	371	0.08
Malaysia	372	0.46	311	0.28	383	0.30
	311	0.18	383	0.20	311	0.29
	331	0.12	372	0.20	331	0.09
	353	0.11	331	0.15	372	0.08
	382	0.02	321	0.03	353	0.05
Thailand	311	0.63	311	0.41	311	0.42
	372	0.24	372	0.18	322	0.11
	321	0.05	321	0.11	383	0.09
	331	0.02	322	0.07	390	0.07
	390	0.02	383	0.07	372	0.06

advantage in a category if the RCA measure is larger than 1 and a comparative disadvantage if it is smaller than 1. Note that measures for RCA are imperfect and may be criticised on several grounds.[4] Therefore such measures may only be used to provide some general information on the industrial categories in which the Latin American countries have a comparative advantage or disadvantage. The export categories included belong to the top twelve categories of manufactured exports from Latin America according to Lord and are divided into three categories of products according to factor intensities (Lord, 1992).

Two observations are in order. First, Latin America's RCA at the end of the 1980s is scattered over the three categories as distinguished according to factor intensity. As shown, the five small economies in Table 10.4 have RCAs > 1 in natural-resource based industries and unskilled-labour intensive industries. Latin America as a whole shows RCAs > 1 in some industries that make intensive use of human capital such as industrial chemicals (ISIC 351/352), plastic products (ISIC 356) and iron and steel industries

Table 10.4 RCAs in twelve major Latin American manufacturing export sectors, 1988–90[a]

ISIC code	Latin America	Asia[b]	Chile	Ecuador	El Salvador	Uruguay	Venezuela
Natural resource-based industries							
341	1.07	0.30	4.67	0.41	5.33	0.65	1.14
369	1.11	0.52	0.68	1.97	0.16	1.06	2.15
Unskilled labour-based industries							
321	1.14	1.78	0.62	3.35	5.83	2.86	0.41
322	0.85	4.23	0.94	0.86	0.90	6.71	0.70
323	5.50	1.02	0.36	0.10	2.65	43.47	1.51
324	3.74	3.40	1.96	0	8.87	2.18	1.29
Human capital and technology-based industries							
351/352	1.98	0.32	5.39	1.89	0.20	0.56	1.78
356	1.12	0.57	0.36	0.13	0.75	1.18	2.31
371	3.42	0.70	1.58	0.32	0.60	0.24	5.98
382	0.75	0.64	0.90	0.15	0.50	0.40	0.27
383	0.43	1.89	0.90	0.56	0.44	0.12	0.22
384	0.83	0.29	0.31	0.31	0.20	0.19	0.30

[a] Note that Lord has calculated the RCAs presented in this table at the SITC two-digits level. The conversion to ISIC three-digits level has been made by the present author.
[b] Asia includes Hong Kong, Singapore, South Korea, Malaysia, Indonesia, Thailand and The Philippines.
Source: Appendix Table 7 in Lord, 1992.

(ISIC 371). However, Latin America as a whole and the selected small countries in particular do not have RCAs > 1 in some human-capital intensive sectors – such as machinery (ISIC 382), electrical machinery (ISIC 383) and transport equipment (ISIC 384) – that have often been regarded as engines for overall economic growth.

Second, the Asian countries have a clear concentration of RCAs > 1 in unskilled labour-intensive industries. The only human-capital intensive industry with RCA > 1 is electrical machinery (ISIC 383). However, as compared to the human-capital intensive industries in which the Latin American countries have an RCA > 1, electrical machinery is a very dynamic sector. Note that the selected Asian countries, some of which started to liberalise substantially at a relatively early stage, show RCAs > 1 for unskilled labour intensive industries. Obviously, trade liberalisation does not bring an economy closer to a production and export structure of non-traditional, high technology products, but to a pattern of production and export that is in line with comparative advantage. The moves towards trade liberalisation in Latin America have also shifted the structure of production and exports towards industries in which these countries have a comparative advantage (Lord, 1992). As was the case in the Asian countries, comparative advantage in Latin America is not so much concentrated in non-traditional, high-technology products. This suggests that an active government policy to stimulate so-called 'high-tech' industries with high value added will bring about a deviation from the structure of comparative advantage. It is of importance to emphasise here that governments must not try to encourage industries in these non-traditional 'high tech' sectors as long as the country does not have a comparative advantage for such industrial activities. Rather, governments should concentrate on the creation of a stable and credible macro-economic climate that stimulates the domestic and foreign investments that are required for the development of comparative advantages.

APPENDIX 10.1   ISIC CATEGORIES

ISIC code

311–312	Food manufacturing	323	Manufacture of leather and products of leather, leather substitutes and fur, except footwear and wearing apparel
313	Beverage industries		
314	Tobacco manufactures		
321	Manufacture of textiles		
322	Manufacture of wearing apparel, except footwear		
		324	Manufacture of footwear,

	except vulcanised or moulded rubber or plastic footwear	362	Manufacture of glass and glass products
331	Manufacture of wood and wood products, including furniture	369	Manufacture of other non-metallic mineral products
		371	Iron and steel basic industries
332	Manufacture of furniture and fixtures, except primarily of metal	372	Non-ferrous metal basic industries
341	Manufacture of paper and paper products	381	Manufacture of fabricated metal products, except machinery and equipment
342	Printing, publishing and allied industries	382	Manufacture of machinery, except electrical
351	Manufacture of industrial chemicals	383	Manufacture of electrical machinery apparatus, appliances and supplies
352	Manufacture of other chemicals	384	Manufacture of transport equipment
353	Petroleum refineries		
354	Manufacture of miscellaneous products of petroleum and coal	385	Manufacture of professional and scientific and measuring and controlling equipment not elsewhere classified, and of photographic and optical goods
355	Manufacture of rubber products		
356	Manufacture of plastic products not elsewhere classified		
		390	Other manufacturing industries
361	Manufacture of pottery, china and earthenware		

Notes

1. Chenery (1960, pp. 643 and 644) emphasises that 'changes in supply conditions are more important in explaining the growth of industry than changes in demand'.
2. Another observation may be made pertaining to the steady increase of the contribution of manufacturing industry to GDP in the Asian developing countries as compared to a declining contribution in several Latin American countries in the 1980s. This may be explained by a decline of relative prices of products from formerly protected manufacturing industries. However, data have not been corrected for relative price changes. This creates an upward bias in the ratios presented in Table 10.1. Consequently, after corrections for price changes, ratios will be even lower.
3. Reduction of disincentives to export does not necessarily imply absence of state intervention. For example, taxes on inputs in the export sector may be neutralised by subsidies on exports.
4. An RCA > 1 may reflect competitiveness, but may also be the outcome of government policy.

11 Chile: from Early Liberalisation to 'Second-phase Export-led Growth'
Anne Theo Seinen

11.1 INTRODUCTION

The Chilean economy displays the weaknesses that the small Latin American countries have in common: low levels of physical and human capital per caput, a small domestic market, and dependence on a single major export product: copper. However, what sets the Chilean case apart from other Latin American countries, are the early and radical liberalisations that have been put into effect since 1973. The import-substitution industrialisation strategy was abandoned radically, and an export-led growth policy was implemented. The government did not assume an active role to stimulate this open industrial development pattern as was the case in the Asian NICs.

The new approach produced a 'Latin American success story' and exports showed unprecedented growth. However, export growth was largely based on a small number of primary products and contributed only little to the strengthening of the economic structure. These limitations have stimulated the debate on the rôle of government in an open industrial development strategy: how actively should the government be engaged in export promotion, and what policies and instruments should be used? The new democratic government in power since 1990 has been trying to change course by taking a somewhat more active stance. Its strategy carries the banner of 'second-phase export-led growth'. This chapter analyses the possibilities for successful implementation of the new concept.

11.2 LIBERALISATION POLICIES

After the 1973 *coup d'état*, the new military government introduced a drastic shift in the economic and political regime. The import substitution strategy, culminating in the socialist experiment of the Allende-government, had failed. An alternative approach was presented by a group of neo-liberal technocrats, the 'Chicago boys', that took over the most important government posts related to the economic sector (Edwards and Edwards, 1987, p. 94). They promoted extremely liberal and monetarist policies and were averse to discriminatory policies. The role of government was to be reduced as much as possible.

The Pinochet Government embarked upon a radical liberalisation programme in real and financial markets. Prices of almost 3000 commodities were decontrolled. Within a few months the thirteen exchange rates were unified into one, tariffs were cut from 105 per cent on an average to a uniform level of 10 per cent in 1979. The fiscal deficit was reduced from over 24 per cent of GDP in 1973 to 2.6 per cent in 1975, and was reversed into a 3.0 per cent surplus in 1981 (Edwards and Edwards, 1987, p. 32).

Privatisation was also radical. By 1980, CORFO had sold nearly 500 firms. This stimulated enormously the creation and expansion of large conglomerates. These *grupos* controlled banks and firms in many different sectors of the economy and had already played an important role in the Chilean economy for a long time. The new *grupos* were modern and technocratic and operated with high debt to equity ratios. Their orientation was on the long run and they anticipated and supported the liberalisation process. They operated successfully in the export sector.

Initially trade unions were dismantled or repressed. The 1979 Labour Law sharply reduced union power. Unions were restricted to individual firms, membership became voluntary, and firms could impose lock-outs and temporarily lay off workers (Edwards and Edwards, 1987, p. 104).

The new policies had a strong dynamic effect on the manufacturing sector: new technologies were introduced, the product composition changed and the quality of products improved remarkably. The number of industrial firms, in particular of small and medium-sized firms, increased. However, owing to tariff reductions, the share of industry in GDP fell from 25 per cent in 1973 to 21 per cent in 1979 (De la Cuadra and Hachette, 1988, pp. 97–150).

Export promotion was the central theme of the new policy, but unlike the south-east Asian NICs, the state did not assume a developmental rôle. The anti-export bias was to be eliminated by trade liberalisation, by elimination of the incidence of indirect taxes on export prices and by the maintenance of a stable real exchange rate. Exports would develop according to comparative advantage, and the government was averse to targeted export incentives, such as fiscal and financial subsidies.

The late 1970s showed high growth rates, but the economic boom was short-lived. Owing to the lack of government control, the financial liberalisation resulted in high interest rates. The 1979 wage indexation made wages extremely sticky. Moreover, in 1978 the government fixed the exchange rate according to a pre-set schedule, the *tablita*, in order to abate inflation. According to the neo-liberal theories, the 'law of one price' would ensure price stabilisation, but actually a serious overvaluation of the peso resulted. The system of large *grupos* with many interrelations initially enabled the banks to roll over bad loans, but the economy worsened. The crisis became acute with the sudden increase in international interest rates and the sharp world recession. A very deep recession followed in 1982: GDP fell by 14 per cent, and unemployment jumped to over 20 per cent.

Despite the crisis, the regime succeeded in sticking to its liberal and indiscriminate approach. Industrial organisations waged a campaign to protect their markets from foreign competition. However, for the new export sector a reversal of the trade liberalisation would bring unfavourable relative prices. The consequent disunion among the entrepreneurial community enabled the government to resist protectionist pressures. Trade tariffs were increased only mildly and indiscriminately to 35 per cent in 1984. The increase did not last long. Since 1985, tariffs have been gradually reduced to 11 per cent (1995).

From 1984 onwards, a stable and coherent macro-economic policy was implemented, based on a stable, competitive real exchange rate. The export promotion instruments were further improved and expanded, though the indiscriminate approach was largely maintained. It took some time before confidence in government policies was restored, but from 1984 onwards investments increased. The second half of the 1980s showed a growing economy as well as growing exports.

The shift in 1990 to a democratic government came with high expectations from the poorer part of the population and with anxiety among capital owners and industrialists. The centre-left government headed by President Aylwin had to manoeuvre carefully. It emphasised repeatedly that it would continue the export-orientated, liberal economic policies of its predecessor, but it also promised to make adjustments in order to come to a more equal sharing of benefits. As the limitations of the 'export success' became clear, policies for further development were sought.

Since 1991, policies carry the banner of a 'second-phase export-led growth' strategy. The goal is real diversification of exports into non-traditional goods with higher national value added and based on higher levels of human and other capital. 'Export substitution' has been promoted, implying substitution of traditional exports by products that make more intensive use of skilled labour and technology. As the urgent need for foreign exchange has declined, exports and investment in the export sector should bear a medium and long-term perspective.

The new stance demands active governmental involvement. The government should develop the industrial export supply. This requires a high degree of selectivity with respect to the choice of industries to be developed. However, until now the degree of selectivity does not seem to have increased very much, and the 'change' seems to be rhetorical rather than substantial. The shift in emphasis has been introduced gradually and rather slowly.

Moreover, a major problem arose: the favourable growth of exports and the weak international position of the $US caused strong upward pressure on the peso. In 1991 the peso was revalued by an estimated 9.4 per cent in real terms and by another 5 per cent in the first months of 1992.

11.3 THE POINT OF VIEW OF INDUSTRIAL EXPORTERS

Successful implementation of 'second-phase export-led growth' policies requires insight into the bottlenecks in the export process and the exporters' perceptions of them. An active export-led growth policy should be a dynamic process of interaction, in which the public and private sectors exchange information on export-related problems and opportunities. This section attempts to identify current, export-related problems by drawing upon some recent questionnaire studies.[1]

Two categories of problems have been investigated:

(i) internal problems of the firm; and
(ii) external problems of the firm at the national level.

Internal problems

The major internal problems are related to finance, international marketing, quality standards, required level of technology, and credit insurance.

Latin American capital markets have failed to supply sufficient credits to exporters and many export firms lack resources for the medium and long term. There is a lack of pre-embarkment and post-embarkment credit lines for working capital, and of risk capital for small and medium-sized exporters and trading companies, and for financing market entrance activities. Also, financial intermediation has been costly, with real spreads up to 15 per cent, as compared with spreads of 3–5 per cent in OECD markets.

Moreover, the range of financial instruments available to Latin American companies is much more narrow than in developed markets. The financial problems are particularly hitting exporters of industrial products, since industrial exports require relatively high investments in fixed and working capital, and relatively large risks are involved.

Owing to the financial liberalisation, the Chilean capital markets are among the most sophisticated in Latin America, but the general diagnosis applies here as well (Schulz, 1992). There is a growing bond market and stock exchange. Leasing-supply is relatively well developed, and other non-traditional financial instruments, such as venture capital, factoring, business credit cards and credit insurance, have been introduced.

However, financial supply is much more limited and real costs of financial resources are much higher for small and medium-sized industrial exporters. This can largely be attributed to management deficiencies, such as lack of accounting control, unreliable financial statements and unfamiliarity with financial alternatives. Training needs to improve financial management are enormous. Another factor is the relatively weak market position of these small and medium-sized firms (Schulz 1992, p. 7). Most of them have to resort to informal supply. Private and family capital are available in sufficient quantities, and supplier credit is widespread in Chile and generous in concession periods, but the implicit costs are high. Therefore, many of the present exporters conduct a very cautious financial policy, and consequently they do not always agree with the contention that lack of finance is a major problem. Whether governmental credit supply should become a major export promotion instrument will be assessed below.

There is a lack of information on international markets. This is partly due to the distance factor, in particular with respect to markets in Europe and east Asia. This makes it more difficult and more costly to locate potential customers and to find information on product requirements and other market characteristics. Marketing of industrial products in particular requires up-to-date information. Industrial markets require more complex and more comprehensive marketing techniques. Market penetration has become very difficult in many markets and requires a consistent and coherent marketing strategy. Firms acknowledge the lack of experience and of specialists in the field of managing foreign operations. Moreover, high marketing costs add to their financial problem.

In the past, inward-orientated policies exacerbated these problems: 'export pessimism' prevailed. Owing to the strategy of export-led growth, cultural attitudes towards exporting have become more positive. Additionally, some Chilean exports were hampered in the past for political reasons.

The public export-promotion organisation, ProChile, has been established to help overcome this kind of marketing problems and its functioning will be assessed below.

In general, modern industrial production processes are complex and require fairly sophisticated technology. Chilean firms do not complain much about the availability and costs of technology. Most technological innovations are generated by continuous experience at the shop-floor level or are being acquired from abroad. Foreign knowledge is usually obtained by foreign investment, joint ventures and licences, and is embodied in imported capital goods. Delivery contracts for capital goods usually include assistance in the learning process. Many firms maintain contacts with external R&D institutions. Imitation of foreign products by own R&D has been relatively unimportant.

One aspect of technology is the capability to comply with all quality requirements. Quality and design, stability of supply, punctual delivery and a broad assortment have increasingly become the competitive edge of industrial products and the markets are much more segmented than markets for primary products, each market segment and country setting its own requirements and quality standards. Chilean exporters are aware of this, but find it difficult to meet foreign standards. The problems vary among sectors but are hardly commented upon in the studies.[2]

Also, the questionnaire studies do not pay much attention to the lack of credit insurance. Moreover, there appear to be no complaints about price to quality ratios. However, this may reflect to some extent a certain lack of awareness of the role credit insurance may have and unfamiliarity with the instrument, rather than satisfaction with the existing situation. A guarantee fund for non-traditional exports was established in 1987 for the purpose of insuring commercial risks, but it is not yet functioning. Political-risk insurance does not exist either.

For all these reasons, industrial exports consist mainly of products for which design is not a major aspect and for which quality standards and marketing techniques are relatively simple. Thus, comparative advantage of the manufacturing sector of Chile is still limited to traditional products and most exports are in markets in which price is the major competitive factor.

External problems at the national level

The major external problems of the firm at the national level are macro-economic instability, an unstable exchange rate, import regulations, transport problems, bureaucracy and lack of adequate government services. In all studies exporters affirm the primordial importance of macro-economic and exchange-rate stability. The 1975 and the 1982 recessions were extremely serious, and the 1978–82 overvaluation was traumatic to exporters: many new export firms went bankrupt. Current macro-economic stability compares favourably with other Latin American countries, but unfortunately for the exporters, the successful growth together with a negative Dutch disease effect owing to high copper prices is causing upward pressure on the peso, resulting in a real revaluation against the $US in recent years. This is considered the major problem at the moment. However, as is apparent from questionnaire studies not all firms were affected to the same degree and much depends on profit margins and the capability to adjust prices or output to exchange-rate fluctuations. Firms that invested recently or which operate in highly competitive markets suffered most. Moreover, there is a significant diversification of markets and the revaluation of the peso relative to currencies other than the $US was less significant. Finally, many industrial exporters are exporting only a small share of their production, which makes absorption of the consequences of adverse exchange-rate movements less difficult.

Thanks to the liberalisations in the 1970s and 1980s, the anti-export bias hardly exists any more. Chilean firms have no problems with the acquisition of necessary investment goods or intermediary inputs. Moreover, the drawback of remaining customs duties is fairly efficient.

The poor functioning of transport and governmental bureaucracy was extremely tedious under the import-substitution regimes. The Pinochet regime modernised and liberalised the customs office and the air and sea transportation system quite successfully. The current transportation system is relatively efficient and customs formalities are simple and flexible as compared to the situation in many Latin American countries. The questionnaire studies show a relatively small number of firms that complain about costs of transportation, not so much about the quality of transportation services. In general, exporters do not see major problems of infrastructure, and agree that the country has a good international position. Nevertheless, one study shows a lack of preparation and interest by the users to achieve optimisation of the distribution system (ECLAC, 1991a). With respect to multimodal container transport, for example, there is a lack of knowledge among exporters, intermediation is informal and operations are not managed very systematically. Also, air transportation to certain destinations lacks capacity, and the necessity of transhipment increases the risks of robbery.

Firms hardly complain about excessive bureaucracy of transport-related formalities. A lot of paperwork is still required, but none of the studies mentioned this as a major obstacle. Exporters do complain about the inadequate supply of government services. It is mentioned by some firms that telephone services are adequate but expensive, while in some cases connecting lines are lacking. Postal services are considered cheap and quite reliable but slow. Telecommunications infrastructure is comparatively well developed. In general, the Chilean position compares favourably with many other Latin American countries.

Almost all of the problems mentioned tend to be larger for small and medium-sized firms than for larger firms. There are economies of scale in many aspects of the export process such as marketing and technology acquisition. Large firms can spread the fixed costs of their export operations over more sales and meet financial requirements more easily. Excessive officialdom and deficiencies in public services have a similar effect. The government has made some efforts to alleviate such problems of small and medium-sized export firms, but this has proved to be rather difficult.

11.4 INDUSTRIAL EXPORT PROMOTION INSTRUMENTS

Export promotion organisations and institutions, fiscal incentives and export credit schemes are used by many governments to support an export-led growth strategy. During the period of import-substitution industrialisation these instruments played a less important role and were, moreover, often rather erratic. The shift towards a liberal, export-led growth policy changed entirely the institutional context of export promotion instruments.

In the south-east Asian NICs an active government co-operates closely with the industrial sector. This requires a highly effective and efficient government and a very warm relationship between the private and public sectors. Both conditions have not been met in present-day Chile. The governmental bureaucracy rather reflects a long-standing tradition of autonomy, exacerbated by dictatorship. This seriously hampers effective and efficient 'second-phase export-led growth' policies.

A serious problem is the scattering of responsibilities and competencies with respect to foreign trade over many ministries and governmental institutions. Four ministries are involved, as well as the central bank, customs office and CORFO.[3] The lack of inter-institutional co-ordination causes confusion regarding responsibilities, duplication of efforts, officialism and even contradictory policies. Improved co-ordination is required (ECLAC, 1990b, p. 89). Inter-institutional rivalry could soar rather than decline, the more the government becomes involved in the economy.

The export sector is well organised. The National Exporters Association represents most of the large agricultural exporters, and the Industrial Exporters Association (ASEXMA) has a membership of about 200 firms, most of them medium-sized. These organisations have direct contacts with the ministries involved, but that does not imply a very large influence. On the contrary, lack of consultation and co-operation remains a problem.

The public export promotion organisation, ProChile, was established in 1974 and has become the most visible exponent of the new export-led growth policy. It was assigned to stimulate growth and diversification of non-traditional exports. ProChile is to play a prominent role in the 'second-phase export-led growth' strategy, but since the new policy has only been pursued since 1992, its impact is hardly perceptible yet. ProChile attempts to assume a catalytic role by bringing exporters together. Export committees are the basic mechanism for contacts between firms and ProChile. Currently, some 60 committees are operational, and about 600 out of the 4000 Chilean export firms (many of which are industrial firms) are participating in the committees. Most of the firms are medium-sized, with exports between $US 100 000 and $US 2 000 000. Large firms have little interest in ProChile and prefer to do it on their own. ProChile has not actively sought the participation of small firms, as the resulting exports would not be worth the expense and trouble. ProChile now has thirteen regional offices, but regional exporters do not rate ProChile's services very high (Escobar and Mizala, 1990, p. 5).

ProChile is performing most of the functions that export promotion organisations usually do, but suffers from a number of deficiencies. First, too much emphasis has been put on short-term export opportunities, and medium-term and long-term incentives have been neglected. This has favoured the fruit, fishing and mining sectors, as compared with manufactures. Promotion of new products, more complex commodities or integrated export-development projects require systematic action rather than isolated efforts, but ProChile does not seem to have a clear policy for such cases. Second, ProChile's officials lack knowledge of the export-supply side and their markets, especially with respect to the industrial sector. This problem has been aggravated by the high turnover of ProChile's staff, caused by low wages as compared with the private sector. Moreover, there is a general lack of control and of effectiveness and efficiency as regards the export promotion activities (Escobar and Mizala, 1990, p. 23).

ProChile's budget is quite small: the current value is approximately $US 7 m. With respect to sectoral activities, resources are only available for co-financing, and this should guarantee optimal use of the budget. The contribution of the private sector is approximately equivalent to

110 per cent of the resources provided by ProChile: if ProChile's role is to be increased, a larger budget is indispensable.

Unsurprisingly, industrial exporters have been pressing for policies more favourable to them. ProChile should become more selective, which is supposed to favour industrial exports (ASEXMA, 1986, pp. 11–13). However, the many suggestions made by ASEXMA have only partly been put into effect. Instead, ProChile has implemented plans designed by itself. Improved co-operation with ASEXMA is highly desirable to avoid further frictions and duplications.

Has ProChile been useful to industrial exporters? Exporters that have participated suggest that the answer is positive: activities such as information services, assistance in trade fairs and trade missions have been useful, although to varying degrees and not too much importance should be attached to them. Much remains to be improved. ProChile's assistance does not eliminate the marketing problems and the lack of information. It seems to benefit firms most in their first stages of exporting, though its success in motivating potential exporters is quite limited as well. Firms that have not participated are less positive and tend to consider ProChile a diplomatic organisation, lacking dynamism and technical knowledge and not suitable for functioning in export markets (Pietrobelli, 1992). It appears to be fairly difficult to implement adequate instruments tailored to the needs of industrial exporters.

In conclusion, there is a role for ProChile to play in the 'second-phase export-led growth' strategy, provided that four changes are introduced.

(i) Emphasis should be shifted to the industrial sector, and the number of industrial participants should increase relative to other participants. This requires larger and more persistent efforts, a broader range of instruments and more operational flexibility. ProChile should actively assist in creating export supply. It should provide technical assistance and should stimulate expansion of capacity in a selective way, although it might be preferable to establish other institutions for these purposes (Pietrobelli, 1992).
(ii) The level of knowledge of ProChile's officials should increase. Higher wages are necessary, and evaluation should become systematic.
(iii) If evaluations are positive, the budget should be increased.
(iv) Co-operation with industrial exporters and ASEXMA has to be improved.

The Chilean system of fiscal incentives reflected the aversion of the military government to preferential subsidies for exporters. The basic instruments were relatively simple and the main objective was to compensate for the anti-export bias that remained after the liberalisations. Most instruments were designed or redesigned after 1973. A restitution of value added tax was introduced and a fiscal credit system was implemented. The fiscal credit is considered fast and easy to obtain, and it can represent a significant part of the financing of fixed assets. In the late 1970s more specific measures were designed, such as regulations for bonded warehouses, a drawback for stamp duties, and a new drawback system for import tariffs. These measures are particularly important for large exporters. In the 1980s many modifications followed, but these mainly concerned the operational effectiveness and efficiency of the system.

The drawback system was relatively complex and small exporters had limited access to its benefits. These firms were also less easily exempted from other indirect taxes. To compensate, a simplified drawback was introduced in 1986, which permits an exporter to obtain repayment of 10-per cent of the fob value of exported goods. This applies to products of which total exports do not exceed $US 8.8 m. A 5 per cent drawback is granted to exporters of products of which total exports amounted to between $US 8.8 m and $US 13.2 m respectively (1988 figures). Figures are adjusted annually. The system has proved very successful and most industrial exporters use the mechanism. Some of them state that it is a decisive factor for their export-activity: 10 per cent of export value is a very significant margin. In 1991 approximately $US 1007 m dollar worth of non-traditional exports benefited from this instrument.

In studies and interviews firms have frequently indicated that the system of fiscal incentives is adequate, efficient and fast. No serious complaints have been ventilated. Minor remarks concern further simplification of the tariff drawback, the need to increase the accessibility of the VAT-restitution, and the systemic bias against national suppliers of capital goods.

Some argue that fiscal incentives should play a more predominant role in the 'second-phase export-led growth' strategy. Selectively targeted subsidies could promote certain industrial exports. However, this is not desirable for four reasons:

(i) for economic and political reasons it is very difficult to select the industries to be subsidised;
(ii) high fiscal costs may make this instrument inefficient;
(iii) selective subsidies easily provoke protectionist measures abroad; and

(iv) fiscal incentives are not directly related to any of the major problems of exporting – it is preferable to use available funds to tackle these problems directly.

Export financing was only implemented in the 1980s and it has never been an important instrument to promote industrial exports. The contribution of export-financing programmes such as under CORFO and the *Fondo de Garantía* is still rather limited. Expansion of the credit incentives system fits conceptually well in the 'second-phase export-led growth' policy. Some minor modifications have already been implemented, but there are no signs of a significant increase in credit programmes. However, in order to solve the financial constraints on small and medium-sized industrial exporters, special measures will be required. A number of measures are suggested: the governmental system should incorporate indirect exporters such as trading companies, post-embarkment credit lines for exports of capital goods should be established, and financing for international marketing should become more widely available (ECLAC, 1990b, pp. 82–3). The financial system itself should also be further improved, in particular with respect to pre-embarkment credits. To increase effectiveness, many of the plans and policies require more financial resources and modifications in their application (Pietrobelli, 1989, p. 42). However, none of these instruments provides a panacea for the structural problems. Coherent and stable macro-economic management, a well developed transportation system and an efficient government apparatus are more important factors than a 'second-phase export-led growth' policy.

Notes

1. These are Pietrobelli (1992), ECLAC (1991a), Ondarts (1991), Baldinelli (1991), ECLAC (1988a and 1988b), Schulz (1992), and Seinen (1992).
2. Product certification is getting more important. Public institutions have implemented several certificates, but these are still inadequate.
3. CORFO was established in 1939. It used to formulate industrial development plans in line with the stategy of import sustitution and controlled state-owned enterprises. Notwithstanding the privatisation process, it is still an important institution.

12 Industrial Competitiveness and Government Policies in Uruguay

Anton Timpers

12.1 INTRODUCTION

After the oil crisis of 1973 the new military government in Uruguay abandoned the industrialisation strategy of import substitution and changed the incentive system to stimulate industrial exports. Growth rates of GDP and exports accelerated, and this revitalisation was sponsored to a large extent by the government by means of subsidised credits and tax exemptions for exporting firms (Corbo and de Melo, 1985, pp. 165–8).

After 1978, economic policy was directed at price stability, but pegging the peso to the $US without the necessary control over the monetary variables led to highly distorted prices and increasing overvaluation of the currency. Growth continued on the basis of rising imports and a huge inflow of foreign capital. At the same time, domestic industry lost its competitiveness due to the overvalued exchange rate (Corbo and de Melo, 1985, p. 160). The increase in domestic demand was not accompanied by an increase in domestic production and this ultimately led to the crisis of 1982 and the heavy burden of foreign debt. The period of crisis ended in 1985, but after two years of renewed growth, stagnation returned once again after 1987. This structural economic instability hampers economic development as it creates uncertainty and passivity among economic agents, and hinders long-term and medium-term planning and optimal investment decisions by private and public enterprises.

Apart from long-term economic instability, three main problems may be identified regarding economic development in Uruguay. First, rather than using domestic fiscal instruments, integrated industrial credit policies, or an industrial development bank, the major policy instruments used by the government were related to the external sector. Industry was stimulated by import barriers, exchange controls and differentiated exchange rates, and at the end of the 1970s the Uruguayan government tried to reach price stability by pegging the peso to the $US. But these *ad hoc* policies were motivated by urgent disruptions and failed to bring about macroeconomic equilibria most of the time.

Second, decisions by economic agents were for a long period made in the context of a strategy of import substitution. This strategy tended to increase the monopolisation of economic activities, and lacked stimuli to enhance efficiency. Thus, economic decisions in Uruguay were often directed towards rent-seeking and the protection of rents rather than towards efforts to increase efficiency. Such a situation continues to exist, but less markedly than in the past.

Third, a long-term development strategy was lacking, and consequently, no significant change occurred in the industrial structure after 1973. Exports increased after the policy shift of 1974, but this increase was based on the traditional industrial structure, shaped in the era of import substitution. By means of export incentives, firms were stimulated to export part of their production, but only a small fraction of manufacturing industry reached the efficiency levels required to compete in world markets (Messner, 1990, p. 54). It is characteristic of the industrial development process of Uruguay that the levels of investment were insufficient to sustain manufacturing growth in 1986 and 1987. In 1988 growth came to a halt not so much because of falling demand, but because installed capacity had reached the level of full utilisation. There is no such thing as a clearly defined sectoral growth path, and growth was often merely the result of favourable external developments (Balcarcel, 1992, p. 19).

The economic crisis at the start of the 1980s had a dramatic impact on the country's economy. Between 1980 and 1990 GDP increased by 5 per cent in real terms, while manufacturing GDP declined by almost 10 per cent. This resulted in a diminishing of the share of gross manufacturing production in total GDP from nearly 30 per cent in 1980 to 25 per cent in 1990. A major cause of the decline of manufacturing output was the low investment ratio in the sector, both in relation to manufacturing output and in relation to total investment in Uruguay. Figure 12.1 shows investment as a share of GDP and industrial production during the 1980s.

Contrary to the development of manufacturing output, manufactured exports increased during the 1980s and the country became increasingly dependent on exports of manufactures, as shown in Figure 12.2.

The decrease of manufacturing output at a time that overall GDP increased is an indication of the inability of manufacturing industry to adjust successfully to the new economic environment of the 1980s. As such the growth of exports suggests the opposite, but these exports were produced by only a few highly specialised manufacturing sectors and firms

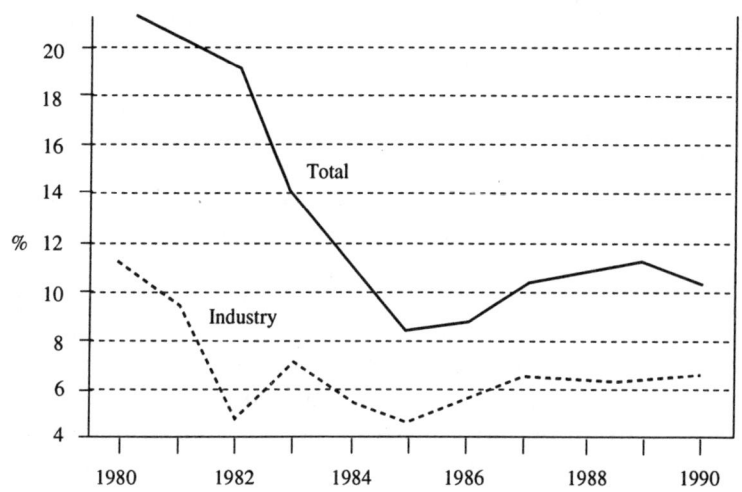

Figure 12.1 Invesment as a proportion of GDP and industrial production, 1980–90(%)
Source: Banco Central del Uruguay

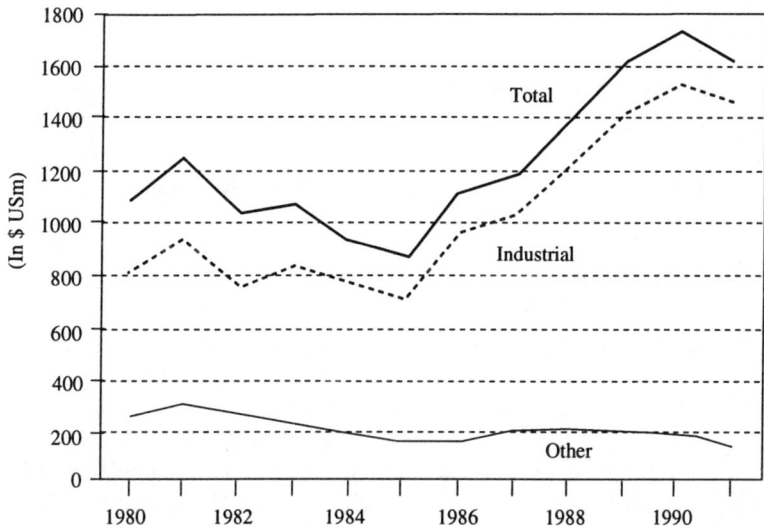

Figure 12.2 Total, industial and other exports, 1980–91 (current $US)
Source: Banco Central del Uruguay

and a large part of manufacturing industry was not capable of penetrating the international market.

12.2 GOVERNMENT POLICY IN THE 1980s

The 1980s showed a clear break with the 1970s. Between 1979 and 1982 the exchange rate was overvalued and huge external deficits were created, but in response the government pursued a more pragmatic policy. The main policy objective became the cultivation and protection of a stable macro-economic environment. It is broadly accepted that a policy of 'getting prices right' is a necessary but by no means sufficient condition for increasing overall manufacturing competitiveness and supporting structural change. The assumption that a successful and rapid insertion in the world economy depends primarily on a change in macro-economic policy ignores the structural deficiencies of the industrial sector that were created during a long era of import substitution. Lack of knowledge of international markets, marketing techniques and quality standards are common problems for industrial firms in Uruguay (Messner, 1992, p. 7).

A summary of the main changes in trade and industrialisation policies in the 1980s, and of the impact they had on manufacturing industry, will be presented below. Policy changes with respect to the exchange rate, the system of protection, regional integration and industrial and export promotion instruments will be presented in order of importance. Note that, unlike countries in south-east Asia, there is no broad consensus in Uruguay on the type of insertion in the world economy, and nor does the government pursue an industrialisation policy which stimulates specifically sectors with a (potential) comparative advantage.

Import tariffs and exchange rates

The policy pursued at the end of the 1970s and the beginning of the 1980s was inspired by the neo-classical tradition. It was expected that by pegging the real exchange rate to the $US, domestic inflation could be cut. However, the law of one price did not hold true. The impact of imports on the domestic price level turned out to be too small to bring inflation down sufficiently. Moreover, inflation was stimulated by $US loans at low interest rates which boosted consumption. This resulted in an overvalued exchange rate which severely impeded the competitive position of manufacturing industry. In November 1982 the government responded with a maxi-devaluation of the currency. In the period after 1982, the exchange rate was determined by market forces. The catastrophic state of the economy after 1982 resulted in an undervaluation of the exchange rate, which stimulated exports. In the second half of the 1980s, a regime of dirty floating was initiated, in which the central bank intervened in the fixed exchange rate with monthly mini-devaluations in a way that kept the real exchange rate fairly stable and generally slightly undervalued as compared to the currencies of the major trading partners. This regime is still pursued, although the exchange rate was no longer undervalued by the end of the decade. The change in exchange-rate policy from overvaluation to a realistic exchange rate was a stimulating development for manufacturing industry and particularly for exports of manufactures.

Table 12.1 shows the changes in import tariffs during the period 1980–93. Different tariffs apply to different stages of the production process. Tariffs at the lower extreme apply to primary products, tariffs at the higher extreme apply to finished products and tariffs in the middle range apply to intermediate products. Some goods are subject to special treatment in the tariff regime. A minimum tariff of 10 per cent applies to capital goods not produced locally or used in the agricultural and livestock sectors.

The programme of tariff reductions was quite impressive, but its impact on the rate of effective protection was controversial, at least until 1986. Macadar (1988) found that tariff reductions until 1986 were ineffective for lowering implicit nominal protection, since previous tariff rates were excessively high. It was also found that the structure of effective protection was not consistent with the objectives of the policy of protection against imports. The objective of the policy was to protect local production of consumer goods more than local production of intermediate or capital goods. However, the structure of effective protection was actually biased in favour of local production of capital and intermediate goods, as shown in Table 12.2.

The highest rates of protection are concentrated in the sectors of capital goods, while the lowest rates are concentrated in the sectors of non-durable consumer goods. The low rate of effective protection for non-durable consumer goods is due to the high value of domestically produced intermediate goods used as intermediate inputs. As intermediate goods are subject to relatively high tariffs, their effective rate of protection is reduced to a level well below the nominal rate of protection.

Moreover, in spite of the reduction of tariff rates, the bias against consumer goods increased between 1981 and 1985. A large part of the exports are non-durable consumer goods, and consequently the bias against consumer goods creates a bias against exports. This bias is not a new

Table 12.1 Import tariffs, 1980–93 (%)

January 1980	January 1982	January 1985	March 1989	April 1992	January 1993[a]
10	10		10	10	10
11					
12					
13					
14					
15	15	15			15
18				17	
22			20		20
26	25	25		24	
30			30		
32	35		35		
35		40	40		
53	45				
55		50			
56	55				
61		60			
64					
65	65				
66					
74					
75	75				
76					
79					
82					
83					
85					
95					
100					
103					

[a] Announced tariff reduction
Source: Lorenzo, et al., 1992.

phenomenon, but its continuation is remarkable in the context of the more recent policy initiatives to open the economy. It reflects the severe shortcomings of the protectionist system and jeopardises the comparative advantages these industries have, or potentially have, in world markets.

Table 12.2 Real effective protection for manufacturing industries, 1981 and 1985 (Corden method, %)

	1981	1985
Consumer goods	46.5	24.1
Durables	316.9	65.5
Non-durables	33.7	21.3
Capital goods	106.6	81.4
Intermediate goods	100.9	83.6
Machinery and transport equipment	286.1	57.4
Average	68.7	45.0

Source: Macadar, 1988, p. 22.

Bilateral trade agreements and regional integration

In the mid 1970s Uruguay signed two bilateral trade agreements: CAUCE with Argentina and PEC with Brazil. Both agreements were revised in the mid 1980s. CAUCE and PEC turned out to be very successful in the stimulation of non-traditional exports (Berretta *et al.*, 1991, pp. 34–42).

Between 1980 and 1990 the percentage share of exports to Argentina under CAUCE increased from 60 to 85 per cent, while the share of exports under PEC increased from 15 to 75 per cent. The value of exports to Brazil increased by 150 per cent, while the value of exports to Argentina decreased by 40 per cent. Total exports to Argentina and Brazil accounted for about 42 per cent of all exports in 1990, and for nearly 90 per cent of exports to Latin America.

The increase in exports to neighbouring countries is not an undistorted reflection of international competitiveness, and it is questionable whether these exports, and particularly non-traditional exports, would have increased without preferential market access. The domestic markets of Argentina and Brazil were highly protected at the time, and most of the products covered by the agreements were not produced domestically. The point is illustrated by the fact that non-traditional exports only increased to the markets of Argentina and Brazil, not elsewhere. Therefore, it is questionable whether these trade agreements can serve as springboards to world markets.

In 1991 Uruguay joined the process of market integration between Argentina and Brazil and signed the Treaty of Asunción. This treaty governs the transition towards the establishment of a common market (Mercosur) between Argentina, Brazil, Paraguay and Uruguay. A major step towards fuller integration has been made by the establishment of a customs union, but the establishment of a common market requires more comprehensive co-ordination of macro-economic policies (Magariños, 1991, p. 101). In the case of the establishment of a common market in the future, bilateral trade agreements will automatically cease to exist. This would affect the favourable position of Uruguay in the markets of Argentina and Brazil and hence the volume of its exports.

Instruments to promote manufacturing competitiveness

In the 1980s, subsidies and incentives to increase manufacturing competitiveness were reduced significantly. Moreover, the government did not pursue a well-defined industrial policy: there were no medium-term or long-term projects to stimulate science and technology and industrial development (Stratta and Halty, 1991, p. 137). This does not imply that there were no projects to promote industrial competitiveness. However, most of these projects did not discriminate between export-orientated and domestic-market orientated sectors and were not specifically related to sectors with comparative advantages.

There are two categories of laws to promote manufacturing industry: laws to promote the competitiveness of manufacturing industry and laws to promote manufactured exports. Two important laws for the promotion of manufacturing industry are the *Ley de Promoción Industrial* (Law of Industrial Promotion) which was replaced by the *Ley de Interés Nacional* (Law of National Interest) in 1986. The objectives of these laws are the increase of efficiency in production on the basis of economies of scale, technology and quality, and the increase and diversification of exports to generate value added in the processing of primary products. Both laws grant permission to industries regarded as being of national interest to import capital goods free of taxes, and assign subsidised credits for productive investments. The second law grants permission to import capital goods to a wide range of exporting sectors and does not require the presentation of an investment project. However, available funds for subsidised credits were diminished drastically.

The most important laws for the promotion of manufactured exports are the *Ley de Admisión Temporaria* (Law of Temporary Admission) and the system of *reintegros,* which was later replaced by a system of restitution of direct taxes. The temporary admission allows companies to import primary products and other inputs free of import tariffs, provided these products are re-exported after domestic processing. This instrument has contributed significantly to the competitiveness of exporting firms.

The system of *reintegros* was established in 1962 and in force until 1982. The system was intended to compensate exporting firms for the negative effects of protectionist measures and granted subsidies to them. The system conflicted with GATT rules and for that reason the USA imposed tariffs on imports of Uruguayan products at the end of the 1970s. Consequently, the system was abandoned in 1982 and replaced by a system of restitution of direct taxes. The system of *reintegros* had a much larger impact on exports than the restitution of direct taxes. The average reimbursement under the system was 14.8 per cent of the fob value of exports in the period 1978–82, but tax restitution constituted only 3.8 per cent of the value of exports in 1985 (Macadar, 1988, p. 12). About 45 per cent of the products exported in 1988 qualified for restitution of direct taxes. The system of restitution of direct taxes was suspended in 1990, but adopted again in 1991, albeit that the percentages of restitution were halved.

The decline in investment ratios is probably strongly related to the reduction of subsidised loans. Tight fiscal policies pursued to bring down inflation required the reduction of funds available for industrial and export promotion. The government is in the difficult position of having to choose between the stimulation of growth and the preservation of a stable macroeconomic environment.

12.3 FIRMS' BEHAVIOUR

In the 1980s, significant efforts were made to create a stable macroeconomic environment and to get prices right. However, this did not result in a more competitive manufacturing industry. This section attempts to identify the reasons why manufacturing firms had difficulties in becoming more competitive and how the policy changes reviewed earlier were appreciated at the level of the firm. Information has been taken from some interviews in the car parts sector at the end of 1992, and studies of industries in the sectors of wearing apparel (Caristo and Terra, 1991), milk products (ECLAC-FAO, 1991), chemicals (ECLAC, 1991b), and leather (ECLAC, 1991c). The use of different concepts and levels of aggregation in these studies make it hard to draw sharp conclusions. Nevertheless, the following observations may be made that help to explain firm behaviour in the 1980s.

According to evidence at the firm level, the overvaluation of the exchange rate between 1979 and 1982 hindered exports in most sectors.

Moreover, most sectors were affected by exchange-rate instability even after the maxi-devaluation at the end of 1982. This may help to explain the lack of long-term strategies and the low investment ratios. Another reason for low levels of investments was economic instability and related changes in profit margins. Changes in demand were usually absorbed by changes in capacity use, not by productive investments.

Firms that produce mainly for the domestic market complained about the speed of import liberalisation and doubted their capability to survive. No study demonstrates the impact on firm behaviour of a bias against exports, except for exchange-rate volatility.

The decline in funds and instruments available for industrial development and export promotion contributed to the decline of investment levels in most sectors in the 1980s. The most important instrument to promote exports was the law of temporary admission, which enhanced significantly the international competitiveness of many firms. This is especially true of the chemical industry: PEC and CAUCE enabled firms in this sector to re-export their products to Argentina and Brazil, often after only marginal processing, whereas competitors in Argentina and Brazil could not benefit from such an instrument. This favourable position, however, will cease to exist when Mercosur imposes similar rules and regulations for firms in all four countries.

Most exports to Argentina and Brazil were favoured by bilateral trade agreements. However, these agreements also create uncertainty, since the volumes of products that qualify for preferential treatment were subject to variations. Establishment of a common market in 1996 is considered unrealistic. Export firms also fear the establishment of a CET of the Mercosur countries, since this would affect the competitiveness now based on the law of temporary admission.

12.4 CONCLUSIONS

The main policy objectives of the 1980s were the creation of a stable macro-economic environment and the reduction of protection. With respect to the liberalisation of trade, significant progress has been made, as shown in Table 12.1. Nevertheless, further policy changes are required. The government must continue and improve its policies to reduce inflation and the bias against exports. Policies must be reliable and predictable to gain the confidence of the private sector. If these conditions are not fulfilled, long-term firm strategies will be deficient and growth of investments and production in Uruguay will remain sluggish.

Moreover, the government should formulate a long-term industrial policy orientated towards technological development and international competitiveness. Such a policy has to be credible, directed at the comparative advantages of the country and supported by effective institutions. Most institutions were established in the era of import substitution and face great difficulties in performing these tasks in an effective and efficient manner. Consequently, they have to be transformed or replaced.

Tightening of monetary policies is required to stabilise the macro-economic environment, but reduces the availability of funds for industrial promotion. The available funds may be used more efficiently if allocated according to a long-term strategy rather than the pressures of individual firms, regardless of comparative advantages and growth prospects. If the private sector has confidence in the feasibility and continuation of such a strategy, investment ratios may rise, the export base may diversify, and renewed and sustained growth may be within reach.

13 The Competitiveness of Manufacturing Firms: the Case of Venezuela
Carla Macario[1]

13.1 INTRODUCTION

This chapter analyses the obstacles to improving their competitiveness faced by Venezuelan industrial firms. Section 13.2 gives a brief overview of export performance. Section 13.3 describes policies that influence the investment and export behaviour of firms, in particular macro-economic policy and trade policy, including export promotion instruments and institutions. Section 13.4 identifies the barriers to export that may be deduced from a survey of Venezuelan manufacturing firms. The section discusses barriers at the level of the firm, as well as in the economic context.

13.2 EXPORT PERFORMANCE

Venezuela has traditionally been an oil-exporting country and was severely hit by the fall in the price of oil. Between 1981 and 1992, the price of crude petroleum exported by this country dropped by 46.4 per cent (ECLAC, 1992e). The decrease in oil export revenues has been a shock to the economy, above all because they are the main source of government income, as well as of foreign exchange. In 1992, 81.2 per cent of export revenues were generated by oil-based products, down from 94.9 per cent in 1980. Although the value of other exports increased throughout this period, this certainly did not compensate for the decline in oil revenues.

In spite of trade-policy reforms undertaken since 1989, the openness of the economy, expressed as the sum of exports and imports over GDP, is not substantially different today from what it was at the beginning of the 1980s. In 1991 the degree of openness was 47 per cent, with exports accounting for 28.2 per cent of GDP and imports equal to 18.8 per cent. Ten years earlier, the degree of openness was 48.5 per cent of GDP, with exports accounting for 30.3 per cent of GDP and imports equal to 18.2 per cent of GDP.

The degree of openness dropped to 30 per cent in 1986, due to the decline in oil revenues (FINEXPO, various years). This openness indicator appears to be more responsive to the availability of oil revenues than to trade liberalisation. However, further analysis requires more recent data to evaluate the impact of trade liberalisation after a few years.

Meanwhile, non-traditional exports increased steadily during the 1980s, but dropped due to the elimination of substantial export subsidies in 1991. The depression in world aluminium markets put an added downward pressure on non-oil exports during 1992. Aluminium is the most important non-traditional export. In spite of the decrease in the price of aluminium, non-traditional exports were relatively stable in 1992, which is generally perceived as a positive development.

The contribution of manufactured exports to total exports is one of the lowest in the region: only 6.3 per cent in 1988. Half of manufactured exports were generated by capital-intensive industries and had a low technological content (ECLAC, 1992f).

Export to output ratios for several manufacturing industries, presented in Table 13.1, show that – with a few exceptions – only natural-resource based sectors exported more than 10 per cent of output in 1989. Moreover, the degree of industrial processing was generally limited. Exceptions are non-electrical equipment and scientific instruments, but their contribution to non-traditional exports was negligible.

The increase of export to output ratios for several sectors between 1988 and 1989 may be an early result of trade liberalisation. However, it is quite likely that the main cause of this increase is the recession that hit the economy in 1989, following a severe stabilisation programme.

Some of the ten major non-traditional manufactured export products are quite sophisticated – for example, vehicles and spare parts – but their share in non-traditional exports is low, as shown in Table 13.2.

Thus, Venezuela has specialised in primary exports, mainly oil-based products. Oil revenues resulted in a Dutch disease syndrome that strongly encouraged investment in tradables with extraordinary competitive advantage, such as oil products, and in non-tradables, and discouraged investment in other exports. In addition to this stifling of export diversification, efforts to increase the degree of processing of exports have also been hindered. The industrial sector produces predominantly for the domestic market.

A positive tendency is the growing participation of private firms in exports: in 1987, 58.6 per cent of goods were exported by state-owned

Table 13.1 Export to output ratios for manufacturing sectors, 1980, 1988 and 1989 (%)

	1980	1988	1989
Food products	0.46	0.58	2.52
Beverage	0.03	0.18	0.70
Tobacco	1.07	2.00	6.61
Textiles	0.29	0.47	4.41
Wearing apparel	0.04	0.69	16.41
Leather products	0.04	1.45	8.87
Footwear	0.17	0.42	6.87
Wood products	0.07	0.34	3.70
Furniture	0.05	0.35	4.77
Paper	1.23	3.46	5.16
Printing and publishing	0.66	0.71	4.13
Chemical industries	12.45	14.20	33.01
Other chemicals	1.30	0.84	4.44
Petroleum and coal products	76.23	4.79	7.07
Rubber products	0.15	0.05	1.03
Plastic products	0.09	0.65	5.79
Pottery, china and earthenware	0.30	5.50	19.48
Glass	0.08	1.46	3.89
Other non-metallic minerals	0.27	4.15	11.98
Iron and steel	7.79	15.71	36.09
Non-ferrous metals	72.85	53.02	62.72
Metal products	1.05	3.00	10.87
Non-electrical machinery	5.03	1.23	14.30
Electrical machinery	1.09	1.39	8.66
Transport equipment	1.43	2.47	8.54
Scientific instruments, etc.	4.70	3.79	20.82
Other manufactures	3.58	10.18	40.34

Source: ECLAC, on the basis of official figures.

firms, and in 1991 51.6 per cent of exports were generated by private firms (FINEXPO, 1992). In 1992, 67 per cent of non-traditional exports were generated by the private sector as compared to 35 per cent in 1988 (ICE, 1993a).

Finally, there has been an extraordinary surge in trade with Colombia, since a free-trade agreement was signed in March 1992. Trade between the two countries has increased from $US 525m in 1990 to $US 932m in 1992,[2] and most estimates assume it will continue to increase.

Table 13.2 Ten major non-traditional manufactured exports, 1992[a]
(as % of non-traditional exports)

Aluminium and aluminium manufactures	27.69
Casting, iron and steel	19.04
Organic chemical products	5.36
Vehicles, tractors, spare parts	3.78
Tobacco	3.58
Mineral fuels	2.95
Plastic and plastic manufactures	2.25
Inorganic chemical products	2.18
Other chemical products	2.08
Casting manufactures, iron and steel	2.07

[a] preliminary estimates up to September 1992.
Source: ECLAC, on the basis of official figures.

13.3 POLICIES

Exchange-rate policy

Venezuela has remained on an expansive course after an abrupt recession in 1989. GDP increased by 8 per cent in 1992 and GDP per caput by 5 per cent. However, the economy is still under the shock of the fall in world oil prices. Though there are other causes that contributed to the economic downturn, the impact of the oil shock is illustrated by the fact that GDP per caput is still below the level it reached at the beginning of the 1980s (ECLAC, 1992b and 1992e).

Recent growth has been fuelled by a growing public-sector deficit, close to 8 per cent of GDP and the highest in the region in 1992. This deficit results from a rigidity of public-sector expenditures, a decrease in fiscal revenue at the end of the Gulf War, and from the refusal by Congress to approve tax reform. The deficit enabled domestic demand to surge. This led to high growth rates in several sectors, particularly in commerce (24 per cent), construction (18 per cent) and manufacturing (10 per cent). High growth allowed the rate of urban unemployment to decrease from 9.6 per cent in 1991 to 7.7 per cent at the end of 1992. However, the public-sector deficit has also fuelled inflation, which climbed to 33 per cent in 1992, in spite of restrictive monetary policies pursued by the central bank.

One of the policy tools used by monetary authorities to stabilise the economy is the exchange rate. The exchange rate was fixed from the late 1960s to 1983, when a system of multiple fixed exchange rates was established. In February 1989 the exchange-rate system was unified and left to fluctuate freely. The central bank has a wide margin for intervention, since it absorbs a substantial share of the foreign exchange that enters the country. The monetary authorities allowed the nominal exchange rate to remain unchanged from the beginning of 1992 until October of that year. Meanwhile, inflation between October 1991 and 1992 amounted to 33.4 per cent.

The appreciation of the bolivar was not the only stabilisation tool used by the central bank. Nominal interest rates rose to 60 per cent at the end of March 1993, which was particularly shocking to a country accustomed to low or even negative real interest rates.

The appreciation of the bolivar put downward pressure on exports and on the expectations of exporting firms. Meanwhile, imports continued to grow, stimulated by increases in domestic demand and by trade liberalisation. For the first time since 1988, the balance of payments showed a current-account deficit. Significant foreign investment flows were attracted by the privatisation of state-owned firms, such as the telephone company, in 1991.

Most estimates assume that uncertainty combined with high interest rates has put downward pressure on domestic private investment and that most private investment is generated by foreign firms. PDVSA, the state oil company, has also made large investments.

Import regulations

Until 1989, the trade regime was made up of a large and intricate series of regulatory instruments that sought to protect domestic industry from import competition through a variety of tariff and non-tariff barriers (ECLAC, 1990a). Nominal tariffs were often quite high and dispersed, with a range of 0–972 per cent. In addition to these tariff barriers, an assortment of NTBs was in use – for example, import quotas, lists of goods forbidden to import, import licenses, tariff exemptions for public-sector imports, as well as multiple exchange rates and preferential exchange rates for specific goods. These types of regulations were a powerful incentive for importers to lobby for exemptions. Numerous exemptions resulted in tariff ineffectiveness. Trade associations could veto the granting of import licenses by government institutions. Thus, although the average nominal tariff rate was 52 per cent, the ratio of tariff revenue to total imports never exceeded 7 per cent (based on cif values).

The government made extensive use of price-setting prerogatives and intervened frequently in a wide range of economic decisions. Imports of equipment were heavily subsidised by low or negative interest rates.

Before 1989 an export diversification policy was pursued, not through direct export-promotion incentives but through the support that state-owned firms engaged in natural-resource based production activities provided for private investment in downstream firms. This policy was to some degree successful, as was the case in the petrochemical and aluminium sectors. However, the intricacy of the regulatory system and the anti-export bias that resulted from it, along with the shock from the drop in the oil price which caused a plunge in export revenues and in public sector income, prompted the government to modify substantially the main policies that had been enforced over several decades.

In 1989, the government launched a widespread reform and eliminated most restrictions that had regulated economic life and had previously set the scene for ample rent-seeking activities. Most of the price-setting interventions were eliminated, but a few interventions remained for basic foodstuffs and medicines. However, prices of a variety of goods produced by state-owned firms are still set by government officials. This is the case for most oil-based products, electricity, steel and aluminium.

Trade liberalisation was far-reaching since most import quotas and nearly all import-licence requirements were eliminated. Nominal tariff rates were reduced and so was their degree of dispersion. Further tariff reductions were planned, according to a progressive schedule over several years, with the goal of achieving moderate and uniform protection levels. The scheduled tariff reductions were effectively implemented, in spite of strong opposition from the business sector.

These reforms were supposedly accompanied by industrial restructuring programmes. However, for all practical purposes, their scope was ultimately quite limited.

Exports were also heavily subsidised by a bond. This export-promotion instrument was eliminated in 1991, due to numerous fraud cases as well as to the public sector's financial difficulties.

Nowadays, the highest nominal tariff for most goods is 20 per cent and average tariff is close to 12 per cent. Vehicles under $US 15 000 pay duties of 25 per cent and those above that price pay 40 per cent. Import licences are required for a few items, mostly basic foodstuffs (Business Latin America, 7 September 1992). Only 2 per cent of imports were subject to NTBs in 1991 (ECLAC, 1992b).

Venezuela belongs to LAIA and since 1973 to the Andean Pact, and has been a contracting party of GATT. Anti-dumping legislation which has been valid since June 1992 is based on the anti-dumping code in GATT and seeks to protect domestic firms from damage arising from dumping or imports that have been subsidised in the country where they were manufactured. An Anti-Dumping and Subsidies Committee is in charge of its enforcement (Capriles, 1992). This legislation does not penalise the import of subsidised goods or dumping under all circumstances but requires evidence of damage to domestic firms.

Following a current trend in Latin America, Venezuela has recently signed bilateral free-trade agreements with several countries in the region. A comprehensive agreement signed with Colombia in 1992 has increased trade between the two countries substantially. Free-trade agreements have also been signed with Chile and the Caribbean countries. Meanwhile discussions are under way between Colombia, Mexico and Venezuela to create a free-trade area that would include those three countries, as well as countries in Central America.

There is also a free port in Isla Margarita, where imported goods may be sold without paying tariffs. These zones are administered by the Urban Development Fund.

Export-promotion incentives

This section describes six export promotion instruments as they appear in official publications. An evaluation of the impact of these incentives, as perceived by manufacturing firms, will be made further on in Section 13.4.

(i) The export bond pays 10 per cent of the fob value of exports. In 1991 this incentive was cancelled except for agricultural products. In order to qualify for this incentive, products must have national value added of over 98 per cent and must also be included in an official list published in June 1991. The list shows that most of the products have very low processing levels.

(ii) A drawback system fully reimburses tariffs paid on imported inputs used to produce exports. It has been included in the customs legislation since 1978, but has not been used, as firms found the export bond more profitable. However, since the export bond was eliminated in June 1991 the drawback appeared to be the most convenient incentive for exporting firms. It seems to have been of special interest to firms that do not export regularly.

(iii) The *Régimen de Admisión Temporal para el Perfeccionamiento Activo* (Special Temporary Admissions System), also known as ATPA, allows firms to be exempted from paying tariffs on imported inputs used for manufacturing exports. Tariffs must eventually be paid if the goods are not re-exported. As was the case with the drawback described earlier, this instrument was introduced in 1978, but has only been used since 1989. Firms have to submit a new application each time they intend to import inputs. Moreover, they are required to provide a detailed description of the production process to avoid omission of tariff payments on inputs used to produce goods sold domestically. Pre-tabulated physical input–output coefficients are not used for this purpose and the administration decides on a case-by-case basis.

(iv) Firms may use the replenishment scheme to replenish imported inputs without paying tariffs. These imported inputs must be identical to previously imported items that were used to manufacture exported goods but did not benefit from any other export promotion incentive. To qualify, a new application has to be submitted for each transaction, and it appears to be more convenient for occasional exporters.

(v) Firms may store imported goods in bonded warehouses, and use them in the production of manufactured exports or export them without further processing. The warehouses are supervised by the customs.

(vi) Venezuela has an EPFZ in Paraguaná.

Export-promotion institutions

Venezuela has the following five export-promotion institutions.

(i) The Instituto de Comercio Exterior (ICE)

This is specifically responsible for the design of trade policies to promote non-oil exports (ICE, 1993b). It plays an important role in negotiating free-trade agreements and is the country's representative in GATT.

Since 1991, ICE has organised *Comités de Promoción Comercial* (CPC) in several manufacturing sectors, such as the chemical and garment industries. These committees consist of private entrepreneurs, trade association delegates and civil servants. One of their objectives is to identify the main obstacles faced by exporting firms and to suggest measures to overcome them. Export-market research and participation in trade fairs abroad, are other areas ICE deals with, often in close collaboration with these committees. ICE is also trying to organise shoe firms to manufacture products for export markets that have uniform standards and measures, to offer a relatively homogeneous export supply.

Since 1992 the institution has assisted exporters by providing them with information on export markets, through the *Centro de Atención Directa al Exportador* (*CADEX*). This centre also issues certificates of origin which allow firms to benefit from preferences negotiated in the Andean Pact,

LAIA and other trade agreements. It has participated in the design of a project to establish a foreign trade bank to consolidate the different institutions which currently offer services to exporters. It is planned to provide commercial banks with export credit, to administer export insurance, to provide information on export markets and to assist firms in selling abroad. This project was approved by the government in 1992, but has not yet been approved by Congress.

(ii)   The Fondo de Financiamiento de las Exportaciones (FINEXPO)

FINEXPO is part of the central bank. It was established in 1973 to provide credit for non-traditional exports at rates competitive with rates on world markets. It supplies pre-shipment export credit for working capital and post-shipment credit for foreign firms buying Venezuelan exports. If the credit application is submitted directly to FINEXPO, the institution charges an interest rate that is 10 per cent below the rate charged by commercial banks. It requires a collateral equivalent to 110 per cent of the loan which must be backed by a bank or an insurance company. Real estate or equipment cannot be used as collateral.

(iii)   La Mundial

Credit insurance for non-traditional exports is provided by only one company, *La Mundial*, established by a pool of private insurance companies. It protects firms against the risk that client firms abroad may go bankrupt. However, it does not protect them against any risk that may arise from political problems in the importing countries.

(iv)   Promexport: Oficina de Promoción de Exportaciones

This is a non-profit institution established by private firms in 1987. Its objective is to promote non-traditional exports. It currently has about ninety members, most of which are large private firms. This institution seeks to promote contacts between domestic and foreign entrepreneurs. However, it has focused on providing firms with information on export markets and the main trends in international trade. With this purpose, it is setting up an information system designed by Wharton Econometrics Forecasting Associates.

(v)   The Asociación Venezolana de Exportadores (AVEX)

This brings exporters together and is their representative in negotiations with government. It organises seminars on export-related topics. It also provides exporters with information on trade fairs abroad. However, it has no budget to finance trade missions overseas.

13.4 FIRMS' BEHAVIOUR AND CONSTRAINTS ON COMPETITIVENESS

A survey of 22 medium-sized and large domestic firms was carried out in Venezuela in March 1993.[3] The survey included 11 firms in the labour-intensive garment sector and 11 firms in the capital-intensive petrochemical sector. Some of the firms were holdings rather than individual enterprises.

The objective of the survey was to investigate the main barriers to enhanced competitiveness, and it focused particularly on factors related to technology, human resources and exports.[4] The main conclusions of this survey with respect to export capabilities are analysed below. The survey investigated obstacles within the firms and factors related to export policies and infrastructure.

Firms' behaviour

Most of the garment firms in the survey do not market abroad but sell small amounts to customers who come from abroad and take merchandise back to their country. Some of the largest garment firms market small percentages of their output abroad, rarely more than 5 per cent. They use personal contact rather than trading companies. Also, imported inputs are obtained through personal contacts. The use of imported inputs was not as significant as might have been expected following liberalisation of trade. Some firms had difficulties in importing inputs of appropriate quality, due to lack of information.

Most garments are exported to countries in the Caribbean or to the Andean Pact countries. Exports to the USA stagnated due to quality problems, changes in the exchange rate and economic recession in the USA. Some of the largest firms are planning to increase their exports to Andean Pact countries before attempting to sell to other countries in Latin America and the USA.

The petrochemical firms in the survey were obviously much larger than the garment firms, when measured according to output values. They often had joint ownership with a TNC that provided them with access to technology. Several firms operated at a scale appropriate to selling on the domestic market but not on world markets. Firms in this sector which do export generally ship abroad between 20 and 50 per cent of their output. However, several firms exported only marginal amounts and many firms imported a substantial part of their inputs. The Caribbean and South American countries are the main markets.

Firms in both sectors often stated that one of their main competitive advantages is Venezuela's geographical location for exporting to the Caribbean, USA, Central and South America. Few firms mentioned the advantage of having access to cheaper inputs. Some of the competitive disadvantages frequently mentioned were related to human-resource development, such as poor education and training institutions that do not prepare students for an industrial working environment. Moreover, labour costs were reported to be high, due to rigid labour legislation and confrontational relationships with trade unions.

The shortage of technicians in the labour market has been assuaged by a regular flow of immigrants, particularly from Europe, and by training offered by bigger companies. However, training efforts in Venezuela are relatively limited and ineffective. Training tends to concentrate on middle and higher-level employees and covers more administrative matters than productive aspects. It has been estimated that the private sector spends 0.2 per cent of its payroll on training; larger companies spend more, but not more than 0.5 per cent of their payroll (Guerguil, 1993).

Some firms stated that the availability of human resources rather than costs was a constraint when buying new technology. This has resulted in overcapitalisation of firms, along with limited investment in human capital and R&D. Due to the overvaluation of the exchange rate, it was relatively easy to import machinery. A few business managers mentioned that the main difficulty was finding qualified technicians able to repair equipment.

In discussing investment decisions, the topic of uncertainty came up repeatedly. The prevailing political and institutional uncertainty complicates decisions on investments in new export-orientated projects and even decisions on the re-orientation of activities that do not entail new investment.

In addition, there is also substantial ambivalence surrounding trade liberalisation. There does not seem to be a consensus about the irreversibility of this process, and there are important political sectors that claim the country should reverse, at least to some extent, the reforms carried out in 1989. Rather, they expect specific exceptions, in the vein of the lobbying tradition.

This uncertainty, along with high interest rates, is an additional constraint on decisions to transfer resources to the production of tradables. Most of the firms stated they had no major investment plans for the near future and that they would only carry out projects yielding profits in the short term. They are generally adopting a wait-and-see attitude before taking decisions about investments.

Moreover, there is a strong distrust between government officials and the private sector. Public officials often believe that import-substitution policies made most entrepreneurs accustomed to rent-seeking. At the same time, business people feel government opened the economy recklessly. They also complain about the lack of industrial restructuring projects to help firms in transition.

As follows from the survey, barriers to export may be classified according to the three groups discussed below:

(i) obstacles within firms;
(ii) obstacles related to export-promotion policies; and
(iii) institutions and obstacles related to export infrastructure.

Obstacles within firms

Most entrepreneurs have been accustomed to producing for the domestic market with only little competition. They are not used to exporting and their firms are not organised to do so. There are serious quality problems, and several firms mentioned having lost export contracts due to difficulties in meeting deadlines.

In the past, many firms could sell their products easily on the domestic market and rarely had to worry about adapting their products to the taste of consumers. They exported only occasionally surplus output. Substantial incentives boosted exports for a few years until subsidies were eliminated in 1991. This firm behaviour was rational at the time the domestic market was heavily protected. However, since the trade liberalisation in 1989 firms have been facing international competition on the domestic market.

Due to suboptimal plant size, the production costs of some large companies are higher than those of comparable firms abroad. A similar problem occurs in firms that are vertically integrated, a strategy that made sense during a policy of extreme import-substitution.

Improvement of export performance seems to be a secondary consideration for most firms. Their first priority is to strengthen their competitive edge in the domestic market and to survive trade liberalisation. This strategy is based, to some extent, on the steady increase in domestic demand in 1991 and 1992, which allowed many firms to survive in spite of strong import competition and decreasing market shares. Sizeable profit rates and a large domestic market, in combination with the abundance of foreign exchange resulting from oil exports, created a powerful anti-export bias. Moreover, the strategy is also based on the belief that their products are inadequate to compete in world markets. The main difficulties appear to be related to quality, adaptation to consumer tastes in export markets and meeting deadlines.

There is a considerable lack of knowledge about potential export markets, procedures and ways to establish contacts with international traders. Firms are also not used to hiring consultants to assist in the production process and the design of products adapted to world-market standards.

Foreign markets are much riskier than the domestic market and the costs of initiating exports are high. So far, firms have not joined together in export associations to produce and export goods of standardised quality, in spite of some efforts by ICE in this direction.

Export-promotion incentives and institutions as viewed by firms

The performance of export-promotion incentives and institutions is assessed below, using the survey and interviews with key informants such as civil servants and representatives of business associations.

The bond to promote agricultural products was unimportant to the firms surveyed. However, this may be the only rebate currently in force. The drawback does not exist for all practical purposes. Export promotion is not a priority for the government and export incentives have a poor reputation due to the substantial abuses by the private sector in the past. The main obstacle to the utilisation of these incentives has been public budget constraints. Many firms are still waiting for the administration to pay the bond from the export subsidies scheme abolished in 1991. Those firms that currently receive payments have seen values dwindle, due to inflation.

An incentive used by some of the firms surveyed is the ATPA. It appears to be the only export-promotion instrument currently employed by firms in the industrial sector. Several entrepreneurs who import inputs under ATPA hold the opinion that the system does not function properly. Moreover, they are discouraged by the red tape required to complete an application. Delays in approval were also a source of complaints, although not so much for firms that submit claims on a regular basis. No data on export values or firm size under ATPA are available, but the survey shows that only larger firms use the system. This may be due to the complicated procedures that require a lot of paperwork and careful accounting procedures. Going through such procedures only makes sense for firms which export large amounts frequently.

The other two export-promotion incentives that are set forth in government publications, the replenishment system and the bonded warehouses, do not seem to be currently in use.

Although the survey did not include EPFZs, it appears that the *Zona Franca de Paraguaná* has been used more as a port of entry for imported goods than as an export platform.

Despite the fact that government did establish an Anti-Dumping and Subsidies Committee, hardly any complaint has been filed. This is due to some extent to lack of knowledge on legislation and to inexperience with the system. Moreover, to gather evidence in a foreign country in order to prove dumping is costly. Also, the distrustful relationship between the private sector and the government contributes to firms' lack of initiative in this matter.

With reference to ICE, some entrepreneurs stated that the limited resources of the trade promotion institution restricts its capacity to help exporters effectively. Exporters claim the annual budget of $US 300 000 to promote products in trade fairs abroad and to finance firms' participation is insufficient. Moreover, many executives complain about the high priority ICE attaches to negotiating free-trade agreements, without consulting the private sector. There is concern about the consequences of a free-trade agreement with Mexico, if not properly negotiated.

FINEXPO extended credits for around $US 66m in 1992, of which 28.6 per cent was spent on direct loans for pre-shipment working capital and on post-shipment credit to import firms overseas. The remaining funds were spent on indirect export financing through foreign banks, and only a very small amount was loaned through domestic financial institutions. FINEXPO has been unable to provide export firms with substantial financial support and its coverage has decreased in recent years. It financed 3.9 per cent of non-traditional exports in 1989 and only 2.9 per cent in 1991. Pre-shipment working capital credit was used by only ten firms in 1991. A few entrepreneurs who had received export credit from FINEXPO complained about the delays between approval and disbursement of loans and claimed the real value of loans is reduced by inflation. Moreover, the interest rate charged by FINEXPO is only slightly lower than the rate charged by commercial banks and substantially higher than international rates. FINEXPO's current situation is uncertain. Since the government has approved the establishment of the Foreign Trade Bank, with which FINEXPO would merge, its financial resources and its capacity to extend larger loans have been reduced. However, Congress yet has to approve the establishment of the foreign trade bank. There have been numerous cases in which Venezuelan firms have won tenders in other

Latin American countries but had to withdraw for lack of financial support.

Export insurance was provided by *La Mundial* to a few of the firms in the survey. These firms were satisfied with the service. In 1991 only 45 firms obtained export credit insurance, down from 79 in 1987. Most of these firms were relatively large and had no problems with providing collateral, many of them being petrochemical industries. According to executives of *La Mundial,* one of the main obstacles to providing services to more firms is the cost involved in checking the credit rating of importing firms.

Promexport is widely known, but the general feeling is that it still has to fulfil its objectives to provide firms with information. Executives claim there is a considerable lack of information on export markets, and that Promexport and ICE are unable to provide substantive support in this matter. Interviews also showed a significant lack of information on government export procedures. Many firm executives believe that exporting still requires special permits. This confusion is not limited to the private sector: public officials themselves are often misinformed and provide incorrect information. Discussions with public officials in export-promotion institutions showed the lack of a clear policy as well as a shortage of funds.

The interviews demonstrated that Venezuela offers inadequate support for non-traditional exports. The few instruments that are of some use are geared towards larger firms.

Customs is undoubtedly one of the main obstacles, being plagued with unpredictable delays that result in shipments being missed, particularly for firms are using ATPA, the only export incentive currently in effect for manufacturing firms.

There is a significant amount of red tape involved in any customs formality. Lack of information among customs officials is widespread, and many of them continue demanding that exporters fulfil requirements that are no longer valid, such as proof of being registered as an exporter. Since there are no clearly established procedures, the level of discretionality is high and allows rampant corruption. The risk of goods being stolen while in customs is quite high. Medium-sized and small firms are particularly vulnerable, as they frequently use boxes rather than containers. Some progress has been made towards automating customs services, but there has been an additional delay owing to the change towards a system compatible with those used by customs in Colombia and the USA.

Communications difficulties are also critical. The national telephone company was privatised in recent years, but its deficient performance has been a significant bottleneck for firms. Company executives often report having lost export clients to foreign competitors.

Transportation networks connecting Venezuela with some of its main markets abroad, such as the Caribbean, are inadequate. Shipping and airline schedules to those destinations are not sufficiently frequent. Connections with Colombia are the exception, since the signing of an open-skies agreement between the two countries. But entrepreneurs complain about crowded roads and long waiting lines at the border.

Public utilities continue to be very inefficient, in spite of price increases in the past years. Firm executives claim they would not mind paying the rates if the services provided were commensurate.

Notes

1. Comments by R. Baumann, R. Ffrench-Davis, M. Guerguil, J. Katz and J. Ramos are hereby acknowledged.
2. *The Economist*, 15 May, 1993, p. 78.
3. The survey was carried out as part of the ECLAC/UNDP Project RLA/88/039 'Policies to promote technological innovation and international competitiveness in Latin American and Caribbean firms'.
4. The survey was carried out by ECLAC staff members Peres, Guerguil and the author. Mr Peres was responsible for technology-related issues, Ms Guerguil for issues related to human resources and the author for export-related issues.

14 Export Promotion in Costa Rica

Geske Dijkstra and Juut van der Wijk

14.1 INTRODUCTION

Costa Rica is a relatively rich Central American country. It is also one of the smallest countries in the region, both in land area and in market size. Foreign trade and aid are therefore of prime importance to the economy.

The country had experienced high growth rates of GDP after the Second World War, at an average 6 per cent per year between 1965 and 1980. This growth was based on exports of traditional goods such as coffee, sugar, meat and bananas. Manufacturing industry was built up in this period and expanded rapidly. It benefited from an expanding domestic market, from state subsidies, and from a high effective rate of protection as a member country of CACM.

In 1980, the economy entered a crisis. Prices for its main agricultural export products had been low in 1979 and interest rates on the substantial foreign debt suddenly increased in 1980. Exports to the region stagnated because of similar economic problems and military conflicts in the other countries.[1] A large balance-of-payments deficit appeared.

Costa Rica managed to recover relatively fast from this economic crisis. Growth rates rose again in 1983. This was accompanied by a policy shift to an outward-orientated policy (Buttari, 1992 and Bulmer-Thomas, 1988). More than before, exports were orientated towards countries outside CACM. These were mainly non-traditional exports, both agricultural and manufactured.

In this chapter, we shall explore the development of manufactured exports in the past ten years and the role macro-economic policies and export promoting policies played in stimulating these exports. We shall also attempt to assess the remaining bottlenecks for the development of manufactured exports, with emphasis on perspectives in the context of new free-trade agreements with third countries and renewed attempts at regional integration.

Manufacturing industry and manufactured exports

During the 1960s and 1970s, manufacturing industry expanded rapidly: the average annual growth rate was 9 per cent in the 1960s, and 8 per cent in the 1970s (IDB, 1992, p. 157). The sector mainly produced non-durable consumer goods for the domestic market and exports to CACM countries. Since most raw materials, intermediate goods and machinery were imported from third countries, manufacturing industry depended to a significant extent on agricultural export performance. In years with relatively little export revenue from traditional agricultural goods, the growth of manufacturing industry was below average.

The CACM provided high levels of effective protection for many manufacturing sectors, by low tariffs on inputs and machinery imported from outside the region and high tariffs on final products. Regional coordination of industrial investment policies was hardly achieved, although some 'regional industries' were established. Manufacturing industry was also promoted by a favourable credit policy, and by corporate tax deductions that formed part of the Central American Agreement on Fiscal Incentives.

The government also stimulated direct investment in manufacturing industry. To foster projects that require a large amount of capital, CODESA was founded in 1973 as the public holding company in the manufacturing sector. It made important investments in sectors such as oil refineries, cement and fertiliser manufacturing, aluminium extrusion, and sugar refining (IDB 1992, p. 168). TNCs also played an important role: they contributed 47 per cent of total investment in manufacturing industry between 1960 and 1983 (ILO, 1987).

During the 1980s, the average annual growth rate of manufacturing industry declined to 2 per cent. In 1989, the manufacturing sector contributed about 19 per cent to GDP. It provided 185 000 jobs, including 75 000 jobs generated by micro-sized firms.

Although some changes in government policies toward manufacturing industry have been introduced in the 1980s, the following five characteristics are still valid and reflect the impact of policies in force in the 1960s and 1970s (IDB, 1992, p. 159):

(i) A relatively low ratio of value added:gross production;
(ii) low capital intensity;
(iii) small size of firms;
(iv) high market concentration; and
(v) high debt to equity ratios.

In 1980, Costa Rican manufacturing industry exported 11.4 per cent of gross output to the CACM and only 2.7 per cent to countries outside the CACM (IDB, 1992, p. 170). Manufactured exports to the CACM decreased dramatically during the 1980s, whereas exports to the rest of the world increased. Total manufactured exports increased at a rate of about 10 per cent per year in the 1980s, reaching $US 574 m in 1989, which is 43 per cent of total exports in that year. Of total gross manufacturing production in 1989, 19 per cent was exported: 5 per cent to the CACM partners, and 14 per cent to the rest of the world. This clearly indicates a marked change for manufactured exports as compared to 1980.

The Caribbean Basin Initiative (CBI) was a prime factor explaining the growth of non-traditional exports to countries outside CACM (see Chapter 6 in this volume). The US market is the most important market for Costa Rica, in particular for non-traditional exports: it accounted for $US 700 m out of $US 1700 m total exports in 1992.[2] Manufactured products exported to that market include textiles, pharmaceuticals, cosmetics, and electronic components (*Latin America Monitor*, 1993).

TNCs played an important role in these exports. The sectoral distribution of FDI between 1986 and 1991 was as follows: 37 per cent was absorbed by textiles, 16 per cent by electrical machinery and 15 per cent by agro-industry, in particular tropical and citrus fruit processing (Vargas, 1993, pp. 40–41). Manufactured exports from Costa Rica to the US market grew relatively fast: the share of exports from Costa Rica in US imports of manufactured products from Caribbean Basin countries increased from 8 per cent in 1985 to 14 per cent in 1989 (IDB 1992, p. 174). However, quotas for most goods are still in place, and there is a continuous danger of more US protection.

Sectoral export to output ratios also changed. They declined in many relatively capital-intensive sectors, such as textiles, paper and paper products, chemical industry and plastics, which used to export a large share of output to Central America. Nowadays, sectors with a higher than average export to output ratio are either based on low wages – for example, clothing, pharmaceuticals, and the assembly-type industries in metal products; or on domestic natural resources – for example, fruit and vegetable canning, wood products, tanneries, aluminium (IDB, 1992, p. 173). Most of these exports are directed to markets outside CACM.

A list of fast-growing export sectors[3] (IDB, 1992, p. 176) also includes some industries that were affected severely by the crisis in the CACM in the early 1980s: paper and paper products, printing and publishing, rubber products, plastics, and glass. Their competitive advantage seems to be based on labour productivity that has grown faster than wages. For these firms, the Central American market may have been a learning ground.

Most of the assembly-type industries seem to be based on new investment and involve the production of specific items with access to the US market. Some of the industries based on raw materials processing also stem from new investment, such as the canning of fruit and vegetables. In other sectors, a redirection of sales seems to have taken place as, for example, in wood products and in cocoa and confectionary.

14.2 MACRO-ECONOMIC POLICIES

Costa Rica reacted relatively rapidly to the balance-of-payments crisis of the early 1980s. It had the advantage over other countries in the region of not being immersed in political and military conflict and therefore had more room for manoeuvre. In addition, there was more disenchantment with the CACM than in some of the other member countries (Bulmer-Thomas, 1988). Although the change to outward-oriented policies is usually said to have begun in 1983, an important measure had already been taken in 1981. Partly in response to IMF pressure, the colon was devalued. In combination with the abolishment of some export taxes, this was important to stimulate exports to countries outside Central America.

The devaluation induced domestic price increases, since many inputs for manufacturing industries are imported. To avoid a decline in production, the government increased expenditure, which increased inflation. A new government introduced a stabilisation policy in 1982 and brought down the budget deficit by lowering expenditure and increasing taxes. This stabilisation programme was not agreed upon with the IMF and there was less conditionality involved. However, it was supported by USAID and some other donors, and was accompanied by foreign aid and an agreement on debt rescheduling and relief (ILO, 1992b).[4]

Partly due to the generous foreign support, the stabilisation programme was fairly successful. However, the current-account deficit remained. In 1985, the country reached an agreement with the IMF and The World Bank on its first Structural Adjustment Programme (SAP). The aim was to raise productivity by reducing import tariffs. Although exports increased, the trade balance worsened and the fiscal situation remained worrisome. A second SAP stressed privatisation of some state-owned enterprises and further tariff reforms. The third SAP included a loan of $US 100 m granted by The World Bank and an IMF stand-by credit of $US 30 m and was agreed upon in 1993 after further privatisations and restructuring of the public sector. The World Bank loan is conditional upon reforms of the financial sector, in particular giving private banks the same rights and obligations as state banks. As yet, this reform has not passed Congress (*Latin America Monitor*, 1993).

Manufacturing industry was particularly hard hit by the economic crisis of the early 1980s. Real wages dropped by 40 per cent in 1981–82 (ILO, 1992b), so the sector lost part of its domestic market. After the stabilisation in 1983, real wages recovered to some extent, but remained below the 1980 levels during most of the decade. Manufacturing industries also lost regional markets due to political, military and economic crises that affected the partner countries. This forced firms to explore extra-regional markets. In addition, manufacturing industry suffered from high import prices of its inputs due to the 1981 devaluation of the colon. This devaluation was followed by a slight appreciation, but after 1981 a crawling peg was maintained and the colon was kept at the relatively low level of the 1970s (Gindling and Berry, 1991).

The stabilisation measures of 1982 included a drop in government expenditure, particularly capital expenditure, which remained low during the decade. Social expenditure was also reduced, particularly expenditures on primary and secondary education. To bring expenditure down further, agreements on the privatisation of state enterprises formed part of the first SAP. Between 1985 and 1989 many CODESA companies were sold, liquidated or transferred. The privatisation process of remaining state enterprises FERTICA (fertiliser plant), CEMPASA (cement works) and some others continued in the early 1990s (*Latin America Monitor*, 1993, p. 1171).

Government revenues increased in the early 1980s due to higher income tax, sales and consumption taxes. Tax income was reduced, however, by exemptions introduced to stimulate non-traditional exports. No important changes were introduced in the tax system. Though official taxes were relatively high, many exemptions remained and there was ample opportunity for evasion. Tax administration remained poor.

In their efforts to control the money supply, the monetary authorities restricted the credit volume and abolished interest subsidies. They also attempted to reduce the government deficit, with apparent success in 1991 and 1992. However, the public deficit remained high until 1991 and most of it was financed with short-term bonds, which resulted in high real lending rates of around 15 per cent (IDB, 1992, p. 179). Interest rates are also high because of the inefficiency of the state banks, which leads to a spread of over 10 per cent. The allocation of credit is another problem: security is often more important than the profitability of the project.

Although private banks have been allowed to operate since the mid 1980s, they have as yet a small part of the market (IDB, 1992, pp. 65–6).

The capital market is still underdeveloped. It did not develop properly as interest rates for investment in manufacturing industry were negative in real terms, and as the tax system allowed for deduction of paid interest but not of distributed profit. Although the country now has a stock exchange, trading is still limited and concentrated on short-term notes and public sector securities (*Latin America Monitor*, 1993, p. 1157). Domestic investors also lack access to international financing (IDB, 1992, p. 63).

In conclusion, it appears crucial to maintain a low public sector deficit in order to prevent capital shortage. Reforms of the financial sector, leading to more competition between private and state banks, are urgently needed. The high domestic interest rate already leads to undesired capital inflows, for example, by ficticious exports, overbilling of exports, and underbilling of imports (IDB 1992, p. 179). This will induce an appreciation of the currency, which in turn will endanger the export prospects.

The IDB conducted a survey among Costa Rican businessmen, based on questionnaires. Most of the businessmen were from manufacturing industry and agro-industry, some from tourism and assembly industry; almost all were exporting abroad. According to the results of the survey, shortage of credit and high nominal interest rates were major constraints on investment (IDB 1992, pp. 63–5). The fact that banks demand security before profitability when judging the creditworthiness of a project also hampered new investment. Another major constraint for investors proved to be the weak infrastructure: deficient ports and airports were mentioned frequently. The decade-long attempts by governments to economise on capital expenditure now proves to be hampering the development of the private sector.

Businessmen also complain about the opaque tax structure. Exemptions from regular tax rules abound, but it often takes enterprises several years to obtain adequate information and qualify for these exemptions.

14.3 TRADE POLICIES

Trade liberalisation

Trade liberalisation started in 1986, with the introduction of a new and lower CET of the CACM. At the same time, import quotas were abolished and import duties were expressed in *ad-valorem* terms. The Central American Agreement on Fiscal Incentives was also abolished (Saborio, 1990).

The CETs continued to differ between goods. In 1987, Costa Rica started to lower its tariffs gradually, on a unilateral basis. By 1989, the effective rates of protection were still very high.[5] Average effective protection for 50 ISIC groups declined from 133 per cent in 1987 to 50 per cent in 1989. Sectors that were most protected at the beginning of the period were so as well under the new tariff scheme.

New negotiations with CACM partners, all of which are now applying for GATT membership, resulted in an agreement according to which all countries would have a maximum nominal rate of 20 per cent and a minimum rate of 5 per cent by January 1993. Costa Rica introduced these rates in April 1993. Spread of tariffs were also to be reduced, but there is still much dispersion between low tariffs on imported inputs and high tariffs on final products.

In addition, some exceptions were allowed: lower tariffs for essential products, rates above 20 per cent for 'fiscal products' (such as motor vehicles) and a series of products including textiles with rates that will be reduced in stages to 20 per cent in 1995. Effective rates of protection in 1993 are still high for some branches, as shown in Table 14.1.

In spite of tariff reductions, very few industries have really been under pressure to reconvert their production and explore new markets. Two exceptions are the carpet industry and vinyl fabrics, which used to be protected heavily. In most other industries, import competition is still moderate (IDB, 1992, p. 166). On the other hand, the government re-introduced import restrictions in 1991, in view of continuing balance-of-payments problems (*Latin America Monitor*, 1993).

More measures to reduce protection depend also on developments in CACM and on other regional negotiations. Costa Rica was hesitant to sign the agreement made early in 1993 by the four other Central American countries on free trade and further economic and political co-operation. It did, however, sign bilateral free-trade agreements with Venezuela, Colombia and Mexico and seeks an agreement with the USA (*Latin America Monitor*, 1993, p. 1171).

Export promotion

The first law to promote exports was introduced in 1972 at a time when Costa Rica was attempting to become less dependent on agricultural exports. This law established, among other incentives, the temporary admission scheme. Temporary admission enables producers to import inputs such as raw materials and semi-finished goods duty free if they are processed for exports (IDB, 1992, Annex 3A, p. 13). The ministry of

Table 14.1 Effective protection in manufacturing sectors, 1987 and 1993 (Balassa method, %)

		1987	1993
3219	Other textiles	3306	199
3833	Domestic electrical appliances	249	129
3233	Leather products, except footwear	236	113
3901	Jewellery	101	101
3819	Various, except machinery	115	93
3523	Soaps and cosmetics	103	80
3215	Cordage, rope, etc.	144	80
3117	Bakery products	133	76
3115	Oils and fats	106	71
3560	Plastic products	83	70
3231	Tannery products	69	70
3240	Footwear	165	67
3119	Cocoa and confectionery	103	66
3513	Synthetic resins	76	65
3829	Other non-electrical machinery	83	65
3320	Furniture	70	65
3812	Metal furniture	74	63
3211	Yarns and fabrics	149	61
3419	Paper and paperboard articles	68	60
3412	Boxes and containers	60	57
3114	Fish processing	83	54
3214	Carpets and rugs	117	52
3213	Knitted and crocheted goods	90	47
3113	Fruit and vegetable canning	59	46
3511	Basic industrial chemicals	44	44
3529	Chemical products n.e.s.	89	42
3832	Radio and television apparatus	32	41
3841	Ship repair	40	40
3909	Industrial n.e.s.	62	39
3903	Sports goods	39	39
3831	Industrial products	55	38
3610	Ceramic articles	41	37
3522	Pharmaceutical products	44	36
3559	Other products	41	35

Source: IDB, 1992, p. 178.

finance might ask for additional guarantees. During the 1970s this scheme was not very important, and only 32 enterprises qualified between 1973 and 1982 (ILO, 1987). However, manufacturing exports to the CACM did increase from $US 44 m in 1970 to $US 250 m in 1980. Rapid growth of the Central American economies was the most important explanatory factor (IDB, 1992, p. 169).

In 1983, some new export promotion measures were introduced to promote non-traditional exports. The emphasis was now on exports to countries outside Central America. The government began to subscribe to 'export contracts' with exporters. These export contracts include special port charges, bank credits with preferential interest rates, tax reductions, and tax certificates. Firms that sign export contracts are exempted from taxes on net earnings which are attributable to non-traditional exports to markets outside Central America. In addition, they do not have to pay import duties on goods used in the production of these non-traditional exports (IDB, 1992, Annex 3A, pp. 14–15). However, firms have to fulfil many and complicated requirements in order to obtain these benefits.

The tax certificates (*Certificado de Abono Tributario*, or CAT), abolished in 1992, constituted a tax credit of 15 per cent of the fob value of non-traditional exports and of 20 per cent of exports to Europe (Hoffmaister, 1992). This subsidy implies high costs for government: in 1988 and 1989, the costs amounted to the equivalent of 1.2 per cent of GDP on an average. Hoffmaister estimated that each dollar spent on subsidies created $US 1.35 in export value. However, duty-free imports of intermediate inputs also increased significantly and consequently net exports increased only by 54 cents. The benefits of the CATs were not distributed evenly: fewer than twenty firms absorbed 60 per cent of the CATs and a total of 362 small enterprises received only 6 per cent (ECLAC, 1990c, p. 151).

The temporary admission scheme was re-activated, and came to benefit only exporters to countries outside Central America. Firms were granted exemptions from import duties if these imports were used to produce non-traditional exports to countries outside Central America. In 1983 and 1984, 46 enterprises started to operate under this scheme, which brought the total number to 78. Most of these firms were textile industries (56), five were in the electronics sector, and four were metal-working industries. However, in 1984 the value of imports of these firms exceeded the value of their exports: $US 38 m versus $US 29 m (ILO, 1987).

In 1985, the government revived two EPFZs on the Pacific and the Atlantic Coast. Only five enterprises had operated in the zones until then. The main reason for the lack of interest was that firms could obtain almost the same benefits by participating in the temporary admission scheme.[6] The government started to improve the infrastructure of the zones, and in 1990 a new law permitted private industrial parks. By 1992, there were

109 enterprises operating in the EPFZs, providing about 15 000 jobs (IDB, 1992). Firms qualifying under the Duty-Free Zones Regime of 1990 are active in export-processing, export-trading, technical and scientific research, services and shipyards activities. Assembly enterprises and the EPFZs generated $US 125 m of exports, which amounts to 28 per cent of total manufacturing exports to countries outside Central America in 1989.

Evaluating export promotion incentives, the first conclusion is that they imply a high cost for the government. Duty-free admission of raw materials and intermediate goods reduces the tax base, and the CATs imply high direct costs. Although non-traditional exports tripled between 1985 and 1991, expenditure on CATs increased tenfold (*Inforpress Centroamericana*, 17 December 1992). Attracting investments to EPFZs implies additional investment in infrastructure in regions previously not particularly attractive for investment. Moreover, the promotion of exports by means of duty-free imports stimulates such imports, and has a dubious impact on the trade balance. With respect to the effect of CATs, Hoffmaister (1992) estimated that the same export level could have been reached at much lower cost by an additional depreciation. On the other hand, Gindling and Berry (1991) argue that the policy of limited devaluations combined with export subsidies helped to avoid social unrest: more depreciation would have increased inflation and decreased real wages. No doubt this policy was facilitated by generous foreign aid.

The government introduced changes in the export-incentive schemes in 1991 and 1992, in order to limit the costs of export subsidies. The IDB reports that the government will put more emphasis on EPFZs in the 1990s (IDB, 1992, p. 268). CATs were modified in 1990 and abolished in 1992 because of disappointing results, and since GATT rules do not allow Costa Rica to maintain them. The export contracts already signed will remain valid until 1996 or 1999, and consequently their fiscal costs will continue for some time (IDB, 1992, p. 268 and *Inforpress Centroamericana*, 17 December 1992). It is difficult to predict the effects of the abolishment of CATs on investment. According to the IDB survey, CATs were not a major factor in deciding whether to invest or not. However, they were regarded as a means of compensating for other unfavourable tax rules and as a source of extra income. Since they could be abolished easily, they did not increase security for investors (IDB, 1992, p. 77).

Other export promotion policies

Several institutions were founded to assist adjustment of the manufacturing sector to the new conditions. The Center for Promotion of Exports and

Investments (CENPRO) had already been created in 1968. It carries out trade missions, provides information to firms, and assists with customs formalities. In 1983, the Ministry of Exports[7] was established to supervise the whole process of non-traditional export promotion and to simplify the procedures (Bulmer-Thomas, 1988, p. 223). It created a 'single window' at CENPRO, where firms can get all information on export procedures, and export contracts are approved and signed (IDB, 1992, Annex 3A p. 20). In spite of this facility, firms selling non-traditional exports to countries outside Central America still face many different incentive schemes. The process of qualifying for a certain scheme may take several years (IDB, 1992, p. 70).

Another problem for firms is the lack of stability of the tax and incentive regime. The recent changes in CATs and finally its abolishment are a case in point. Sometimes government policies are not consistent: on the one hand, the government announces the reduction of trade barriers and the promotion of exports. On the other hand, due to fiscal problems and balance-of-payments difficulties, it recently re-introduced import surtaxes and prior deposit requirements for imports (IDB, 1992, p. 180).

With respect to industrial reconversion, some funds were created to finance projects in experimental research and development. The Technology Development Fund (FODETEC) uses resources from an IDB loan. It finances research and development in determined areas. Another case is the Incentives Fund that was established by the 'Law to Promote Scientific and Technical Development' and financed by the federal budget available for technology-based companies (IDB, 1992, Annex 3A, pp. 17–20).

However, there still remains a large gap between some well-equipped universities and institutions that carry out basic research, and the needs of enterprises (IDB, 1992, p. 59). In the chemical industry, firms lack the technical capability to appreciate and assimilate technology developed in local research institutes. Notwithstanding attempts to strengthen the links with universities, such links are still insufficient (Arguedas Chaverri, 1989, pp. 14–15). In the capital goods branch, only a minority of firms apply scientific principles in a systematic way, introducing new products on local markets and improve quality on the basis of research and development efforts. However, most firms use their own experience and intuition to develop products and control processes (UNIDO, 1987, pp. 11–12).

In sum, although a range of funds and institutions was created to support technological development, results are not yet satisfactory. Research efforts do not seem to result in improvements in industrial processes or in the introduction of high technology in production.

To develop the skills required for working in exporting firms, the government has supported training programmes for workers and management, respectively, by the *Instituto Nacional de Aprendizaje* (INA) and the *Instituto Centroamericano de Administración de Empresas* (INCAE) (IDB, 1992, p. 168). It seems that INA training programmes do not respond sufficiently to market demand, and that no systematic programme for development of skills is defined, so that INA programmes are relatively ineffective (ILO, 1992b). This is more serious, as the reduction of spending on education has led to reduced secondary school enrolment.

Until now, the government has invested very little in assisting firms to penetrate export markets. Although some institutions have been established in recent years to provide training and information on marketing, firms still face serious difficulties in this respect (IDB, 1992, p. 61). There is also a lack of co-ordination between the Ministries of Industry and of External Relations and Trade. According to the IDB survey, firms have great troubles in getting information of all kinds: on available facilities, market conditions, infrastructure, and technological development (IDB, 1992, pp. 61–3).

The Costa Rican Development Initiatives Coalition (CINDE) is a private institution that provides technical assistance and assists enterprises in exploring foreign markets. It attempts to identify companies in the USA which are willing to reduce labour costs by becoming partners of Costa Rican firms (IDB, 1992, pp. 166–7). According to the IDB, the limited industrial reconversion that did take place in Costa Rica is induced by CINDE and not by active government policies. However, the government-supported training facilities and technology programmes were probably important in persuading the private sector that the government was determined to promote export-orientated development (Bulmer-Thomas, 1988).

Evaluation

During the 1980s, a striking change in market orientation took place. Sales in domestic and Central American markets were substituted by sales in the rest of the world. In addition, during the second half of the 1980s total exports increased remarkably. These changes can hardly be ascribed to an overall shift from import-substitution policies towards export promotion. The shift in market orientation was introduced as early as 1983, whereas trade liberalisation policies started only in 1986. In addition, effective protection was still high in 1987, and has only slowly decreased since then.

In order to assess the role of export-promotion policies as compared to protectionist policies, Bulmer-Thomas (1988) calculated the effect of the different incentives on the profit rate per unit of output, and made a comparison with the incentives provided by tariffs. Under the assumptions that domestic inputs constitute 50 per cent of output and imported inputs 20 per cent, the export-promotion incentives – exemptions from corporate taxes and tariffs on imports and exports – resulted in a subsidy of 30 per cent per unit of output. The CATs were not included in these calculations. However, under the same assumptions, an industry producing for the CACM – 50 per cent corporate tax, 60 per cent tariff on final products and 20 per cent tariff on inputs – enjoyed a subsidy of 43 per cent per unit of output. The conclusion is that in 1986, export to the Central American market was more supported than exports to other countries. Yet, export incentives did give some compensation for the bias toward domestic and regional sales that still existed.

In sum, the shift in markets seems to have been the result mainly of the devaluation in the early 1980s and the recession in domestic and regional markets. Preferential access to the US market under CBI was also of importance. The Costa Rican export-promotion incentives, as well as the other export promoting policies, such as technology programmes and training facilities, probably played a minor role. The same factors were important in stimulating export growth from 1986 onwards.

An attempt has been made to assess the impact of the new tariff structure of 1993 on the market orientation of production. Using the same assumptions as Bulmer-Thomas did with respect to the share of domestic and imported inputs in gross production, but lowering the external tariff on inputs to 5 per cent and the final good tariff to 20 per cent, the subsidy per unit of output for the domestic or regional market decreased from 43 per cent to 25 per cent.[8] Since the incentive for extra-regional markets remains 30 per cent, investment in the latter type of production now enjoys a higher government subsidy per unit of output. However, since the CATs have been abolished, the overall incentive structure has probably not changed very much.

14.3 CONCLUSION

Costa Rica has increased its manufacturing exports considerably during the 1980s, most of these exports being destined for markets outside Central America. Among the factors that induced this performance are the recession in domestic and regional markets, the CBI, the maintenance of a low exchange rate, tax exemptions and other export promotion incentives, and some supporting government measures in the areas of technological development and training. The effect of the last was in part psychological: they showed private investors that the government was determined to stimulate exports.

The change in markets was not a result of overall trade liberalisation. Since 1986 tariffs have been reduced, but by 1993 many manufacturers still enjoyed comfortable protection. On the other hand, export subsidies and exemptions from import taxes and income taxes are a heavy burden for the government budget. These costs have been affordable thanks to generous foreign aid, but this aid is decreasing. Costa Rica will therefore be forced to maintain a more depreciated exchange rate, gradually to reduce tariffs further, and to abolish export subsidies and exemptions from corporate taxes. At the same time, this will provide fewer possibilities to protect wages and to maintain employment in less competitive branches and firms.

Most successful exporters are in the natural-resource based and labour-intensive manufacturing sectors, and their sales are directed to the US market. However, the domestic value added of these exports is low, and the contribution to net exports is also low in the case of the labour-intensive industries. The list of successful exporters also includes some other industries with promising indicators: strong production growth and a strong growth of labour productivity. In some of these branches, firms re-orientated successfully sales from the protected Central American market to markets outside the region. In terms of long-term development objectives, it seems more promising to stimulate such capital and technology-intensive industries with higher domestic value added. Costa Rica has a relatively high level of development as compared to other countries in the region, and as a result, has a potentially favourable position in the regional market. For these reasons, striving for renewed Central American integration as a stepping stone for a good position in the world market offers good perspectives for the development of manufacturing industry in Costa Rica. However, this seems to contradict the prevailing political disenchantment with the CACM.

To continue stimulation of manufacturing exports and to achieve technology-based competitive advantage, government policies must also address the following five issues:

(i) reform of the financial system, in order to increase financing for private investment projects;
(ii) the building up of physical and social infrastructure: in particular ports and airport capacity must be improved and secondary school enrolment must be increased;

(iii) adapting existing technological research and training programmes to fit the needs of firms;
(iv) more efforts in the area of export marketing and marketing research; and
(v) increased availability of information to firms, a more transparent tax structure and fewer bureaucratic procedures for qualifying for export promotion schemes.

Notes

1. In 1980 there was a temporary revival due to the reconstruction policy in Nicaragua, but since then they decreased dramatically.
2. In 1992, the EU accounted for $US 400 m of exports (mainly traditional exports), and Central America for $US 300 m of exports (mainly manufactured exports) (*Latin America Monitor*, 1990).
3. From 1987 through 1989 (IDB, 1992, p. 176).
4. In general, IMF, The World Bank, IDB and USAID imposed less severe conditionalities upon Central-American countries othet than Nicaragua. These countries were supported to strenghthen the 'anti-communist bloc'. See also Saborio, 1992.
5. According to a study by Ulate, cited in IDB (1992).
6. In fact, most enterprises that adhered to the temporary admission scheme were located in the Meseta Central, the centre of the country.
7. Later called Ministry of External Relations and Trade.
8. See Bulmer-Thomas (1988, p. 226).

$$\pi^{i_{ROW}} = \left[P^i e - \left(\sum_J ad^{ji} + \sum_j m^{ji} \right) \right]$$

$$r^{i_{CACM}} = (1-t) \left[P^i e (1+p^i) - \left[\sum_j ad^{ji} + \sum_j m^{ji} (1+p^j) \right] \right]$$

π: profit per unit of output on exports
ad: domestic inputs per unit of output
m: foreign inputs per unit of output.

15 The Systemic Weakness of Guatemala's Competitiveness
Juan Alberto Fuentes K.

15.1 INTRODUCTION

In response to disequilibria, traditional economic theory tends to concentrate on stabilisation and adjustment through exchange-rate policy that favours the production of tradables, fiscal policy that reduces deficits, and trade reforms that eliminate anti-export biases or which favour exports outright. However, it has become increasingly clear that the development of international competitiveness goes beyond this simple recipe, and that it has additional 'systemic' requirements (ECLAC, 1990a). Guatemala's experience, especially from 1987 to 1992, illustrates how the initial contribution of stabilisation and exchange-rate policy to growing exports may be threatened by the weakness of these other requirements. These include physical infrastructure, education, and institutional arrangements. In Section 15.2 a description is presented of basic exchange-rate policies and trade reforms adopted from 1980 to 1992 and attempts to determine their effects on export and investment performance. Section 15.3 deals with export performance, in particular with the development of non-traditional and manufactured exports. Section 15.4 reviews systemic obstacles to the further development of these exports. In Section 15.5 the main conclusions are summarised.

15.2 TRADE POLICY

Exchange rate policy and stabilisation

The economic crisis and negative growth rates of GDP between 1981 and 1986 were triggered by four types of shocks:

(i) deteriorating terms of trade, including rising oil prices and falling prices of traditional export commodities such as coffee, cotton, sugar, bananas and meat;
(ii) capital flight due to political uncertainty;
(iii) declining exports, particularly of industrial products to other Central American countries;
(iv) plummeting tourist receipts (from $US 82 m in 1979 to $US 7 m in 1983) due to increasing political violence and internal war.

However, the foreign external debt that amounted to 61 per cent of GDP in 1980, had not reached the same level as in other Latin American countries and there was no net negative transfer of resources abroad. Consequently, the country was still in the position to finance its current-account deficit by increasing its level of public debt during the first half of the 1980s. Thus, whereas highly indebted countries in Latin America were forced to devalue during the first half of the 1980s, Guatemala did so only during the second half of the decade (ECLAC, 1992c). Furthermore, psychological and political obstacles to devaluation were strengthened by the remarkable stability of the currency, which had been pegged to the $US on a one-to-one basis since 1926 (Bulmer-Thomas, 1989, p. 40). Historically, adjustment to external shocks had taken place basically by changes in the level of domestic activity and in reserves, rather than by changes in relative prices.

This orthodox adjustment mechanism no longer functioned during the 1970s and particularly the 1980s. The basic pillar under the exchange rate ceased to exist with the collapse of traditional agricultural exports. An initial indicator of this process was the double-digit inflation experienced in most years from 1973 to 1981. This phenomenon, not observed since the 1920s, gradually appreciated the exchange rate in real terms and contributed to external imbalances that were aggravated by increased public expenditures to compensate for falling domestic activity.

Initially, stabilisation programmes in the period 1982–4 attempted to balance the economy without modifying the exchange rate. Attempts were made to reduce domestic absorption by lowering government expenditure and particularly investment, the introduction of a value-added tax and the use of strict import quotas. Although the trade balance and current account improved in 1983, GDP, exports and investment fell without prospects for improvement, and the real effective exchange rate continued to appreciate during the first half of the 1980s, as shown in Table 15.1.

Adjustment of the exchange rate proved to be a drawn-out, complex and uncertain process. In 1984 a multiple exchange-rate system was intro-

Table 15.1 Macro-economic indicators, 1980–92 (%)

Year	CA:GDP[a]	Inflation (Dec.–Dec.)	PD:GDP[b]	REER	GDP per caput[c]
1980	−2.1	9.1	n.a.	124.9	1.1
1981	−6.7	8.7	7.2	110.9	−1.8
1982	−4.9	−2.0	4.5	113.5	−6.1
1983	−3.0	15.4	3.3	113.6	−5.4
1984	−5.0	7.2	4.3	113.1	−2.7
1985	−3.3	27.9	5.5	100.0	−3.4
1986	−0.6	21.4	5.7	141.8	−2.6
1987	−7.0	9.3	3.1	185.2	0.7
1988	−6.0	12.3	5.4	186.1	1.0
1989	−5.1	20.2	5.6	187.9	0.8
1990	−2.5	59.8	3.2	220.4	0.0
1991	−1.9	10.0	0.8	192.6	0.3
1992	−8.8	14.3	n.a.	190.6	1.7

[a] current account balance as a proportion of GDP.
[b] global public deficit, including fiscal deficit and central bank losses as a share of GDP.
[c] annual growth rate at constant prices.
Source: ECLAC. Data on the global deficit of the public sector taken from The World Bank, 1987 and SEGEPLAN, 1991 and 1992.

duced: one rate at the official parity with the $US, and another depreciating parallel rate. Different export proceeds were compensated at different rates. Although the parallel exchange rate was allowed to devalue sharply in 1985, various regulations limited the inducement to export. Moreover, the commitment to maintain an official rate applicable to certain imports – including oil – and to debt-service payments resulted in losses for the central bank: foreign-exchange receipts obtained at the official rate were smaller than obligations at that same rate. This gap increased with the growing differential between the official and the parallel rates, and contributed to a higher overall public sector deficit. In combination with the devaluation of the quetzal, this resulted in higher rates of inflation in 1985 and 1986, as indicated in Table 15.1.

Consequently, the newly elected Christian-Democrat government that took office in 1986 faced, in practice, thirty-three different exchange rates (SEGEPLAN, 1991, p. 38) and mounting inflation. In June 1986 the new government proceeded to simplify the exchange-rate system and introduced three rates: for official transactions at 1 quetzal per $US, on the regulated market at

2.50 quetzal per $US, and a rate in the free banking market. However, the elimination of exchange-rate regulations, pent-up demand and renewed growth in 1987 and 1988 resulted in a surge of imports, which the failed tax reform of 1987 was unable to dampen.[1] The surge of imports could not be compensated by coffee exports at declining prices. Consequently, the central bank devalued the currency by 8 per cent in June 1988. Also, the regulated and banking markets were merged and the exchange rate was set at 2.7 quetzal per $US. In theory, the exchange-rate regime was conceived as a crawling-peg but the internal political opposition to devaluations resulted in the rate being fixed until July 1989. In the face of continuing and unsustainable current-account deficits, and a growing public sector deficit of including significant losses of the central bank, the quetzal was devalued by an insignificant 3 per cent. This merely exacerbated devaluation expectations and reduced international reserves until the monetary authorities decided to liberalise the exchange rate.

Consequently, the value of the quetzal in terms of the $US plunged by 26 per cent, to a rate of 3.5 quetzal per $US. Exchange-rate instability was exacerbated in 1990. An attempt to establish a band was abandoned due to insufficient liquidity of the central bank, and an informal agreement with the commercial banks in April 1990 resulted in the establishment of a new rate, at 4.25 quetzal per $US, that was supposedly fixed. At the same time interest rates were liberalised to reduce excess demand, facilitate capital inflows and improve the efficiency of financial intermediation. However, the cartelised commercial banks agreed among themselves to keep interest rates fixed and allowed the exchange rate to sink even further, resulting in a clearly inequitable adjustment process: bank profits increased and real wages fell. Subsequently, the central bank established a system of auctions, which finally resulted in a new rate of 5.8 quetzal per $US, representing a nominal devaluation of more than 100 per cent in less than a year.

The new government that took over in 1991 faced internal and external imbalances: the highest inflation in modern history of the country – 60 per cent (comparing end-periods) – and arrears with The World Bank and other financial institutions. A new stabilisation package was introduced, including restrictive credit policy, reduction of government expenditure in real terms, and increased government receipts due to improvements in tax administration and to the sale of emergency bonds, which is the equivalent of a once-and-for-all tax increase. Massive capital inflow was sterilised through open market operations, but at the cost of significant losses to the central bank of 1.5 per cent of GDP. The accumulation of reserves in combination with other fiscal and monetary measures helped in stabilising the exchange rate. The exchange rate was conceived as an anchor to reduce inflation, its continued devaluation was halted and the rate appreciated somewhat in real terms. This policy was maintained in 1992. Relatively expansionary fiscal and monetary policies in combination with higher overall economic growth contributed to a deterioration of the trade balance. Private and public capital inflows that were stimulated by the elimination of arrears were sufficient to compensate the much wider current-account deficit of 9 per cent of GDP without significant changes in the international reserves of the country. At the same time, it became clear that the external adjustment of the country still had a long way to go. Nevertheless, a tax reform that was approved in 1992 provided more possibilities for keeping the fiscal deficit under control subsequently.

Tariff and NTBs

The evolution of the exchange rate from 1986 to 1992 clearly favoured relative prices of tradables *vis-à-vis* non-tradables. However, the anti-export bias resulted from tariff rates that were not significantly altered during this period. The main objectives of the Central American CET were to facilitate trade among CACM members and to avoid trade deflection. At the same time, it promoted import substitution, favoured greater fiscal revenues, took into account balance-of-payments concerns and was conceived of as a common bargaining instrument. The industry most protected was non-durable consumer goods, the most important industrial sector in the region. Raw materials and intermediate products were protected at a lower rate and capital goods industries were least protected of all. Moreover, the need to collect sufficient revenues and to assist in maintaining balance-of-payment equilibrium resulted in higher tariffs for non-essential and luxury products.[2]

Fiscal incentives that were stimulated by competing efforts to attract foreign investment – so-called 'incentive wars' – such as the exemption of tariff payments for imports of capital goods and other inputs, increased effective protection of final goods, particularly of non-durable consumer goods. Consequently, the structure of incentives favoured investment in the production of final goods, which were often import-intensive or of a 'final-touch' nature, at the costs of regional production of raw materials and intermediate inputs. It may also be argued that an anti-export bias was introduced, although this did not apply to intra-regional exports, which expanded at a rapid though declining rate from the late 1950s until 1980. Moreover, rates of effective protection tended to be significantly lower in Central America than in other developing countries during the 1960s and 1970s (Rapoport, 1978).

Recognition of problems related to the structure of protection and particularly fiscal incentives, resulted in a revision of the Central American CET in 1986. Although overall effective protection was only reduced from 46 to 38 per cent, the rate of dispersion was reduced substantially from 62 to 29 per cent, and the anti-export bias remained largely unchanged (The World Bank, 1987, pp. 37 and 38). Only in 1990 did a gradual reduction of tariff rates start, until a new CET with a maximum rate of 20 per cent was adopted in early 1993. This process of tariff reduction was partly due to the conditions attached to entry into GATT in 1991 and to the structural adjustment loans negotiated with The World Bank. Consequently, the impact of tariff changes on the development of extra-regional exports was not significant from 1986 to 1990. Also, the large devaluation in 1990 more than compensated for the effect of reduced protection on import substitutes.

Guatemala did not rely to a significant extent on quantitative restrictions during most of the import-substitution industrialisation period, although such restrictions were applied in the agricultural sector. However, a system of quota allocation to repress import demand was in use from 1982 to 1984 as a response to deteriorating exports and capital flight that were due to the economic and political crisis in Guatemala and Central America in general. External credit arrears and multiple exchange-rate regulations restricted imports further until 1986.

Export incentives

The absence of a clear trade strategy follows from the brief review of trade legislation, particularly regarding non-traditional exports, applied since 1980. In addition to a rather ineffective EPFZ (ITC, 1989, pp. 52 and 53) established in the port of Santo Tomás de Castilla during the early 1970s, a special regime was introduced in 1983 which involved tariff exemptions for inputs utilised by firms exporting non-traditional products outside Central America (DL 80–82). However, the export-promotion agency GUATEXPRO that was in charge of the evaluation of applications to benefit from this special regime, was dismantled at the same time. In 1984 this scheme was replaced by an allegedly more precise new regime for industrial exports (DL 21–84) destined to countries outside Central America. This regime included income tax and tariff exemptions for ten years for firms which export all of their production, but excluded income tax and tariff exemptions applied to fixed capital and fuels for firms that exported only part of their production.

A subsidies scheme involving tax credits (*certificados de abono tributario*, or CATs) for non-traditional exports in general was also established

(DL 73–83 and 22–84). However, little use was made of these subsidies, as the scheme was suspended in 1986, with the argument that the newly established exchange-rate system provided sufficient incentives.

Furthermore, a fund to guarantee bank credit for agricultural exports was established in 1982 (DL 35–82), but was converted in 1983 into a fund to guarantee credit for agricultural activities in general, excluding commercialisation activities (DL 22–83).[3] In 1986 the new government, which was allegedly in favour of integration into the world economy, imposed taxes on exports, including a 4 per cent tax on non-traditional exports, on customs services and on the use of international telecommunication services.

In 1989 more significant progress was made by replacing the regime covering industrial exports (DL 21–84) by a more general and comprehensive law to promote and development export and *maquila* activities (DL 29–89). The law distinguishes more precisely different types of exporters and regimes, such as temporary admission, duty drawback, indirect exporters, and exporters using wholly national inputs, and establishes in each case the corresponding coverage of exemptions that apply to imported inputs, capital goods, value-added taxes and income taxes. An open foreign investment regime was also consolidated two years earlier by simplifying procedures for the application of a bilateral investment agreement signed with the USA in 1969.

15.3 EXPORT PERFORMANCE

As shown in Table 15.2, the average annual growth rate of all major categories of exports – traditional agro-exports, industrial products sold in Central America and non-traditional exports to the rest of the world – was negative from 1981 to 1986. The real devaluation begun in 1985 and the simplification of the exchange-rate system in 1986 have been the major determinants of growing exports since then. After a gradual appreciation in real terms until 1985, the REER was devalued by nearly 100 per cent in the years following 1986–7. For the first time in the 1980s all categories of exports increased in 1987, and only traditional exports experienced negative growth rates thereafter, due to exogenous terms of trade variations, as shown in Table 15.2. Therefore, the 'late' increase in exports, when compared to most other Latin American countries, can be attributed mainly to the late devaluation of the currency.

The effects of devaluation on trade were partly neutralised by the deterioration of terms of trade, crucial in the decreasing share of traditional export products such as cotton, sugar, bananas, coffee, cardamom and meat. The

Table 15.2 Traditional and non-traditional exports, 1981–92
(annual growth rates, %)

Year	Manufactured exports outside CACM	Non-traditional agro-exports outside CACM	Total exports to CACM countries	Traditional exports to all markets
1981	7.9	−19.7	−14.1	−24.4
1982	−28.0	−8.2	−11.1	−4.8
1983	−13.6	6.3	−4.7	2.0
1984	19.6	−13.4	−9.3	0.5
1985	9.8	−13.6	−28.5	15.2
1986	4.5	−34.8	−11.1	−15.1
1987	57.1	5.2	24.9	7.2
1988	10.0	19.7	2.2	−10.0
1989	13.2	17.8	5.5	7.4
1990	9.5	24.4	15.7	−2.7
1991	20.0	12.1	12.5	−6.5
1992	7.8	5.8	21.9	0.2

Source: Own estimates on the basis of data from the Banco de Guatemala. Estimates are based on data in current $US.

share of these products in total exports decreased from 74 per cent in 1986 to 43 per cent in 1992. Sugar, however, benefited from a rather perverse and selective policy that sets it apart from other traditional exports. In addition to the exchange-rate devaluation, sugar producers – a powerful oligopoly consisting of a limited number of sugar refineries – benefited from an internal guarantee price which can be considered equivalent to a subsidy. Thus, in spite of uncertain prospects in world markets, sugar exports increased continuously in the period 1987–92, and nearly doubled their share in total exports from 6.5 per cent in 1987 to 12.2 per cent in 1992.

Non-traditional exports

The strongest initial response to devaluation came from non-traditional industrial and agricultural exports orientated to non-Central American markets. They increased their share in total exports from 17 per cent in 1987 to 25 per cent in 1992. Manufactured exports had been growing since 1984. Real wages, already at a low level, were reduced further by devaluation. Low wages are one of the primary – and in some cases, sole – sources of competitiveness in this sector. The devaluation coincided with a significant increase in apparel assembly activities taking advantage of US policy pertaining to its tariff heading 9802.00.80, that provides tariff relief for goods imported by the USA which were assembled in foreign location and that contain US-made products. In 1989 Guatemala entered the list of principal sources of US imports under heading 9802.00.80, exporting $US 80 m in that year and $US 118 m in 1990, approximately half of which duty-free, corresponding to US components (USITC, 1989). This is partly due to FDI by South Korean firms specialising in exports of textiles and apparel to the US market while taking advantage of close links with South Korean families who emigrated earlier to the USA (ECLAC, 1992c).

Unlike the situation in Mexico, the Dominican Republic and Haiti, exports under US tariff heading 9802.00.80 do not account for most exports of manufactures to non-Central American countries. Until 1989, approximately 200 firms benefited from the special regime for non-traditional industrial exports (DL 21–84), but only 80 of these firms were involved in *maquila* activities (ITC, 1989, p. 52). Exports not benefiting from the special US tariff regulation have included other textile and apparel products and agro-industrial products, the production of which is intensive in the use of labour and natural resources, such as processed food products, wood products and tobacco products.

The borderline between agro-industrial products and other agricultural non-traditional exports is not very clear, and trade policy usually makes no distinction. This is consistent with the view that attaches greater priority to the search for international competitiveness in general, rather than to the promotion of industrialisation *per se*. More specifically, it takes into consideration that the stimulation of technical progress should not be restricted to manufacturing industry, and that it should be promoted in all facets of economic activity (ECLAC, 1990a, ch. IV).

Furthermore, non-traditional agricultural exports, which increased significantly from 1987 to 1992, may have a more favourable impact on income distribution than have traditional exports. Specifically, small-scale production for export and co-operatives of vegetable exporters have been heralded as a success story (ECLAC, 1990a, p. 137). Moreover, the associative nature of these organisations may facilitate articulation with agro-business and the diffusion of technology required to meet standards in world markets.

Export orientation of manufacturing industry

Available evidence suggests that in Guatemala some manufacturing industries established during the era of import-substitution have provided a basis for exports to markets outside Central America. Manufacturing sectors, established to produce for the Central American market, are relatively capital-intensive and lack backward linkages with the rest of the economy, and so have not been able to benefit from comparative advantages associated with the availability of low-skilled labour and natural resources. Combined with the absence of a demanding and competitive market, this has hampered their international competitiveness. However, in other sectors input requirements and relative factor availability have coincided, which has facilitated international competitiveness.

The sectors of chemicals (ISIC 35) and machinery and equipment (ISIC 38) are among the sectors with the highest shares of intra-Central American exports in output and fit in the first category of sectors, as shown in Table 15.3. Both sectors have significantly lower shares of exports to the rest of the world in output.[4] On the other hand, the sectors of wood products (ISIC 33), textiles (ISIC 32) and processed food (ISIC 31) have more backward linkages and are more labour-intensive, and the shares of their output that are exported to the rest of the world are close to, or above, the corresponding shares of output exported to Central America. Previously established plants or entrepreneurial experience may explain the increase of manufactured exports by these sectors to the rest of the world. Gradual reduction of effective protection, complemented by other measures, may favour future investments in these sectors rather than in the former group of sectors.

Table 15.3   Export:output ratios in manufacturing sectors, 1989 (%)

ISIC code	Ratio of exports to CACM countries to production	Ratio of exports to the rest of the world to production
3. Total manufacturing industry	9	6
31. Foodstuffs, beverages and tobacco	5	7
32. Textiles, apparel and leather products	11	10
33. Wood products	11	39
34. Paper and printing	7	1
35. Chemicals	15	6
36. Non-metallic minerals	9	3
37. Steel and iron, metals	7	4
38. Machinery and equipment	11	4
39. Other manufacturing	49	29

Source: Estimates based on data from UNIDO and Banco Central de Guatemala.

Furthermore, there are more possibilities of generating additional value added when backward linkages of some activities, arising from established but competitive industrial firms and services such as tourism, can coincide with forward linkages of other sectors including agro-exports. In such cases there may be possibilities to improve the export and investment performance of a limited number of 'clusters', to the extent that other determinants of competitiveness could be strengthened (Buitelaar and Fuentes, 1991; ECLAC, 1990a; Porter, 1990).

15.4 SYSTEMIC OBSTACLES FOR EXPORTERS

The uncertainty that arises from frequent modifications of legislation and changes in the exchange rate, combined with deficiencies in technological diffusion and infrastructural support, have been significant obstacles for exporters and could bring growth of exports to a halt, as observed in the period 1987–92. According to a survey of non-traditional exporters undertaken in the late 1980s, the main obstacles were supply-related and policy-related (ITC, 1989, pp. 53–5). They identified deficiencies in terms of quality and volumes of inputs and output, in addition to high energy and transport costs. Also, they complained about the absence of clear incentives and expressed concern regarding the lack of adequate financial resources. Inadequate information about foreign markets and export procedures was also pointed out. Some of these issues are dealt with below.

The performance of private investment

One indicator of the systemic obstacles faced by exporters is the performance of investment. Private investment in particular is a proxy of business expectations. Poor performance of investment suggests that export expansion has not yet entered a sustainable phase. The decline of the overall investment to GDP ratio in LDCs during the 1980s has been explained by the positive relationship between the overall investment ratio and the growth of output and public investment, and its negative relationship with macro-economic instability, deteriorating world economic conditions and foreign-debt burdens (Serven and Solimano, 1993). A similar development took place in Guatemala, where the overall investment to GDP ratio was approximately 20 per cent during the second half of the 1970s and subsequently declined to approximately 11 per cent in the early 1990s. The private investment to GDP ratio declined from approximately 15 per cent

218 The Systemic Weakness of Guatemala's Competitiveness

Table 15.4 Private investment, 1980–91 (%)

Year	Ratio of private investment to GDP[a]	Private investment growth rates[b]	Rate of growth of imports of capital goods[b]
1980	7.2	−22.5	n.a.
1981	6.5	−9.8	6.6
1982	6.6	−1.5	2.1
1983	5.2	−23.6	−59.4
1984	5.3	2.6	26.3
1985	5.5	3.2	5.9
1986	5.7	3.7	8.4
1987	6.2	12.6	92.2
1988	6.7	12.2	6.7
1989	6.7	4.7	2.5
1990	5.8	−10.4	−10.7
1991	6.2	10.1	0.0

[a] based on figures in current prices.
[b] based on figures in constant prices.
Source: Estimated on the basis of data from CACM (several years).

during most of the second half of the 1970s to 5–7 per cent in the 1980s and early 1990s, as shown in Table 15.4. No obvious trend is observable after 1986, in spite of growing exports. Negative growth of output, falling public investment, and instability related to political events and to the exchange rate may explain the negative growth of private investment during the first half of the 1980s and in 1990. Growth rates of private investment were high in 1987, 1988 and 1991, but growth in 1987 may be seen as the once-and-for-all effect of a surge of imports of capital goods that resulted from pent-up demand. Moreover, high growth rates of private investment in 1988 and 1991 were to a large extent the result of a boom in the construction sector, the most dynamic sector in the economy during both years.

Moreover, financial markets did not favour investment in new export-orientated activities. In spite of recommendations (ITC, 1989, pp. 64–6), financial mechanisms or instruments specifically designed to favour non-traditional exporters have not been established, and there is no scheme of export-credit guarantees. Export credit is granted almost exclusively by commercial banks, known for their conservatism and the high concentration of their loan portfolio (IPC, 1991). Commercial banks have granted credit to exporters on terms that are equivalent to credit for production oriented towards the domestic market, and they have favoured traditional exporters, their stock-holders or traditional clients (ITC, 1989, p. 63). Furthermore, legislation has required guarantees that new exporters can often not provide.

Education and technological diffusion

Quality control and its relationship with technological diffusion and education has appeared to be crucial for export success. Under conditions that prevent widespread technological diffusion, the larger the extent of linkages of an export activity with the rest of the economy, or the less 'self-contained' it is, the less likely it is that such an activity becomes competitive, since it will not benefit from modern techniques (Clague, 1991). In other words, only assembly or enclave-type activities may be competitive in economies where technological difusion is limited. Vulnerability related to heavy reliance on locally provided inputs, may be illustrated by the case of one of the most successful non-traditional agro-export products, 'Chinese pea'. This product was temporarily barred entry into the USA in 1992 due to the excessive use of pesticides by its small-scale producers. In this particular case, inadequate technological diffusion may be attributed to low levels of education. More generally, problems of employing adequately trained workers and technical personnel have been a frequent complaint of exporting firms (ITC, 1989, p. 44).

The clearly inadequate levels of education, in terms of coverage and quality, are linked to the weak public sector and cannot be understood without taking into account the weak basis of taxation. The country has one of the lowest taxation ratios in the world. During the 1980s the tax ratio was kept below 10 per cent and reached nearly 5 per cent in 1984, which is in contrast to the situation in most Latin American countries that had a tax ratio between 13 and 20 per cent at the end of the 1980s (ECLAC, 1992d, p. 92).

The deterioration of the economic situation, the low tax ratio and growing employment in unproductive public activities weakened the small and inefficient public sector even further during the 1980s. During the first half of the 1980s the situation came close to civil war, and the expenditure of the central government on defence and internal security increased from 12 per cent of the total government budget in 1980 to 21 per cent in 1985, surpassing expenditures on education.

The Systemic Weakness of Guatemala's Competitiveness

Table 15.5 Public investment, 1980–92 (%)

Year	Ratio of public investment I_g GDP[a]	Public investment growth rates[b]
1980	6.7	n.a
1981	8.4	33.6
1982	6.3	−20.1
1983	4.6	−33.3
1984	3.8	−25.5
1985	2.7	−20.3
1986	2.0	−1.6
1987	2.8	24.2
1988	n.a.	16.9
1989	3.6	12.3
1990	3.4	0.0
1991	3.2	5.9
1992	3.1	4.9

[a] based on data in current prices.
[b] based on constant prices.

Public infrastructure

Public investment as a share of GDP declined continuously from 8.4 per cent in 1980 to 2.7 per cent in 1985, as shown in Table 15.5. After 1986, public investment as a share of GDP increased slightly and followed a trend similar to that of private investment, which provides evidence for a crowding-in rather than a crowding-out effect. Investment in roads, telecommunications and energy during the first half of the 1980s illustrates the problems faced by public investment, as well as the ways in which these problems weakened the capability of the country to develop its international competitiveness in more recent years. In 1987 The World Bank stated that 'two-fifths of paved roads and three-quarters of unpaved roads are now in poor condition, twice as high as comparable rates in Latin America' (The World Bank, 1987, p. 6). In 1988, 132 out of 304 municipalities did not have any telecommunication services, and in 1987 approximately 60 per cent of demand for telephone services was not met. The delay in the investment plan of the national telecommunications agency GUATEL for the period 1984–7 exacerbated the weakness of the export infrastructure (The World Bank, 1987) and was an illustration of the serious problems that were due to the limited executing capability of the public sector.[5]

Moreover, the main hydropower project, Chixoy, which absorbed approximately one-third of total public investment in the period 1980–5 and accounted for approximately 60 per cent of total generating capacity in 1990, suffered since its inception from a series of technical and financial problems that were allegedly linked to corruption. These problems contributed to a complete breakdown of the system of electricity generation and distribution in the third quarter of 1991, when rainfall was below the predicted level. This gave rise to blackouts and severe rationing, resulting in estimated losses equivalent to 0.2 per cent of GDP (SEGEPLAN, 1992, p. 21).

The government that was elected in 1986 increased public investments but not in basic infrastructure and the social sectors (SEGEPLAN, 1992, pp. 25–6). Two fundamental problems remained. First, limited savings by the public sector constrained public investment, which tended to depend on the availability of foreign funding. Second, the executing capability of government agencies remained limited. For example, in 1991 only 14 per cent of resources earmarked for investment in the health sector and 50 per cent for investment in education were utilised that year (SEGEPLAN, 1992, p. 35).

The institutional framework

The institutional framework has become precarious. Regarding support for non-traditional exports, it should be noted that the efficiency of the public sector in general deteriorated during the 1980s. Moreover, GUATEXPO, an agency of fundamental importance to export promotion that was established in 1971, was closed down in 1983. This has been compensated to some extent by the chamber of non-traditional exporters, which has actively lobbied for the creation of adequate domestic conditions for exports, and has promoted sales in foreign markets.

More fundamentally, however, Guatemala experienced a continuous deterioration in the respect for rules, ranging from contracts to the most basic human rights. Without commonly accepted rules it is not possible to build the social cohesion and co-operation required as part of the 'systemic' nature of international competitiveness. Polarisation resulting from extreme income inequality and massive poverty has aggravated the situation. The high degree of confrontation also weakened the country's capability to export goods and services more directly because of its negative effect on national and foreign investment and tourism, and because of direct foreign government pressures to reduce market access – for example, threats to eliminate the GSP of the USA – or official development assistance. Guatemala provides a clear example of how an unusually high degree of confrontation is ultimately self-defeating. A long history of violation of workers' rights led eventually to an alliance of Guatemalan labour leaders and labour leaders from the USA that in 1992 came close to achieving the exclusion of Guatemalan exports from benefiting from the preferences granted by the USA under the GSP (*Inforpress Centroamericana*, 1993). The resulting uncertainty was widely seen in the private sector as having a decidedly negative effect on future investment and exports.

15.5 CONCLUSIONS

Guatemala has undertaken far-reaching stabilisation and adjustment measures in ways that do not differ significantly from adjustment processes in other Latin American countries. However, the adjustment process in Guatemala, which has not yet ended, started later than in most other countries in the region. Moreover, a reactive rather than a coherent long-term strategy has predominated, although the trend to stabilise and 'get prices right' has been clear. In general, it would appear that the absence of a clear perception of the economic crisis, and the continuous political crises, have not favoured the formulation and implementation of a long-term development strategy.

The most important instrument of adjustment during the 1980–92 period was the exchange rate. The REER was high from 1986 to 1992, although with significant variations. Some progress has been made to eliminate the anti-export biases in specific sectors by means of tariff exemptions for non-traditional exports. However, significant reduction of external tariffs only started in 1990, mostly as a consequence of conditions attached to entry into GATT (1991) and to structural adjustment loans granted by The World Bank.

However, the extremely polarised society and the absence of a solid rules-based economic and social system, have increased rather than reduced transaction costs and undermined the social cohesion that is required for sustainable international competitiveness. Weak public institutions, insufficient public savings and poor executive capabilities have resulted in inadequate physical infrastructure and public education.

Due to these systemic weaknesses low wages and natural resources are the main sources of competitiveness. The low level of private investment, which should accompany growing exports, undermines prospects for sustainable export growth. The creation of clear rules system and a government capable of enforcing these rules remain challenges that must be met.

Notes

1. The extreme opposition of the private sector is particularly remarkable, given the low tax burden, due in part to a long history of failed tax reforms. Best (1976) found that in most cases in Central America the actual composition of taxes corresponded to the preferences of landowners, and was the reverse of the preferences of the majority of the population.
2. Most of these factors were already implicitly incorporated in the national tariff structure of each country. Consequently, it is not surprising to find that the average tariff structure of the five individual countries in 1959, before the CET was introduced, was not very different from the structure of the CET finally agreed upon.
3. Two additional decrees applied to the industrial sector, although without favouring exports specifically. In the late 1970s, a law was passed to promote industrial decentralisation through partial income-tax exemptions and preferential financial assistance to be channelled through CORFINA, a public financial institution. However, the financial crisis of CORFINA and the restricted nature of other income-tax incentives limited the effects of this law. At the same time a decree to promote small-sized firms included partial exemptions from income taxes and tariffs on raw materials and equipment, as well as pre-investment credit and credit guarantees.
4. The relatively high ratio for chemical industries (ISIC 35) can be explained by the activities of subsidiaries of TNCs in pharmaceuticals. These firms were established in Guatemala because of its relatively large market, and exported to Central America, the Caribbean and other small South American countries. However, the production process is highly import-intensive and its 'final-touch' nature generates limited employment effects.
5. A specific case of communications deficiencies linked to international trade is the situation of the main northern border post. This should have been a gateway to Central America, but in fact poses a series of obstacles: there are no import lots, there is only one old bridge connecting Mexico with Guatemala and there are hardly any telecommunications facilities (*The Journal of Commerce*, 1993).

16 Conclusions
Ruud Buitelaar and Pitou van Dijck

This volume has analysed the contributions governments in small and medium-sized countries in Latin America can make to the strengthening of the international competitiveness of the economy. The study has focused in particular on the role government may play in enhancing in a systemic manner the capabilities of domestic manufacturing firms to penetrate international markets by improving the macro-economic context, adjusting the incentive structure for manufacturing industries and improving institutional support for export industries.

As shown throughout this volume, many of the selected Latin American countries have made significant progress in policy reform, particularly from the second half of the 1980s onwards. The new priorities in the region reflect the Washington agenda, and during a relatively brief time span trade regimes have been liberalised and exchange-rate regimes have become more supportive for the tradables sectors. Notwithstanding these far-reaching changes and the significant achievements that have been made, the domestic industrial basis for a new insertion in international markets is still weak in most of the selected countries. The manufacturing sector is relatively small and its share in overall production has hardly increased in many countries over a long period of time. As shown in the Introduction and in Chapter 10, the manufacturing sector has become more export-orientated and contributes more substantially to the overall export performance of most countries than was the case in the past, but it is also true that comparative advantages are still very much concentrated in only some primary sectors and resource-based industries as well as some labour-intensive sectors. Moreover, the contribution of domestic firms to exports is still relatively limited.

The chances of a successful new insertion in world markets depend critically on the relationship between government and the private sector and in this regard the study has distinguished some challenges ahead. The main findings of the theoretical, cross-country and country-specific studies may be grouped together in the following five areas:

(i) liberalisation of the trade regime;
(ii) priority for a supportive exchange-rate policy;

(iii) stimulation of investment and an appropriate industrial policy;
(iv) reform of export-support institutions and mechanisms;
(v) improvement of the social and political acceptability of the economic reform strategy.

16.1 LIBERALISATION OF THE TRADE REGIME

Many countries in Latin America have made significant progress in liberalising the trade regime: NTBs have been abolished and maximum and average tariff rates, as well as the variation of the rates, have been reduced substantially. Most countries have become contracting parties of GATT and participate in one or more regional preferential system that aims at co-ordinated liberalisation in order to foster open regionalism. The process of liberalisation has been further supported by the region-wide drive towards a preferential trading system as announced during the Miami Summit of December 1994.

As Linnemann has argued in Chapter 2 of this volume, policy should aim at reducing the bias against trade, not necessarily at free trade. Statistical studies indicate that exports may function as a handmaiden of growth, not so much as an engine for growth. Trade liberalisation is not the magic key to economic growth but is part of a broad package of policy reforms, including sound macro-economic policies, a supportive exchange-rate policy, reduction of domestic rigidities and imbalances, and policies to stimulate investment as well as supportive institutions. Against this background, the wisdom may be questioned of a general assertion made by The World Bank that 'trade reforms are successful if they are bold and extensive' (Alam and Rajapatirana, 1993, p. 47).

Different strategies may be pursued to liberalise the trade regime. Most of the free-trade areas and customs unions that were established in the era of predominantly inward-orientated industrialisation policies were not supportive in integrating economies in the region and stimulating a dynamic pattern of industrial development in Latin America based on potential comparative advantages. However, more recent initiatives aim to support the new insertion of Latin American countries in world markets by co-ordinating the reduction of trade barriers, and not so much to seclude regional markets from the world market as used to be the case before. To the extent that these initiatives foster open regionalism and are trade-creating rather than trade-diverting, such a drive towards more substantial policy co-ordination may strengthen the process of policy reform and liberalisation.

It is not possible to generalise on the optimal speed of liberalisation, as this depends very much on specific circumstances. Crucial factors in this regard are the efficiency of domestic industry and its capability to transform itself into an internationally competitive sector in the short term, producing product categories and qualities that are in demand abroad, and the expectations of the private sector with respect to the sustainability of a policy mix that is required to operate in open markets. A shockwise reform may be warranted to reduce possibilities for pressure groups to block or retard reforms, but such a strategy may bring about high economic and social costs. If a shockwise approach is required, additional measures may be needed to reduce its negative effects on employment and the current account of the balance of payments during a transitional stage.

16.2 A SUPPORTIVE EXCHANGE-RATE POLICY

Growth and diversification of the export sector in many Latin American countries was hampered in the past by systematic overvaluation of the domestic currency. Moreover, the experience of countries in the Southern Cone in the 1970s showed that liberalisation of the trade regime is unsustainable if the exchange rate is overvalued and undermines the competitiveness of export-oriented and import-substituting industries. To avoid unsustainable imbalances on the current account and an inefficiency illusion or, more seriously, industrial decline, a high RER is required. The particular choice of exchange-rate regime depends in particular on the structure of production and exports, as indicated by Visser in Chapter 3. A pegged exchange rate may be an attractive option for small countries that have a dominant relationship with only one trading partner, as is the case in many small Latin American countries. Countries with a more diversified export sector in terms of trading partners may opt for pegging the value of their currency to a basket of international currencies. Countries with an export structure dominated by only one or a small number of commodities and widely fluctuating international prices, may require a floating nominal exchange rate. The availability of abundant natural resources and dependence on only a few export commodities may cause Dutch disease effects that hamper export diversification and export-oriented industrialisation. Cases in point are Colombia with coffee and illegal exports, Venezuela and Ecuador with oil exports. Dutch disease effects may also be caused by an abundant inflow of foreign aid, as was the case in Central America. In such circumstances a stable RER is called for to promote non-traditional exports.

A stimulating exchange-rate regime requires liberalisation of the foreign-exchange market and lifting of restrictions that keep the exchange rate at an artificially low level. Moreover, systems of dual and multiple exchange rates may be abused for political motives and may reduce overall welfare. If a government wants to limit non-essential imports, domestic taxes are to be preferred to multiple exchange rates.

A crucial question in this context is how to bring about the liberalisation of the exchange-rate regime. A simultaneous liberalisation of the capital and current account, or a liberalisation of the capital account prior to the liberalisation of the current account, may seriously jeopardise efforts to implement exchange-rate regimes that support insertion in the international economy. Whether there is net capital inflow or outflow, there may be a need for authorities to maintain control over it. As suggested by Visser, there is a case for easing restrictions on capital imports at the time the current account is liberalised.

The experiences of Latin American countries indicate that adjustments in the exchange rate may have a significant impact on the value of exports, in particular non-traditional and manufactured exports. However, to respond adequately to supportive price signals, additional investments and marketing efforts by domestic firms and support by export-promotion institutions may be required.

Moreover, FitzGerald argues in Chapter 4 that the exchange rate is not an instrument that can be controlled easily by local monetary authorities. A stable RER is not easy to come by, and wide fluctuations from year to year may have a negative impact on the profitability of the sectors of tradables. In most countries in the region the nominal exchange rate is not under direct control of the central bank and open market operations are constrained by the need to maintain minimum reserve levels.

16.3 STIMULATION OF INVESTMENT AND AN APPROPRIATE INDUSTRIAL POLICY

The structural adjustment programmes that were implemented in Latin America during the 1980s did not include specific provisions to promote industrial investment and to stimulate industrial development. Rather, the programmes assumed implicitly that trade liberalisation, stabilisation and devaluation would stimulate private investment in the sectors of tradables and that competitive industries would emerge. Industrial policy and investment stimulation policies were not on the Washington agenda.

New investments are required to support the process of structural adjustments and the expansion of the sectors of tradables, but the shares of private investment in GDP decreased significantly in Peru, Colombia and Venezuela during the 1980s, due to high real interest rates. The opposite holds true of Chile. Moreover, public investment declined at the same time. FitzGerald notes that the lack of public investment in infrastructure such as transportation and telecommunication facilities reduced private investment, suggesting that crowding-in rather than crowding-out effects occurred. Moreover, reduction of public investment in technological development, R&D, education and training, has a negative impact on the capability of domestic firms to compete internationally. Finally, elimination of specific credit and technical assistance programmes for small firms has reduced their capability to compete. The main challenges to stimulate investment are: the creation of favourable expectations for private investors; the implementation of tax reforms in favour of re-investments; the provision of long-term credit; and technological and infrastructural support by government.

Tavares de Araujo has argued in Chapter 5 that traditional instruments of industrial policy have become obsolete in this age of rapid globalisation and technological progress. Although domestic pressure groups may lobby strongly for the use of traditional instruments such as barriers to international trade and constraints on the international movements of factors of production, protectionism is not a viable option for stimulating domestic industry. A minimum package to stimulate investments in the manufacturing sector contains the following three elements:

(i) a high and stable RER that is in equilibrium;
(ii) efficient public spending on R&D and on technological infrastructure, to be financed by increased domestic taxes; and
(iii) an institutional framework to improve the functioning of competitive markets by the strengthening of discipline, facilitating mobility and improving resource availability.

Moreover, a system of domestic taxation should be established that is compatible with the levels of public investments that are required to sustain the international competitiveness of domestic industry in an open economy.

Many countries in Latin America have established special industrial zones, EPFZs. These attract foreign investors and contribute in a significant way to export diversification and manufactured exports in many Central American and Caribbean countries. In Chapter 6 Weersma-

Haworth has distinguished some recent changes in the modes of operations of these zones and some of these changes are illustrated in the case study of the San Bartolo EPFZ in El Salvador, presented in Chapter 7. The zones are becoming more specialised and some zones have moved away from low-tech and footloose activities that were typical of the zones in the past, towards more skill-intensive activities. Also, the management and ownership of EPFZs have been privatised in some cases. Moreover, significant investments by firms other than US firms, including domestic investors, have been registered. Finally, alternative ways of financing have been explored and a wide range of incentives and sophisticated support services have been developed to attract foreign investors.

The contribution of EPFZs to overall industrial development and the creation of manufacturing capacities has been questioned frequently in the literature. Available evidence suggest that the contribution of the zones to industrial development and the current account is positive, but in most cases very limited. As such, the establishment of EPFZs cannot be thought of as an alternative industrialisation strategy. Their contribution to the diffusion of technological capabilities, upgrading of the labour force, and the development of an internationally competitive domestic cluster of industries has so far been fairly limited in most cases. The major contribution of the zones to the host country is the creation of employment for low-skilled labour.

16.4 REFORM OF EXPORT-SUPPORT INSTITUTIONS AND MECHANISMS

To strengthen the international competitiveness of domestic firms, a re-organisation or re-creation is required of economic institutions that were established to support the import-substitution strategy in previous decades. Most of the country studies included in this volume reviewed three areas of institutional reform:

(i) direct financial support;
(ii) fiscal incentives; and
(iii) a cluster of export promotion mechanisms and instruments.

In the area of direct financial support, all country studies refer to the inadequate functioning of domestic capital markets. High interest rates and a sub-optimal allocation of credit were major constraints on domestic investment. Additionally, domestic investors have only limited access to international financial resources.

In the case of Costa Rica, it was reported that security was more important to banks than the profitability of the projects. Two specific issues have been commented upon in the country studies: the low level of development of export financing schemes and the poor results achieved with special industrial reconversion funds. Part of the explanation is that only a few firms were under pressure to reconvert. Improvement of the functioning of domestic capital markets should get priority over the establishment of special reconversion funds.

Regarding fiscal incentives, the experience in Costa Rica with the CAT system provides some important insights. The system was costly to government and benefited only a small number of firms, including some TNCs. It is doubtful whether the incentives stimulated investments that would otherwise not have taken place. If so, the CAT system is nothing but a rent.

The case of Chile is an illustration of fiscal incentives that reportedly function efficiently and effectively. The Chilean system is automatic and a ceiling of total value of exports per product category is set, beyond which the incentive is no longer provided. In that way, the system mainly stimulates newly developed and predominantly non-traditional export categories and is more appropriately linked to the needs of small firms. As indicated in this case study, the incentives have been a decisive factor for firms to develop export activities, which is in contrast with the findings reported in the case study of Costa Rica.

According to the case study of Uruguay, fiscal incentives are the only export-promotion instrument actually in use, and much the same type of problems have occurred as was the case in Costa Rica. The system was revised several times in the past decade.

In Venezuela, ATPA is the fiscal incentive regime used by some industrial exporters. The effective functioning of the system has been hampered by red tape. Apparently, large exporters in particular benefited from the system, as was also the case in Costa Rica.

The experiences indicate that fiscal incentives for non-traditional exports should be an integral part of an export-orientated growth strategy to be successful, but practical implementation problems have limited the contribution of the systems actually in use, with the exception of the system in Chile. Further efforts should be made to simplify the systems, to limit red tape and to facilitate access for small exporters.

Chile – the country in this survey that first introduced economic reform – has most experience in institutional restructuring and its export promotion institute ProChile is an interesting case. Notwithstanding some achievements, the impact of ProChile's activities has been limited by the distribution of responsibilities and authorities in the area of foreign trade between many ministries and governmental institutions. Lack of interinstitutional co-ordination has been a major problem. According to firms, the impact of ProChile is hardly perceptible, as the institution reportedly has a short-term orientation, a limited budget and little competence. Promotion of new products, commodities that require a sophisticated marketing approach, and integrated export-development projects require a systemetic, comprehensive and longer-term approach rather than isolated activities, but ProChile does not have a clear policy for such cases.

In Costa Rica, government has invested very little in assisting firms to penetrate export markets. In spite of the single window created by CENPRO, non-traditional exports to countries outside Central America still face many different incentive schemes and to qualify for incentives may take several years. Major problems reported by firms are the lack of a stable and consistent regime of taxes and incentives. As in the case of Chile, co-ordination between the Ministry of Economy and Industry and the Ministry of External Relations and Trade is inadequate.

In Venezuela also a number of institutions have been established, some with overlapping responsibilities. The effectiveness of ICE has been hampered by a severe budget constraint and CADEX is not yet operational, as Congress delayed approval of the budget.

As follows from these experiences, budget constraints, lack of competence and inadequate co-ordination have limited the effectiveness of export-promotion institutions in most cases. Improved co-operation between the private and public sectors is required to support exports in a more efficient way.

16.5 IMPROVEMENT OF THE SOCIAL AND POLITICAL ACCEPTABILITY OF THE ECONOMIC REFORM STRATEGY

During the 1980s social condition deteriorated significantly in several respects. As shown by Van der Hoeven and Stewart in Chapter 9, average urban unemployment increased to over 10 per cent by the mid 1980s. The contribution of the manufacturing sector to total employment declined. In particular, employment in large manufacturing establishments declined rapidly, while employment in small enterprises as well as in the informal sector increased. Also, wage indicators for the manufacturing sector show a sharper decline than overall GDP per caput. Moreover, government spending on health and education as a share of overall government spending declined in Bolivia, Chile, Costa Rica, Ecuador and El Salvador.

However, the relative contribution of these spending categories was stable or increased in Uruguay, Venezuela and Peru. Primary enrolment declined or was stable in seven out of fourteen countries. This trend is worrying in view of the critical role of education and skill formation in income generation and overall economic growth. Lack of progress towards both universal primary education and significant increases in secondary school enrolment is an obstacle to a more equal distribution of income and welfare. There is evidence that in the 1980s expenditure on education was directed more towards lower income groups than before, but the opposite holds true of expenditure on health.

During the 1980s compensatory programmes and social investment funds were established to mitigate the social costs of adjustment. Van der Hoeven and Stewart suggest several ways of strengthening the focus of public expenditure on low income groups: by targeting expenditure on the poor, diverting public expenditure to social expenditure, and by increasing the overall level of public expenditure.

In conclusion, it may be observed that the strengthening of the international competitiveness of domestic firms in order to realise a more economically sustainable and socially acceptable type of insertion in international markets involves learning processes at the levels of domestic firms, support institutions and the government level. Moreover, such a regime change requires private and public investments that may only be generated in a macro-economic policy context that is supportive and predictable in the longer term.

An irreversible liberalisation of the trade regime in combination with a supportive exchange-rate policy is a necessary but not a sufficient condition for the success of regime change. At the same time, the functioning of domestic capital markets will have to be improved to stimulate public and private investment. Moreover, small and medium-sized firms need better access to the domestic capital market in order to increase their capability to export. In addition to changes in incentives and improvements in the functioning of markets, the effectiveness and efficiency of institutions to support technological development and export marketing will have to be improved.

References

Aghevli, B. B., M. S. Khan and P. J. Montiel (1991) *Exchange Rate Policy in Developing Countries: Some Analytical Issues*, Occasional Paper no. 78 (Washington, DC: IMF).
Alam, A. and S. Rajapatirana (1993) 'Trade Reform in Latin America and the Caribbean', *Finance and Development*, vol. 30, no. 3.
Albañez, T., E. Bustelo, G. A. Cornia and E. Jespersen (1989) *Economic Decline and Child Survival: The Plight of Latin America in the Eighties*, Innocenti Occasional Papers no. 1 (Florence: UNICEF).
Alter, R. (1991) 'Lessons from the Export Processing Zone in Mauritius', *Finance and Development*, vol. 28, no. 4.
Arguedas Chaverri, E. (1989) *Reconversión de la Industria Química, Celco de Costa Rica S. A.*, San José, mimeo.
Arriagada, P. (1985) 'Adjustments by Agricultural Exporters in Chile during 1974–82', in V. Corbo and J. de Melo.
Arriola, J., C. Alemán and R. Rivera (1993) *Los Procesos de Trabajo en la Zona Franca de San Bartolo,* Documentos de Trabajo, IIES-UCA, no. 93-2. (San Salvador: Universidad Centroamericana).
ASEXMA (1986) *Políticas de Fomento a la Exportación de Productos Manufacturados*, (Santiago de Chile).
Athukorala, P. (1989) 'Export Performance of "New Exporting Countries": How Valid is the Optimism?', *Development and Change*, vol. 20, no. 1.
Atiyas, I., M. Dutz and C. Frischtak (1992) *Fundamental Issues and Policy Approaches in Industrial Restructuring*, Industry and Energy Department Working Paper, Industry Series Paper no. 56 (Washington, DC: The World Bank).
Bacha, E. (1990) 'A Three-Gap Model of Foreign Transfers and the GDP Growth Rate in Developing Countries', *Journal of Development Economics*, vol. 32.
Balassa, B. (1965) 'Trade Liberalisation and "Revealed Comparative Advantage"', *The Manchester School of Economic and Social Studies*, vol. 33.
_____ (1989) *Comparative Advantage, Trade Policy and Economic Development* (London: Harvester Wheatsheaf).
Balcarcel, E. (1992) *Uruguay 1950–1990: Búsqueda de la Sustentabilidad* (Montevideo: ECLAC, mimeo).
Baldinelli, E. (1991) 'Inversiones para Exportar', in *Integración Latinoamericana*, vol. 16, no. 173.
Banco Central de Reserva de El Salvador (1992) *Estadísticas Varias 1991–92* (San Salvador: BCR).
Baumol, W. (1982) 'Contestable Markets: an Uprising in the Theory of Industry Structure', *American Economic Review*, vol. 72, no. 1.
Baumol, W., J. Panzar and R. Willig (1982) *Contestable Markets and the Theory of Industry Structure* (New York: Harcourt Brace).
Bautista, R. M. (1982) 'Exchange Rate Variations and Export Competitiveness in Less Developed Countries under Generalized Floating', *Journal of Development Studies,* vol. 18, no. 3.

References

Beers, C. P. van (1991) *Exports of Developing Countries* (Amsterdam: Tinbergen Institute).
Berretta, N., F. Lorenzo and C. Paolino (1991) 'En el Umbral de la Integración', *Estudios CINVE*, no. 14.
Bertola, G. and R. Caballero (1994) 'Irreversibility and Aggregate Investment', *Review of Economic Studies*, vol. 61.
Best, M. H. (1976) 'Political Power and Tax Revenues in Central America', *Journal of Development Economics*, vol. 3, no. 3.
Bhagwati, J. N. (1978) *Foreign Trade Regimes and Economic Development: Anatomy and Consequences of Exchange Control Regimes* (Cambridge: NBER).
____ (1982) 'Directly Unproductive, Profit-Seeking (DUP) Activities', *Journal of Political Economy*, vol. 90, no. 5.
____ (1990) 'Export-Promoting Trade Strategy: Issues and Evidence', in C. Milner (ed.) *Export Promotion Strategies. Theory and Evidence from Developing Countries* (New York: New York University Press).
Bianchi, A. (1993) '"Overabundance" of Foreign Exchange, Inflation and Exchange Rate Policy: The Chilean Experience', in C. I. Bradford Jr (ed.) *Mobilising International Investment for Latin America* (Paris: OECD-IDB).
Bianchi, A. and T. Nohara (1988) *A Comparative Study on Economic Development between Asia and Latin America*, Joint Research Programme Series no. 67 (Tokyo: Institute of Developing Economies).
Birdsall, N. (1993) *Social Development is Economic Development*, Policy Research Working Paper, no. 1123 (Washington DC: The World Bank).
Bitar, S. and C. I. Bradford, Jr (1992) 'Strategic Options for Latin America in the 1990s', in C. I. Bradford, Jr (ed.) *Strategic Options for Latin America in the 1990s* (Paris: OECD).
Bruno, M. *et al.* (eds) (1991) *Lessons of Economic Stabilization and its Aftermath* (Cambridge: MIT Press).
Buitelaar, R. and J. A. Fuentes (1991) 'The Competitiveness of the Small Economies of the Region', *CEPAL Review*, no. 43.
Bulmer-Thomas, V. (1988) 'The New Model of Development in Costa Rica', *Studies in the Economies of Central America* (Basingstoke: Macmillan).
____ (1989) *La Economía Política de Centroamérica desde 1920* (San José: BCIE and EDUCA).
Business Latin America, various issues, Washington DC.
Buttari, J. J. (1992) 'Economic Policy Reform in Four Central American Countries: Patterns and Lessons Learned', *Journal of Interamerican Studies and World Affairs*, vol. 34, no. 1.
CACM (various years), *Boletín Estadístico* (San José: CACM).
Calvo, G. A. (1986) 'Fractured Liberalism: Argentina under Martínez de Hoz', *Economic Development and Cultural Change*, vol. 34, no. 3.
Capriles, G. (1992) *Dumping y Subsidios* (Caracas: Instituto de Comercio Exterior).
Cardoso, E. (1993) 'Private Investment in Latin America', *Economic Development and Cultural Change*, vol. 41, no. 4.
Caristo, A. and I. Terra (1991) *La Industria de la Vestimenta Exterior de Tejidos Planos: Rentabilidad y Exportaciones 1978–1990*, Documento 5/91 (Montevideo: Universidad de la República).
Chenery, H. B. (1960) 'Patterns of Industrial Growth', *American Economic Review*, vol. 50, no. 2.

References

Clague, C. (1991) 'Relative Efficiency, Self-Containment, and Comparative Costs of Less Developed Countries', *Economic Development and Cultural Change*, vol. 39, no. 3.

Cline, W. R. (1982), 'Can the East Asian Model of Development be Generalized?', *World Development*, vol. 10, no. 2.

___ (1984) *Exports of Manufactures from Developing Countries: Performance and Prospects for Market Access* (Washington, DC: Brookings Institution).

Coase, R. (1937) 'The Nature of the Firm', *Economica*, vol. 4, no. 16.

___ (1988) *The Firm, the Market and the Law* (Chicago: Chicago University Press).

Congdon, T. (1990) 'Export Promotion and Trade Liberalization in Latin America', in C. Milner (ed.) *Export Promotion Strategies. Theory and Evidence from Developing Countries* (New York: New York University Press).

Connolly, M. and D. Taylor (1976) 'Testing the Monetary Approach to Devaluation in Developing Countries', *Journal of Political Economy*, vol. 84, no. 4, part 1.

Cooper, R. N. (1973) 'An Analysis of Currency Devaluation in Developing Countries', in M. B. Connolly and A. K. Swoboda (eds) *International Trade and Money* (London: George Allen & Unwin).

Corbo, V. (1985) 'Reforms and Macroeconomic Adjustments in Chile during 1974–84', *World Development*, vol. 13, no. 8.

Corbo, V. et al. (1992) *Adjustment Lending Revisited* (Washington, DC: The World Bank).

Corbo, V., and J. de Melo (1985) (eds) *Scrambling for Survival; How Firms Adjusted to the Recent Reforms in Argentina, Chile, and Uruguay*, World Bank Working Paper no. 764 (Washington: The World Bank).

___ (1987) 'Lessons from the Southern Cone Policy Reforms', *World Bank Research Observer*, vol. 2, no. 2.

Corbo, V. and J. M. Sanchez (1985) 'Adjustments by Industrial Firms in Chile During 1974–82', in V. Corbo and J. de Melo (eds) *Scrambling for Survival; How Firms Adjusted to the Recent Reforms in Argentina, Chile, and Uruguay*, World Bank Working Paper no. 764 (Washington: The World Bank).

Corden, W. M. (1984) *Booming Sector and Dutch Disease Economics: Survey and Consolidation*, Oxford Economic Papers, vol. 36, no. 3.

___ (1991) 'Macroeconomic Policy and Growth: Some Lessons of Experience', *World Bank Annual Conference 1990* (Washington, DC: The World Bank).

___ (1993) 'Exchange Rate Policies for Developing Countries', *Economic Journal*, vol. 103, no. 416.

Dahlman, C. (1979) 'The Problem of Externality', *The Journal of Law and Economics*, vol. 22, no. 1.

De la Cuadra, S. and D. Hachette (1988) *The Timing and Sequencing of a Trade Liberalization Policy: the Case of Chile*, Documento de Trabajo no. 113 (Santiago de Chile: Instituto de Economía, Universidad Católica).

De Melo, J. and S. Dhar (1992) *Lessons of Trade Liberalization in Latin America for Economies in Transition*, World Bank Staff Working Paper (Washington, DC: The World Bank).

Denoon, D. B. H. (1986) *Devaluation under Pressure: India, Indonesia, and Ghana* (Cambridge, Mass.: MIT Press).

Dijck, P. van (1986) *Causes and Characteristics of Export-Oriented Industrialization in Developing Countries* (Amsterdam: Free University Press).

―― (1989) 'Análisis Comparativo entre América Latina y el Este Asiático. Estructura, Política y Resultados Económicos', in *Pensamiento Iberoamericano*, vol. 16.

―― (1992) 'The Empty Box Syndrome' in *CEPAL Review*, no. 47.

―― (1995) *Sustainable Outward-Oriented Industrialization Policies*, IDB Working Paper Series 202 (Washington, DC: IDB).

Donovan, D. J. (1981) 'Real Responses Associated with Exchange Rate Action in Selected Upper Credit Tranche Stabilization Programs', *IMF Staff Papers*, vol. 28, no. 4.

Dornbusch, R. (1980) *Open Economy Macroeconomics* (New York: Basic Books).

―― (1991) 'Policies to Move from Stabilization to Growth', *Proceedings of the World Bank Annual Conference on Development Economics 1990* (Washington: The World Bank).

Dornbusch, R. and S. Fischer (1993) 'Moderate Inflation', *The World Bank Economic Review*, vol. 7, no. 1.

Dornbusch, R. and F. Helmers (eds) (1988) *The Open Economy: Tools for Policymakers in Developing Economies* (Washington, DC: EDI, The World Bank).

Dornbusch, R. and L. Tellez Kuenzler (1993) 'Exchange Rate Policy: Options and Issues', in R. Dornbusch (ed.) *Policymaking in the Open Economy* (New York: Oxford University Press).

ECLAC (1988a) *Los Servicios al Productor en la Industria Chilena de Textiles y de Confecciones: un Estudio Piloto* (Santiago de Chile: ECLAC, LC/R.673, mimeo).

―― (1988b) *Los Servicios al Productor en la Industria Textil Latinoamericana: Informe Consolidado de Cuatro Estudios de Caso* (Santiago de Chile: ECLAC, LC/R.709, mimeo).

―― (1990a) *Transformación Productiva con Equidad* (Santiago de Chile: ECLAC).

―― (1990b) *El Esfuerzo Exportador de América Latina. Experiencias y Políticas en Brasil, Chile y Costa Rica* (Santiago de Chile: ECLAC, LC/R.930, mimeo).

―― (1990c) *Estudio Económico de América Latina y el Caribe* (Santiago de Chile: ECLAC).

―― (1991a) *Obstáculos al Transporte por Contenedor, Perspectiva de los Usuarios* (Santiago de Chile: ECLAC, mimeo).

―― (1991b) *La Química Fina: las Empresas y sus Principales Características* (Montevideo: ECLAC, mimeo).

―― (1991c) *La Industria del Cuero en el Uruguay. Competividad, Tecnología y Medio Ambiente* (Montevideo: ECLAC, mimeo).

―― (1992a) *Estudio Económico de América Latina y el Caribe* (Santiago de Chile: ECLAC).

―― (1992b) *Estudio Económico 1991, Venezuela* (Santiago de Chile: ECLAC).

―― (1992c) *La Politica Cambiaria en América Latina a Comienzos de los Años Noventa* (Santiago de Chile: ECLAC, LC/R.1193, mimeo).

―― (1992d) *Equidad y Transformación Productiva: un Enfoque Integrado* (Santiago de Chile: ECLAC).

―― (1992e) *Preliminary Overview of the Latin American and Caribbean Economy 1992* (Santiago de Chile: ECLAC).

_____ (1992f) *El Comercio Exterior de Manufacturas de América Latina, Evolución y Estructura 1962–1989* (Santiago de Chile: ECLAC).

_____ (1992g) *La Cuenca del Pacífico y América Latina: de la Inserción Comercial hacia la Integración Productiva* (Santiago de Chile: ECLAC, LC/L. 704, mimeo).

ECLAC-FAO (1991) *La Industria Láctea en el Uruguay: Su Potencialidad Exportadora* (Montevideo: FAO).

Edwards, S. (1984a) *The Order of Liberalization of the External Sector in Developing Countries*, Essays in International Finance no. 156 (Princeton: Princeton University).

_____ (1984b) 'Coffee, Money and Inflation in Colombia', *World Development*, vol. 12, no. 11/12.

_____ (1986a) 'The Order of Liberalization of the Current and Capital Accounts of the Balance of Payments' in A. M. Choksi and D. Papageorgiou (eds) *Economic Liberalization in Developing Countries* (Oxford: Basil Blackwell).

_____ (1986b) 'Stabilization with Liberalization: An Evolution of Ten Years of Chile's Experience with Free Market Policies', in A. M. Choksi and D. Papageorgiou (eds) *Economic Liberalization in Developing Countries* (Oxford: Basil Blackwell).

_____ (1989a) 'Structural Adjustment Policies in Highly Indebted Countries', in J. D. Sachs (ed.) *Developing Country Debt and Economic Performance*, vol. 1 (Chicago: Chicago University Press).

_____ (1989b) 'Exchange Controls, Devaluations, and Real Exchange Rates: The Latin American Experience', *Economic Development and Cultural Change*, vol. 37, no. 3.

_____ (1990) 'The Sequencing of Economic Reform: Analytical Issues and Lessons from Latin American Experiences', *The World Economy*, vol. 13, no. 1.

_____ (1992) 'Trade Orientation, Distortions and Growth in Developing Countries', *Journal of Development Economics*, vol. 39, no. 1.

_____ (1993) 'Openness, Trade Liberalization, and Growth in Developing Countries', *Journal of Economic Literature*, vol. 31, no. 3.

Edwards, S. and A. C. Edwards (1987) *Monetarism and Liberalization: the Chilean Experience* (Cambridge, Mass.: Ballinger).

_____ (1992) 'Markets and Democracy: Lessons from Chile', *The World Economy*, vol. 15, no. 2.

EIU (1989) *Colombia, Country Report no. 4* (London: *The Economist* Intelligence Unit).

Escobar, L. and A. Mizala (1990) *Promoción de Exportaciones: el Desafío de ProChile* (Santiago de Chile: Ministerio de Economía, mimeo).

Esfahani, H. S. (1991) 'Exports, Imports, and Economic Growth in Semi-Industrialized Countries', *Journal of Development Economics*, vol. 35, no. 1.

Fajnzylber, F. (1988) 'International Competitiveness: Agreed Goal, Hard Task', *CEPAL Review*, no. 36.

_____ (1992) 'Technical Progress, Competitiveness and Institutional Change', in C. I. Bradford Jr (ed.) *Strategic Options for Latin America in the 1990s* (Paris, OECD).

Falvey, R. and Cha Dong Kim (1992) 'Timing and Sequencing Issues in Trade Liberalisation', *Economic Journal*, vol. 100, no. 413.

Felix, D. (1994) *Industrial Development in East Asia: What are the Lessons for Latin America?* Discussion Paper no. 84 (Geneva: UNCTAD).
FINEXPO (various years) *Anuario Estadístico del Sector Exportador No Tradicional* (Caracas: FINEXPO).
Fishlow, A. (1972) 'Origins and Consequences of Import Substitution in Brazil', in L. E. Di Marco, *International Economics and Development: Essays in Honor of Raúl Prebisch* (New York: Academic Press).
―― (1990) 'The Latin American State', *Journal of Economic Perspectives*, vol. 4, no. 3.
FitzGerald, E. V. K. (1992) 'Private Sector Investment and Savings Behaviour: The Policy Implications of Capital Account Disaggregation', *Pakistan Development Review*, vol. 31, no. 4.
―― (1994a) 'ECLA and the Formation of Latin American Economic Doctrine', in D. Rock (ed.) *Latin America in the 1940s: War and Postwar Transition* (Los Angeles: California University Press).
―― (1994b) 'The Impact of NAFTA on the Latin American Economies', in V. Bulmer-Thomas (ed.) *Mexico and the North American Free Trade Agreement* (London: Macmillan).
FitzGerald, E. V. K., K. Jansen and R. Vos (1994) 'International Constraints on Private Investment and Economic Adjustment in Developing Countries', in J. W. Gunning and H. L. M. Kox (eds) *Trade, Aid and Development* (London: Macmillan).
FitzGerald, E. V. K. and G. Mavrotas (1994) *The Implications of Recent Changes in International Capital Flows of Structural Adjustment, Private Investment and Employment Creation in Developing Countries*, Interdepartmental Project on Structural Adjustment Occasional Paper no. 23 (Geneva: ILO).
Fleming, J. M. (1974) 'Dual Exchange Markets and Other Remedies for Disrupted Capital Flows', *IMF Staff Papers*, vol. 21, no. 2.
Fonseca, G. (1992) 'Economie de la Drogue: Taille, Caractérisques et impact Économique', *Revue Tiers Monde*, vol. 33, no. 131.
Frenkel, J. A. and M. L. Mussa (1985) 'Asset Markets, Exchange Rates and the Balance of Payments', in R. W. Jones and P. B. Kenen (eds.) *Handbook of International Economics*, volume II (Amsterdam: Elsevier).
Fröbel, F., J. Heinrichs and O. Kreye (1987) *Export Processing Zones in Developing Countries. Results of a New Survey*, Working Paper no. 43 (Geneva: ILO).
Fuentes, J. A. (1989) 'La Erosión y Desviación del Comercio Intracentroamericano', in J. A. Fuentes, *Desafíos de la Integración Centroamericana* (San José: FLACSO and ICAP).
FUSADES (1991a) 'Zonas Francas en El Salvador', *Boletín Económico y Social*, no. 64.
FUSADES (1991b) 'La Industria Manufacturera en El Salvador', *Boletín Económico y Social*, no. 65.
Galvez, J. and J. Tybout (1985) 'Microeconomic Adjustments in Chile during 1977–81: The Importance of Being a Grupo', *World Development*, vol. 13, no. 8.
Gibson, H. and E. Tsakalotos (1992) *Financial Liberalization and Economic Integration: Prospects for Southern Europe* (London, Macmillan).
Gindling, T. H. and A. Berry (1991) 'Costa Rica', in S. Horton, R. Kanbur and D. Mazunder (eds) *Labor Markets in an Era of Adjustment*, EDI Symposium Volume (Washington: The World Bank).

Ginneken, W. van and J. G. Park (1984) *Generating Internationally Comparable Income Distribution Estimates* (Geneva: ILO).

Goldsmith, R. W. (1951) 'A Perpetual Inventory of National Wealth', *Studies in Income and Wealth*, vol. 14.

Greenaway, D. and G. Reed (1990) 'Empirical Evidence on Trade Orientation and Economic Performance in Developing Countries', in C. Milner (ed.) *Export Promotion Strategies. Theory and Evidence from Developing Countries* (New York: New York University Press).

Greene, J. and D. Villanueva (1991)'Private Investment in Developing Countries: An Empirical Analysis', *IMF Staff Papers*, vol. 38, no. 1.

Grunwald, J. and K. Flamm (1985) *The Global Factory* (Washington: The Brookings Institution).

Guerguil, M. (1993) *Human Resources and Competitiveness in Selected Latin American Countries* (Santiago de Chile: ECLAC).

Gupta, S. (1984) 'Unrecorded Trade at Black Exchange Rate: Analysis, Implications and Estimates', *Aussenwirtschaft*, vol. 39, no. 1–2.

Haggard, S. (1990), *Pathways from the Periphery – The Politics of Growth in the Newly Industrializing Countries* (Ithaca: Cornell University Press).

Harberger, A. C. (1986) 'A Primer on the Chilean Economy, 1973–1983', in A. M. Choksi and D. Papageorgiou (eds) *Economic Liberalization in Developing Countries* (Oxford: Basil Blackwell).

Havrylyshyn, O. (1990) 'Trade Policy and Productivity Gains in Developing Countries: A Survey of the Literature', *World Bank Research Observer*, vol. 5, no. 1.

Heitger, B. (1987) 'Import Protection and Export Performance – Their Impact on Economic Growth', *Weltwirtschaftliches Archiv*, vol. 123, no. 2.

Helleiner, G. K. (1986) 'Outward Orientation, Import Instability and African Economic Growth: An Empirical Investigation', in S. Lall and F. Stewart (eds) *Theory and Reality in Development: Essays in Honour of Paul Streeten* (London: Macmillan).

—— (1990) 'Trade Strategy in Medium-term Adjustment', *World Development*, vol. 18, no. 6.

Hirschman, A. O. (1981) *Essays in Trespassing: Economics to Politics and Beyond* (Cambridge, Mass.: Cambridge University Press).

Hoffmaister, A. (1992) 'The Cost of Export Subsidies: Evidence from Costa Rica', *IMF Staff Papers*, vol. 39, no. 1.

Hoffmann, J. and S. Homburg (1990) 'Explaining the Rise and Decline of the Dollar', *Kyklos*, vol. 32, no. 1.

Hofman, A. A. (1991) *The Role of Capital in Latin America: A Comparative Perspective of Six Countries for 1950–89*, Working Paper no. 4 (Santiago de Chile: ECLAC).

—— (1992) 'Capital Accumulation in Latin America: A Six Country Comparison for 1950–89', *Review of Income and Wealth*, vol. 38, no. 4.

—— (1993) 'Economic Development in Latin America in the 20th Century – A Comparative Perspective' in A. Szirmai, B. van Arkand, D. Pilat (eds) *Explaining Economic Growth, Essays in Honour of Angus Maddison* (Amsterdam: Elsevier/North-Holland).

Hogan, P. et al., (1991) *The Role of Support Services in Expanding Manufactured Exports in Developing Countries* (Washington, DC: EDI).

Hoeven, R. van der and F. Stewart (1993) *Social Development during Periods of Structural Adjustment in Latin America*, Interdepartmental Project on Structural Adjustment Occasional Paper no. 18 (Geneva: ILO).
Hommes, R. (1990) 'Colombia and Venezuela', in J. Williamson (ed.) (1990).
ICE (1993a) *Venezuela: Exportaciones No-Tradicionales, 1992* (Caracas: ICE)
____ (1993b) *Trustuna C.A., Premio Venezuela Exportadora 92* (Caracas: ICE).
IDB (various years) *Economic and Social Progress in Latin America* (Washington: IDB).
____ (1992) *Socioeconomic Report Costa Rica*, no. DES-13 (Washington: IDB).
ILO (1987) *Employment Effects of Multinational Enterprises in Developing Countries* (Geneva: ILO).
____ (1992a) *13th Conference of American States: Report of the Director-General* (Geneva: ILO).
____ (1992b) *Stabilization, Structural Adjustment and Social Policies in Costa Rica: The Role of Compensatory Programmes*, Interdepartmental Project on Structural Adjustment Occasional Paper no. 1 (Geneva: ILO).
IMF (1983) *World Economic Outlook*, Occasional Paper no. 21 (Washington, DC: IMF).
____ (various years) *International Financial Statistics* (Washington, DC: IMF).
Inforpress Centroamericana, several issues.
IPC (1991) *Consideraciones sobre la Reforma del Sistema Financiero en Guatemala* (Guatemala: IPC, mimeo).
ITC (1989) *Propuestas de Medidas Comerciales Complementarias para el Ajuste Estructural en Guatemala* (Geneva: ITC).
Journal of Commerce (1993) 'Guatemalan Border Poses Traffic Hurdle', March 23.
Jung, W. S. and P. J. Marshall (1985) 'Exports, Growth and Causality in Developing Countries', *Journal of Development Economics*, vol. 18, no. 1.
Kamin, S. B. (1988) *Devaluation, External Balance, and Macroeconomic Performance: A Look at the Numbers*, Studies in International Finance no. 62 (Princeton University).
Kavoussi, R. M. (1985) 'International Trade and Economic Development: The Recent Experience of Developing Countries', *Journal of Developing Areas*, vol. 19, no. 3.
Khan, A. H. and N. Saqib (1993) 'Exports and Economic Growth: The Pakistan Experience', *International Economic Journal*, vol. 7, no. 3.
Khan, M. and M. Knight (1985) 'Fund-supported Adjustment Programmes and Economic Growth', *IMF Occasional Paper*, no. 41.
Knight, M., N. Loayza and D. Villanueva (1993) 'Testing the Neoclassical Theory of Economic Growth', *IMF Staff Papers*, vol. 40, no. 3.
Krueger, A. O. (1978) *Foreign Trade Regimes and Economic Development: Liberalization Attempts and Consequences* (Cambridge, Mass.: Ballinger).
Krugman, P. R. (1984) 'Import Protection as Export Promotion: International Competition in the Presence of Oligopolies and Economies of Scale', in H. Kierzkowski (ed.) *Monopolistic Competition and International Trade* (Oxford: Oxford University Press).
____ (1994) 'Competitiveness, A Dangerous Obsession', *Foreign Affairs*, vol. 73, no. 2.
Lal, D. (1983) *The Poverty of 'Development Economics'* (London: Institute of Economic Affairs).

References

Lall, S. (1992) 'The Structural Problems of African Industry', in F. Stewart, S. Lall and S. Wangewe (eds) *Alternative Development Strategies in Sub-Saharan Africa* (London: Macmillan).

Latin America Monitor (1993).

Leff, N. and K. Sato (1988) 'Estimating Investment and Savings Functions for Developing Countries, with an Application to Latin America', *International Economic Journal*, vol. 2, no. 3.

Liang, N. (1992) 'Beyond Import Substitution and Export Promotion: A New Typology of Trade Strategies', *Journal of Development Studies*, vol. 28, no. 3.

Lin, Ching-yuan (1988) 'East Asia and Latin America as Contrasting Models', *Economic Development and Cultural Change*, vol. 36, no. 3, supplement.

Linnemann, H. (1993a) 'Internationale Handel en Economische Groei in Ontwikkelingslanden', *Maandschrift Economie*, vol. 57, no. 2.

―― (1993b) 'Economic Cooperation among Developing Countries: Global or Regional?', in K. Ahuja, H. Coppens and H. van der Wusten (eds.) *Regime Transformations and Global Realignments* (New Delhi: Sage).

Liuksila, C. (1992) 'Colombia: El Ajuste Económico y los Pobres', *Finanzas y Desarrollo*, vol. 29, no. 2.

Lord, M. J. (1992) 'Latin America's Exports of Manufactured Goods' in IDB, *Economic and Social Progress in Latin America* (Washington, DC: IDB).

Lorenzo, F., R. Osmani and S. Laens (1992) *Itinerario de la Apertura y Condiciones Macroeconomicas: El Caso de Uruguay*, Working Papers no. 103 (Washington: IDB).

Lucas Jr, R. E. (1988) 'On the Mechanics of Economic Development', *Journal of Monetary Economics*, vol. 22, no. 1.

Macadar, L. (ed.) (1987) *Industria frente a la Competencia Extranjera*, Estudios CINVE no. 7 (Montevideo: CINVE).

―― (1988) 'Protección, Ventajas Comparadas y Eficiencia Industrial', *SUMA*, vol. 3 no. 5.

Maddison, A. (1989) *The World Economy in the 20th Century* (Paris: OECD).

―― (1991) *Dynamic Forces in Capitalist Development* (Oxford: Oxford University Press).

Magariños, G. (1991) *Uruguay en el Mercosur* (Montevideo: UITGEVER).

Mathieson, D. J. and L. Rojas-Suárez (1993) *Liberalization of the Capital Account*, IMF Occasional Paper no. 103 (Washington DC: IMF).

McKinnon, R. I. (1973) *Money and Capital in Economic Development* (Washington: Brookings Institution).

―― (1979) *Money in International Exchange, the Convertible Currency System* (New York: Oxford University Press).

Messner, D. (1990) *Uruguay: El Sector Industrial ante la Apertura Externa* (Berlin: German Development Institute).

―― (1992) *Uruguay: El Sector Industrial en el Umbral de la Apertura Externa* (Montevideo: CIESU).

Mezzera, J. and J. de Melo (1985) 'Adjustments by Industrial Firms in Uruguay during 1974–82', in V. Corbo and J. de Melo (eds) *Scrambling for Survival; How Firms Adjusted to the Recent Reforms in Argentina, Chile, and Uruguay*, World Bank Working Paper no. 764 (Washington: The World Bank).

Michaely, M. (1984) *Trade, Income Levels and Dependence* (Amsterdam: North Holland)

Michaely, M., D. Papageorgiou and A. M. Choksi (eds) (1991) *Liberalizing Foreign Trade: Lessons of Experience in the Developing World* (Cambridge, Mass: Basil Blackwell).

Mill, J. S. (1848) *Principles of Political Economy* (London: Penguin Books, 1970 edn).

Mills, C. A. and R. Nallari (1992) *Analytical Approaches to Stabilization and Adjustment Programs* (Washington, DC: EDI, The World Bank).

Milner, C. (ed.) (1990) *Export Promotion Strategies. Theory and Evidence from Developing Countries* (New York: New York University Press).

Ministerio de Trabajo y Previsión Social (1991) *Estadísticas del Trabajo 1990* (San Salvador: MTPS).

MIPLAN (1989) *Plan de Desarrollo Económico y Social 1989-1994*. (San Salvador: MIPLAN).

MIPLAN (1992) *Indicadores Económicos y Sociales, 1991-92*. (El Salvador: MIPLAN).

Morawetz, D. (1977) *Twenty-five Years of Economic Development 1950 to 1975* (Baltimore: Johns Hopkins University Press).

Morriset, J. (1993) 'Does Financial Liberalization Really Improve Investment in Developing Countries?', *Journal of Development Economics*, vol. 40, no. 1.

Nelson, R. and S. Winter (1982) *An Evolutionary Theory of Economic Change* (Cambridge, Mass.: Harvard University Press).

Nowak, F. (1989) *Auswirkungen der Aussenhandels-und Kapitalverkehrsliberalisierung auf den Realen Wechselkurs und die Produktion von Gütern* (Göttingen: Schwartz).

OECD (1987) *Structural Adjustment and Economic Performance* (Paris: OECD).

——— (1988) *The Newly Industrialising Countries: Challenge and Opportunities for OECD Industries* (Paris: OECD).

——— (1990) *Economic Outlook, Historical Statistics* (Paris: OECD).

Ondarts, G. (1991) 'Exportaciones y Crecimiento, una Encuesta a Firmas de Argentina, Brasil, Chile, Paraguay y Uruguay', *Integración Latinoamericana*, vol. 16, no. 173.

Pastor, M. and E. Hilt (1993) 'Private Investment and Democracy in Latin America', *World Development*, vol. 21, no. 4.

Pavez Hermosilla, G. (1987) *Industrias de Maquila, Zonas Procesadoras de Exportación y Empresas Multinacionales en Costa Rica y El Salvador*, Documento de Trabajo, no. 48, ILO/Programa de Empresas Multinacionales (Geneva: ILO).

Pfefferman, G. and A. Madrassy (1992) *Trends in Private Investment in Developing Countries*, Discussion Paper no. 14 (Washington, DC: IFC, The World Bank).

Pietrobelli, C. (1992) *El Proceso de Diversificación de Exportaciones en Chile de 1960 a 1980* (Santiago de Chile: ECLAC, mimeo).

Porter, M. (1990) *The Competitive Advantage of Nations* (New York: The Free Press).

Psacharopoulos, G. et al. (1992) *Poverty and Income Distribution in Latin America: The Story of the 1980s*, Latin America and the Caribbean Technical Department Report no. 27 (Washington, DC: The World Bank).

Putnam, R., R. Leonardi and R. Nanetti (1993) *Making Democracy Work: Civic Traditions in Modern Italy* (Princeton: Princeton University Press).

Quinn, J. (1992) *Intelligent Enterprise* (New York: The Free Press).

Quirk, P. J., B. V. Christensen, K.-M. Huh and T. Sasaki (1987) *Floating Exchange Rates in Developing Countries*, IMF Occasional Paper no. 53 (Washington, DC: IMF).

Rapoport, A. I. (1978) 'Effective Protection Rates in Central America', in W. R. Cline and E. Delgado (eds) *Economic Integration in Central America* (Washington: The Brookings Institution).

Reich, R. (1984) 'Small State, Big Lesson', *Boston Observer*, vol. 3.

____ (1991) *The Work of Nations* (New York: Vintage Books).

Ribe, H. et al. (1990), *How Adjustment Can Help the Poor: The World Bank's Experience*, Discussion Paper no. 71 (Washington, DC: The World Bank).

Riedel, J. (1992) Public Investment and Growth in Latin America, internal document (Washington, DC).

Romer, P. (1986) 'Increasing Returns and Long-Run Growth', *Journal of Political Economy*, vol. 94, no. 5.

____ (1990) 'Endogenous Technological Change', *Journal of Political Economy*, vol. 98, no. 5.

Rondinelli, D. A. (1987) 'Export Processing Zones and Economic Development in Asia: a review and reassessment of a means of promoting growth and jobs', *American Journal of Economics and Sociology*, vol. 46, no. 1.

Saborio, S. (1990) 'Central America' in J. Williamson (ed.) *Latin American Adjustment: How Much Has Happened?* (Washington, DC: Institute for International Economics).

Sabre Foundation, *Free Zones in Developing Countries: Expanding Opportunities for the Private Sectors*, Program Evaluation Discussion Paper no. 18 (Washington: AID).

Sachs, J. D. (1987a) 'The Bolivian Hyperinflation and Stabilization', *American Economic Review*, vol. 77, Papers and Proceedings.

____ (1987b) 'Trade and Exchange Rate Policies in Growth-Oriented Adjustment Programmes' in V. Corbo, M. Goldstein and M. Kahn, *Growth-Oriented Adjustment Programmes* (Washington, DC: IMF/ The World Bank).

Sachs, J. D. (ed.) (1989) *Developing Country Debt and Economic Performance*, vol 1 and 2 (Chicago: Chicago University Press).

Schadler, S. (1992) *Recent Experience with Surges in Capital Inflows*, Occasional Paper no. 108 (Washington, DC: IMF).

Schloss, M. and V. Thomas (1986) 'Ajuste con Crecimiento: la Experiencia de Colombia', *Finanzas y Desarrollo*, vol. 23, no. 4.

Schulz, H. U. (1992) *Financing for Small and Medium-Sized Industry* (Santiago de Chile: ECLAC, mimeo).

SEGEPLAN (1991) *Programa de Estabilización y Ajuste Estructural. Un Proyecto Nacional de Corto y Mediano Plazo* (Guatemala: SEGEPLAN and GTZ).

____ (1992) *Informe Económic y Social 1991–1992: El Reto de la Inversión* (Guatemala: SEGEPLAN).

Seinen, A. T. (1992) *Industrial Export Promotion in Chile and Colombia* (Groningen, mimeo).

Serven, L. and A. Solimano (1992a) 'Private Investment and Macro-economic Adjustment: A Survey', *World Bank Observer*, vol. 7, no. 1.

―― (1992b) 'Economic Adjustment and Investment Performance in Developing Countries', in Corbo *et al.* (1992).
―― (1993) 'Debt Crisis, Adjustment Policies and Capital Formation in Developing Countries: Where Do We Stand?, *World Development*, vol. 21, no. 1.
Singer, H. W. and P. Gray (1988) 'Trade Policy and Growth of Developing Countries: Some New Data', *World Development*, vol. 16, no. 3.
Solow, R. (1993) 'Policies for Economic Growth' in A. Knoester and A. Wellink (eds) *Tinbergen Lectures on Economic Policy* (Amsterdam: North Holland).
Stewart, F. (1992) *Protecting the Poor during Adjustment in Latin America and the Caribbean in the 1980s: How Adequate was the World Bank Response?*, Working Paper no. 44, (Oxford: Queen Elizabeth House and Centro Studi Luca d'Agliano).
Stolwijk, H. J. J. (1992) *De Nederlandse Landbouw op de Drempel van de 21ste Eeuw*, Onderzoeksmemorandum no. 95 (The Hague: CPB).
Stratta, N. and M. Halty (1991) 'Políticas Públicas e Innovación Industrial', in ECLAC, *Competividad, Políticas Tecnológicas e Innovación Industrial en Uruguay* (Montevideo: ECLAC).
Summers, L. H. and V. Pritchett (1993) 'The Structural Adjustment Debate', *American Economic Review*, vol. 83, no. 2.
Supelano, A. (1992) 'The Political Economy of Latin America: The Colombian Experience during the 1980s', *Journal of Economic Issues*, vol. 26, no. 3.
Tavares de Araujo, J. (1992) *Latin American Trade Policies: Issues and Options* (Washington: ECLAC, mimeo).
Thomas, V., J. Nash *et al.* (1991) *Best Practices in Trade Policy Reform* (New York: Oxford University Press).
Tinbergen, J. (1975) *Income Distribution* (Amsterdam: North Holland).
Tybout, J. R. (1992) 'Linking Trade and Productivity: New Research Directions', *World Bank Economic Review*, vol. 6, no. 2.
Tyler, W. G. (1981) 'Growth and Export Expansion in Developing Countries: Some Empirical Evidence', *Journal of Development Economics*, vol. 9, no. 1.
UNCTAD (1983) *Export Processing Zones in Developing Countries: Implications for Trade and Industrialization Policies* (Geneva: UNCTAD).
UNIDO (1971) *Industrial Free-Zones as Incentives to Promote Export-Oriented Industries*, (Geneva: UNIDO).
―― (1987) *Situación y Perspectivas de las Industrias de Bienes de Capital en América Latina: vol. III, Costa Rica*, Serie de Documentos de Trabajo Sectoriales no. 63 (Santiago de Chile: UNIDO).
United States Department of Commerce (1987) *Comparative Guide to Caribbean Basin Free Trade Zone* (Washington: Caribbean Basin Division, Department of Commerce).
USITC (1989) *Product Sharing: US Imports Under Harmonized Tariff Schedule Subheadings 9802.00.60 and 9802.00.80, 1987–1990* (Washington, DC: USITC).
Vaessen, T. (1990) 'De "Witte Motor" van de Colombiaanse Economie', *Internationale Samenwerking*, vol. 5, no. 9.
Vargas, L. A. (1993) 'Productividad y Recomposición Industrial: El Caso de Costa Rica', *Serie Política Económica*, no. 7 (Heredia: EFUNA).

Verbruggen, H. (1985) *Gains from Export-Oriented Industrialization in Developing Countries: With Special Reference to South-East Asia* (Amsterdam: Free University Press).

Vogel, R. and S. Buser (1976) 'Inflation, Financial Repression and Capital Formation in Latin America' in R. McKinnon (ed.) *Money and Finance in Economic Development* (New York: Marcel Dekker).

Warr, P. G. (1989) 'Export Processing Zones and Trade Policy', *Finance and Development*, vol. 26, no. 2.

Williamson, J. (ed.) (1990) *Latin American Adjustment: How Much Has Happened?* (Washington, DC: Institute for International Economics).

Williamson, J. (1993) *The Emergent Development Policy Consensus: The Market-oriented Model*, Paper presented at the seminar on 'Sustainable Development with Equity in the 1990s: Policies and Alternatives, (Madison, Wisconsin, mimeo).

Willmore, L. (1989) 'Export Promotion and Import Substitution in Central American Industry', *CEPAL Review*, no. 48.

World Bank, The (1987) *Guatemala, Economic Situation and Prospects* (Washington, DC: The World Bank).

____ (1989) *Guatemala, Public Sector Expenditure Review* (Washington, DC: The World Bank).

____ (1990) *Trends in Developing Economies 1990* (Washington, DC: The World Bank).

____ (1992a) *Trade Policy Reforms Under Adjustment Programs*, World Bank Operations Evaluation Study (Washington, DC: The World Bank).

____ (1992b) *World Tables* (Baltimore: The Johns Hopkins University Press).

____ (1993) *Latin America and the Caribbean a Decade After the Debt Crisis* (Washington, DC: The World Bank).

____ (1994) *World Debt Tables 1994–95* (Washington, DC: The World Bank).

____ (various years) *World Development Report* (New York: Oxford University Press).

Zahler, R. (1980) 'The Monetary and Real Effects of the Financial Opening Up of National Economies to the Exterior; The Case of Chile 1975–1978', *CEPAL Review*, no. 10.

Index

accounting, growth *see* growth accounting
Admisión Temporal para el Perfeccionamiento 181–2, 187, 189, 231
Agency for International Development 97, 100
aid 95, 191
aluminium 176, 180
Andean Pact 180, 182, 184
anti-dumping legislation 180–1, 188
anti-export bias 6, 20, 28, 152, 155, 157, 161, 180, 211, 212
anti-trade bias 26
Argentina 55–6, 106
   devaluation 45
   exchange rates 32
   income per caput 124
   industrial development 2
   regional integration 169–70, 172
Asia
   manufacturing production 2, 137, 144–6
   newly industrialising countries 2, 19, 23, 106, 110, 112, 118, 158
Asociación de Exportadores de Manufacturas (ASEXMA) 159, 160
Asociación Venezolana de Exportadores 183–4

balance of payments
   Chile 50
   Colombia 52–3
   Costa Rica 191, 197
   problems 18
banks, long-term support 70
Barbados 124
Baumol, W. 78–9, 82, 83 n2
bilateral trade agreements 169–70, 172, 177, 181
black market, foreign exchange 40
Bolivia 124, 232
bonded warehouses, imported goods 182, 188

Brazil 65, 106, 129
   EPFZs 88
   industrial development 2
   manufactured exports 60
   regional integration 169–70, 172
Bretton Woods 108
Buitelaar, R. 225
Bulmer-Thomas, V. 191, 201, 202–3, 208

Canada 92
capital account, liberalisation 42–3
capital exports, regulation 43–4
capital flight 208
capital flows 56–7
   control 40–1
   liberalisation 27
   medium-term 49
capital goods, imports 218
capital inflows 18, 36, 38, 39, 42–3, 50, 51, 57 n1, 71
capital markets
   Costa Rica 196, 231
   deregulation 62, 155
   Latin America 154–5, 230–1
capital stock, Latin America 112–13, 119–20
Caribbean 85, 184, 185, 189
   EPFZs 89–93
Caribbean Basin Initiative 92, 98, 193, 203
Caribcan 92
CEMPASA 195
Center for the Promotion of Exports and Investments 200–1, 231
Central America 85, 193
   EPFZs 89–93
Central American Agreement on Fiscal Incentives 196
Central American Common Market 191, 192, 193, 194, 196, 197, 198–9, 203, 204, 211
central banks
   autonomy 71
   Venezuela 183

Centro de Atención Directa al Exportador 182–3, 232
Certificado de Abono Tributario 199, 200, 201, 212–13, 231
chemical industry 201
Chenery, H. B. 139, 140
Chicago boys 48, 152
Chile 1, 6, 7, 45, 81, 181, 231, 232
  capital stock 113
  case study 2, 15
  economic growth 105, 115
  exchange rates 32, 48–52
  export-led growth 151–62
  income per caput 124
  liberalisation 24, 151–4
  natural resources 121 n4, 144
  private investment 229
Chixoy 221
clothing industry
  EPFZs 87
  exports 127–8
  Guatemala 214
  Venezuela 184
coal, exports 47
Coase, R. 76, 77–80
cocaine 53
Codetel 90
coffee
  exports 47, 210, 227
  prices 52, 53
Colombia 6, 7, 125, 189, 190
  bilateral trade agreements 177, 181
  capital stock 113, 119
  economic growth 105, 115
  exchange rates 10, 52–4
  exports 128, 227
  income per caput 124
  private investment 229
Comités de Promoción Comercial 182
commodities, export 2
common external tariffs 196–7, 211, 212, 223 n2
competition
  regulation 82
  Schumpeterian 79–80
construction industry
  investment 56
  wages 125

consumer goods, protection 167–8
contestable markets 78–9, 83 n2
Convenio Argentino-Uruguayo de Cooperación Económica 169, 172
convertibility, foreign exchange 31
copper
  exports 47
  prices 48, 157
CORFINA 223 n3
Corporación de Desarrollo Industrial S.A. 192, 195
Corporación de Fomento 158, 162
corruption 189, 221
Costa Rica 7, 125, 128, 130, 191, 231, 232
  case study 2, 15
  EPFZs 90, 104, 199–200
  export promotion 197–202, 232
  macro-economic policies 194–6
  manufacturing industry 6, 192–4, 195
  trade liberalisation 196–7
Costa Rican Development Initiatives Coalition 202
costs, reduction 50
credit allocation 71
credit insurance 155, 156, 183, 188
credits
  agricultural exports 213
  exporters 163, 188, 218–19
  subsidised 7, 10
current account
  Colombia 52–3
  deficit, Chile 50
  equilibrium 34
  liberalisation 42–3
customs, procedures 189
customs duty, EPFZs 85
customs unions 28

de-industrialisation 46, 47
debt 130
  crisis 60, 66, 141
  reduction 62
deflation 48
demand, contraction 69
dependent-economy model, exchange rates 32, 33–9, 50–1

Index

devaluation 23, 30 n5, 35, 44–6, 48, 51, 55, 56, 61–2, 65, 107, 123, 172, 194, 195, 200, 209, 213, 214
development strategies, long-term 164
Dijkstra, G. 14, 95, 191
direct investment, foreign 18, 90
direct taxes 134
   restitution 170, 171
domestic market
   preference for 186–7
   production 7, 19
Dominican Republic 128
   EPFZs 87, 89–90, 98
doubly augmented joint factor productivity 115–18, 120 n5
drugs, illegal 47
drugs trafficking, Colombia 53–4
dumping, legislation 180–1, 188
Dutch disease 12, 46–7, 95, 157, 176, 227
Duty-Free Zones regime 200

Economic Commission for Latin America and the Caribbean 69, 120, 121
economic development, national competitiveness paradigm 142–3
economic growth
   export promotion and 23–6
   Latin America 105, 109
   world 107–9
   see also growth accounting
economies, small 59–60
Ecuador 7, 10, 105, 227, 232
education 110, 120–1, 129, 137, 185, 202, 219, 229
   expenditure 131, 134, 202, 232–3
effective exchange rates 19–22, 23, 29 n1
Egypt 87
El Salvador 10, 232
   export processing free zones 95–104, 230
electronics, EPFZs 87
employment
   creation 68, 104
   effects of structural adjustment 124–7

   growth 110
   impact of EPFZs 87–8, 102–4
   Latin America 120
   public service 219
   see also labour
environment, effects of industrial production 14
European Union 90, 92
exchange controls 63, 163
exchange rates 14, 157, 203, 213
   Chile 32, 48–52
   Colombia 52–4
   dependent-economy model 32, 33–9
   depreciation 127
   effective 19–22
   El Salvador 95
   equilibrium 81, 83
   export promotion 32–3
   fixed 31, 34–5, 44, 167
   floating 31, 35–6, 48
   Guatemala 10, 207–11, 222
   liberalisation 42–4
   multiple 21, 41–2, 48, 54, 163, 208–10
   nominal 64, 73 n5
   overvaluation 71, 163, 166, 171–2, 185, 227
   policy 18, 22, 31–3, 226, 227–8, 233
   reform 1, 10–11
   unified 26, 39–41, 61, 152, 179
   Uruguay 54–6
export bonds 181, 187
export contracts 199, 200, 201
export processing free zones 6, 14, 85–9, 229–30
   Central America and the Caribbean 89–93
   Costa Rica 199–200
   El Salvador 95–104, 230
   employment effects 102–4
   forward and backward linkages 100–2
   Guatemala 212
   private ownership and management 90
   Venezuela 182, 188

export promotion 18–22, 28, 96, 180, 230–2
  Chile 156, 158–62
  Costa Rica 197–202
  economic growth and 23–6
  exchange rates 32–3, 52
  firms' views on 187–90
  manufactures 170–1
  Venezuela 181–4
exportables, prices 38–9
exports 12, 17, 107, 127–8
  agricultural 191, 208, 213
  Colombia 52–4
  contribution of EPFZs 88, 100
  diversification 153–4, 180, 227
  effective exchange rates 19–22, 23
  Guatemala 213–17
  illegal 53–4
  incentives 212–13
  labour-intensive 127–8
  manufactures 6, 19, 60, 139, 140–1, 144–8, 176, 193–4, 198–9, 203
  non-traditional 169, 176, 183, 189, 199, 201, 212–13, 214–15, 221, 227
  primary commodities 18–19, 46–7, 176
  problems 154–8
  structure 143–8
  subsidies 186, 200, 204
  traditional 41, 191
  Venezuela 175–8

factor prices 19
Fajnzylber, F. 46, 142
FERTICA 195
finance, export industries 154–5
financial intermediaries, relationship with firms 70, 154–5
financial markets
  Guatemala 218–19
  liberalisation 66
financial reform 62
firms
  competitiveness 171–2, 184–90
  exporting 154–5
  small and medium 72, 75, 78, 79, 155, 158
  under structural adjustment 70–1

fiscal credits 161
fiscal deficits 152
fiscal policy 81, 123
fiscal reforms 62
FitzGerald, V. 14, 59, 137, 228, 229
fixed assets, acquisition 70
fixed exchange rates 31, 34–5, 44
floating exchange rates 31, 35–6, 48
Fondo de Financiamiento de las Exportaciones 183, 188
food subsidies 68
footwear, exports 127, 128
foreign aid 95, 191
foreign debt 217
  Guatemala 208
  Uruguay 163
foreign direct investment 18, 62, 72, 215
  EPFZs 90
foreign exchange 130, 186–7
  allocations 20
  contribution of EPFZs 88, 100
  convertibility 31
  liberalisation 40
  restrictions 39–42
foreign trade zones *see* export processing free zones
France 106, 113, 119
free economic zones *see* export processing free zones
free trade 17, 20, 26, 28, 75
Fuentes K, J. A. 207
FUSADES 97

garment industry *see* clothing industry
GDP
  effects of export growth 24–6
  growth 7, 105
  Latin America 119–20
General Agreement on Tariffs and Trade 68, 75, 171, 180, 197, 200, 212, 226
General Motors 79
General System of Preferences 92, 222
Germany 106, 119
globalisation 75–6, 229

Index

government expenditure 35, 37, 194
government intervention 71
  export promotion 23
  international trade 17
  selective 13
growth accounting 14, 109–19
  sources of data 119–21
grupos 152
GUATEL 220
Guatemala 130
  case study 2, 15
  EPFZs 212
  exchange rates 10, 207–11
  export performance 213–17
  exports, systemic obstacles 217–22
  trade policy 207–13
GUATEXPRO 212
Guyana 124

Haïti 92, 124, 215
health 129–30
  expenditure 131, 134, 232–3
high-technology, EPFZs 90
Hoffmaister, A. 199, 200
Hofman, A. A. 14, 105
Honduras, EPFZs 98
Hong Kong 57
hours worked 110, 119, 120
household incomes 124
human resources 13, 142, 143, 185
hydropower 221

IBM 79
Ilopango airport 96
import licenses 20, 52, 179, 180
import-substitution 18, 19, 20, 23, 28, 52, 60, 108, 139, 157, 164, 186, 202, 211, 215
  industrialisation 141, 151, 158, 163, 212
importables, prices 38–9
imports 210
  barriers 23, 24, 163
  capital goods 218
  effective exchange rates 19–22, 23
  EPFZs 102
  inputs 181–2, 184, 187, 195, 197–8, 199, 211

liberalisation 7–10, 18, 69
  primary products 170–1
  restrictions 7, 44, 48, 55
  tariffs 166–9
incentive structures 19–22, 29 n1
Incentives Fund 201
income distribution, Latin America 128–9, 134, 137
incomes policies 137
indirect taxes 134
Industrial Exporters Association (ASEXMA), Chile 159, 160
industrial monocultures, EPFZs 87
industrial parks, private 199
industrial policy 14, 75–6, 228–30
  consistency and efficacy 80–2
  El Salvador 95–8
  Uruguay 170
industrialisation 139, 226
  export-oriented 227
  future strategy 71–3
  import-substitution 141, 151, 158, 163, 212
  policy 19
  private investment 59–63
  role of EPFZs 86
industry
  profitability 66
  restructuring 134–7
  sustainable configurations 78–9
  under structural adjustment 59–63
infant industries, protectionism 80
infant mortality 129–30
inflation 35, 43, 127, 134, 178, 187, 194, 208, 210
  Chile 48, 50
  Colombia 52
  domestic rate 64
  Uruguay 166
  use of exchange rates 32, 44
informal sector, employment 125
information, markets 155, 183, 187, 189, 202
infrastructure 69, 72
  development 13
  EPFZs 102
Instituto Centroamericano de Administración de Empresas 202

Instituto de Comercio Exterior 182–3, 187, 189, 232
Instituto Nacional de Aprendizaje 202
Inter-American Development Bank 196, 201, 205 n4
interest rates 230
  Chile 153
  Costa Rica 195
  deregulation 71
  real *see* real interest rates
international markets
  competitive edge 13
  information 155
International Monetary Fund 26–7, 68, 137 n2, 194, 205 n4
international payments
  liberalisation 42–4
  restrictions 39–42
investment 14
  industrial 70
  manufacturing industry 192
  private *see* private investment
  public 14, 66, 69, 72, 81, 220–1
  share in GDP 12
  stimulation 228–30
  Venezuela 185–6

Jamaica 90, 92, 128
Japan 106, 119
joint factor productivity 115–18, 121 n5
just-in-time production 104

Korean War 60

La Mundial 183, 189
labour 47
  costs 202
  deregulation 85–6, 123, 124
  EPFZs 90, 103
  growth accounting input 110–12, 118–19
  leaders, Guatemala 222
  productivity 57 n4, 110, 112, 194
  skilled 88
  unskilled 104, 125, 230
  see also employment
labour market, legislation 185

land, availability 113–15, 120
Las Americas, EPFZ 89–90
Latin America
  capital stock 112–13, 119–20
  economic growth 105, 106, 107, 109
  foreign trade 26–7
  GDP 109, 119–20
  income distribution 128–9, 134, 137
  income per caput 124
  land availability 113–15
  revealed comparative advantage 67, 145–8
  social development 123–30
  trade policies 141–3
Latin American Integration Association 180, 183
law of one price 32, 55
less developed countries 80, 217
  EPFZs 86
  GDP growth 35–6
  liberalisation 13–14, 54, 55, 56, 157, 225
  trade 172
Linnemann, H. 14, 17, 139, 226
Lomé Convention 92

Macario, C. 175
macro-economic policies 1, 12, 27, 81, 83, 108, 131, 157, 194–6, 226
Maddison, A. 105, 106, 108, 119, 120
Malaysia 87, 144
manufacturing industry 149 n2
  Chile 152
  contribution to exports 6, 19, 60, 139, 140–1, 144–8
  Costa Rica 6, 191, 192–4
  development 47
  employment 124–5, 232
  export-oriented 1, 19, 86, 215–17, 225, 227
  Guatemala 215–17
  performance 2–7
  Uruguay 163–5, 170–1
  value added 100
marketing, techniques 166

Index

markets
  contestable 78–9
  functioning 143
  information 155, 183, 187, 189, 202
  international 13, 155, 166
Martínez de Hoz, J. 32
maternal mortality 130
Mercosur 170
Mexico 2, 65, 106, 130, 181, 188
  EPFZs 87, 88
  manufactured exports 60, 144, 215
Mill, J. S. 82–3
minimum wages 123, 125, 129
monetary policy 37, 69, 107, 123, 173
money supply 35, 195
Montego Bay, EPFZ 90
moral hazard 71
mortality 129–30

nation states 75
national competitiveness paradigm 142
National Exporters Association, Chile 159
natural resources 109, 121 n4, 142, 144
neo-liberalism 152
Netherlands 106, 119
newly industrialising countries 2, 19, 23, 106, 110, 112, 118, 158
Nicaragua 124, 205 n1
non-tariff barriers 10, 11, 14, 20, 21, 27, 46, 179, 180, 211–12, 226
non-tradables, prices 32–3, 35–8, 43, 51, 61–2, 211
North American Free Trade Area 74 n25

OECD 68, 69, 80, 81, 106, 108
Oficina de Promoción de Exportaciones 183, 188
oil
  exports 47, 175, 176, 187, 227
  prices 48, 107, 178, 180
OPEC 108

Pacific Rim 2
Panama 128, 130

Paraguaná 182, 188
parastatals 70
PDVSA 179
Peru 229, 233
petrochemical sector, Venezuela 184–5
plant size 186
population 120
Portugal 106, 119, 120, 121
poverty 125, 130, 131, 134
  Guatemala 221
  Latin America 128–9
prices
  copper 48, 157
  decontrolled 152
  oil 48, 107, 175, 178, 180
  regulated 11
  relative 50, 64
  structure 19
  tradables 32–3
primary education 129, 134, 137
primary products
  dependence 12
  exports 18–19, 46–7
  processing 170–1
private investment 14, 66–7, 229
  Guatemala 217–19
  industrialisation 59–63
  industry 71, 72
  LDCs 70
  stimulating 12
  Venezuela 179
private sector
  exports 176–7
  incentives 22
privatisation 62, 64, 66–7, 70, 71, 152, 179, 194, 195
ProChile 156, 159–60, 231–2
product prices 19
production, domestic market 7, 19
production costs 77–80
profits, repatriation 90
Promexport 183, 188
protectionism 1, 18, 21, 48, 68, 75, 76, 80, 102, 167–8, 171, 197, 202–3, 211, 229
Protocolo de Expansión Comercial 169, 172

public expenditure 124
  cuts 64
  education 131, 134, 202, 232–3
  health 131, 134, 232–3
  social 131–4
public investment 14, 66, 69, 72, 81
  Guatemala 220–1
public sector
  deficit, Venezuela 178
  weakness, Guatemala 219
Puerto Rico, EPFZs 90, 92
purchasing power parity 32

quality requirements, exporters 156, 166

real effective exchange rate 13–14, 213, 222
real exchange rates 32–3, 41, 47–8, 51, 52, 53, 54, 56, 61, 64–6, 71, 81, 166, 227, 228, 229
real interest rates 12, 45, 51, 62, 66, 229
real wages 13, 37
  reduction 61, 64, 109, 123, 195, 214
recession 51, 125, 157, 178
regional integration 169–70
Reich, R. 75, 77–8, 80
rent-seeking 27, 31, 55, 76, 164, 180, 186
research and development 81, 156, 185, 201, 229
resources, re-allocation 62
revaluation, Chile 157
revealed comparative advantage 67, 145–8
risk capital, access to 62
Rivera Alemán, C. 95
roads, investment 220

Salvador, El see El Salvador
Salvadorean Development Foundation 97
San Bartolo, EPFZ 96, 98–104, 230
San Cristobal, EPFZ 90
San Isidro, EPFZ 89–90
San Salvador 96
Santo Tomás de Castilla 212

savings, domestic 12
secondary education 129, 202
Seinen, Anne Theo 151
service industries, EPFZs 90
Singapore 57, 88
skilled workers, EPFZs 88
social costs 68
  industrial policy 10
  transformation 13–14
social deprivation 130
social development, Latin America 123–30
social policies, and industrial restructuring 134–7
social unrest 65
South Korea 24, 52, 57, 88, 90, 106, 113, 118, 119, 120, 121, 144, 214
Spain 106, 119, 121
special economic zones see export processing free zones
Sri Lanka 87, 129
Stewart, F. 14, 109, 123, 232, 233
stock exchanges 62
structural adjustment 14
  consequences 64–7
  dealing with the consequences 130–4
  loans 212, 222
  social effects 123–30
structural adjustment programmes 61, 141–2
  Costa Rica 194–5
  gap between model and experience 67–71
  industry under 59–62
subcontractors 72
subsidies, exports 161–2
sugar, guarantee prices 214
sustainability, industrial policy 80–2

tablita 48, 50, 55
Taiwan 52, 57, 90, 106, 113, 119, 212
tariffs 7, 10, 11, 24, 27, 44, 51, 72, 95–6, 153, 170, 179, 194, 197, 203, 211–12, 226
  cuts 152
  drawback system 181
  imports 166–9
  reduction 20, 62

Tavares de Araujo, J. 14, 75, 229
tax certificates 199, 200, 201, 212–13
taxation 81, 134, 204, 219, 223 n1, 229
  Costa Rica 195
  EPFZs 97
technical progress 118
technicians, shortage 185
technology, assimilation 201
Technology Development Fund 201
technology transfer 62
telecommunications
  Chile 158
  Guatemala 220–1
  Venezuela 189–90
Teleport International 90
terms of trade 208, 213
textile industry
  EPFZs 87
  exports 127–8
Thailand 106, 119, 121, 144
Timpers, A. 163
tourism 208, 221
tradables 225
  prices 32–3, 35–8, 43, 48, 50, 51, 55, 61–2, 211
  sector 63, 229
trade
  gains from 17–18
  patterns of 143–8
  world 24
trade agreements, bilateral 169–70, 172, 177, 181
trade liberalisation 14, 18–22, 24, 52, 63, 96, 123, 144, 148, 152, 153, 172, 176, 180, 185, 186, 226–7, 233
  Costa Rica 196–7
  implementation 26–9
  Venezuela 184
trade policies 1, 139–43
trade restrictions, dismantling 50
trade unions 104, 152, 185
traditional exports 41
training 185, 202, 229
transaction costs 77–80
transnational corporations 79–80, 102, 184, 192, 223 n4
  EPFZs 86

transportation 157
  Venezuela 190

unemployment 13, 37, 39, 47
  industrial 72, 124–5
  urban 124, 178, 232
United Kingdom 106, 113, 119
United States 90, 92, 97, 106, 113, 119, 171, 185, 189, 202, 219, 222
  access to markets 60, 92, 97, 98, 185, 193, 194, 214
United States Agency for International Development 205 n4
universities 201
unskilled workers
  EPFZs 104, 230
  wages 125
Uruguay 7, 45, 231, 233
  case study 2, 15
  economic policy 163–71
  exchange rates 10, 32, 54–6
  regional integration 169–70, 172
Uruguay Round 72

value added, manufacturing industry 100
value added tax 62, 161
van Beers, C. 14, 139
van der Hoeven, R. 14, 109, 123, 232
van der Wijk, J. 191
van Dijck, P. 1, 225
Venezuela 121, 144, 229, 231, 233
  bilateral trade agreements 177, 181
  case study 2, 15
  competitiveness of firms 184–90
  economic growth 105
  exchange-rate policy 10, 178–9
  export performance 10, 175–8, 227
  export promotion 181–4, 232
  import regulations 179–81
Visser, H. 14, 22, 31, 227

wage controls 65
wages 13
  indexing 68
  low 193, 214, 222
  real *see* real wages

Washington agenda 1, 11, 12, 129, 225, 228
Weersma-Haworth, T. W. 14, 85, 229–30
women, employment, EPFZs 87, 104
working conditions, unregulated 104

World Bank 12, 50, 68, 69, 82, 138 n2, 194, 195, 210, 212, 220, 222, 226
World Development Report 1987 141
world trade, conditions 24

DATE DUE

OCT 15 2001	
DEC 07 2001	
JAN 07 003	
MAY 02 9	
NOV 2 06	

HIGHSMITH #45230